LONDON

JOHN RUSSELL

LONDON

HARRY N. ABRAMS, INC., PUBLISHERS

For Nick Grimshaw
An exemplary Londoner

Project Manager: Robert Morton
Editor: Ruth A. Peltason
Designer: Dirk Luykx
Photo Editor: Catherine Ruello

Front cover: *The Queen's Return from the House of Lords*. 1839. Private collection

Back cover: François Xavier Vispré. *Portrait of John Farr* (before restoration). c. 1765–70.
Ashmolean Museum, Oxford

Frontispiece: Thomas Rowlandson. *The Band*. c. 1780. Pen and ink and watercolor over pencil,
9¹⁄₁₆ × 10¾″ (23 × 27.3 cm). Collection Peter Fry, Esq., London

Endpapers: John Rocque (engraved by John Pine). *A Plan of the City of London and Westminister*.
1744–46. Facsimile published by London Topographical Society 1913–18

Library of Congress Cataloging-in-Publication Data
Russell, John, 1919–
   London / John Russell.
     p.   cm.
   Includes index.
   ISBN 0–8109–2673–3 (pbk.)
   1. London (England) — Description and travel.   I. Title
DA684.25.R87   1994
942.1′2—dc20   94–1528

Contents

Acknowledgments

WHILE WRITING THIS BOOK, I was conscious throughout of the debt beyond computation that I owe to contacts first made in London during World War II and prized ever after. There was Nikolaus Pevsner, an émigré historian of architecture whose dream it was to list and comment upon every building of consequence in the whole of London. There was John Betjeman, a poet who explored the hidden life, by turns poignant and hilarious, of many a disregarded quarter of London. There was John Piper, a painter and topographical writer who taught me to see the merits of an anonymous vernacular architecture. There was John Summerson, a social and architectural historian who was a master of understated English prose.

There was William Plomer, a novelist and poet who, already in the 1930s, knew how life in Bayswater and Notting Hill Gate was lived by marginal men and marginal women. And there was P. D. Whitting, schoolmaster and historian, who taught me to see the incorporation of the Royal Society in London in 1662 as a key event in the intellectual history of Europe.

Directly or indirectly, singly or collectively, these people caused me to make a six-word entry in the Victorian ledger that I used as a notebook. "One day," it said, "do something about London."

I took forever to act upon that injunction. But as of 1974, when I left London and came to live in New York, a certain idea of London took hold of me and wouldn't let go. Never did a day pass without my reading, hearing, thinking, remembering, or looking at something that reminded me of London. And when I was asked by my longtime friends at Harry N. Abrams, Inc., to write a book about London my hand seemed to reach out and sign the contract of its own accord.

I have tried in the text of this book to give due credit to the sources that I have drawn upon from time to time. Apart from those already named, they include Bridget Cherry (Pevsner's lieutenant and successor in the Buildings of England series), Anne Saunders, Gavin Stamp, Colin Amery, Andrew Saint, Elain Harwood, and Gavin Weightman.

Thereafter, as in many another undertaking, large and small, Rosamond Bernier has been my one-person court of appeal. Every page of *London* is the better for her mastery of the illustrated book, past and present, the stringency of her line editing, her lifelong delight in London, and the stimulation of her company, there and elsewhere.

In times of puzzlement, and even more so in times of crisis, I never failed to find in Celina Fox, then of the London Museum, a veritable geyser of knowledge, discrimination, and wit. Her two major exhibitions, "Londoners" (1987) in the London Museum and "London: World City" (1992) in the Villa Hügel in Essen, had a galvanic effect upon me. So did the books that came with them. It was also thanks to Dr. Fox that in the last stages of the book I was able to draw, however briefly, on the experience and ingenuity of Juliet Brightmore as picture researcher in London.

For other kindnesses rendered to me in England, I remember especially Dr. John Hayes and Sarah Kemp at the National Portrait Gallery. Mr. Piers Gough gave me a memorable account of early days in the Docklands. For help with permissions and transparencies that I should have hated to be without, I remember the owners of *The Sharpe Family* by Zoffany, now on loan to the National Portrait Gallery, Mr. Peter Fry for Rowlandson's *The Band* that opens the book in such glorious style, and the Marquess of Zetland for my all-time favorite among London interiors.

Thanks to two dauntless automobilists, Lavinia Grimshaw and Natalia Jimenez Fawcett, I was able to explore the Docklands in some depth.

In New York, Maurice Tempelsman sent me a whole slew of invaluable books on subjects of which I would otherwise have known nothing. Peter Brown interceded for me with Sir Andrew Lloyd Webber for the right to reproduce his Canaletto of *The Old Horse Guards*. Until his death in 1987, the gravelly, well-measured utterances of Henry-Russell Hitchcock often set both the virtues and the follies of London's architecture in a cosmopolitan perspective.

Since it opened in 1977, I have regarded the Yale Center for British Art in New Haven as my second home. I owe many a happy day to its first director, Edmund Pillsbury, to his successor Duncan Robinson, to Constance Clement, its assistant director, and to Patrick Noon, its curator of prints and drawings and rare books.

About Harry N. Abrams, Inc., with whom I have been publishing off and on for nearly thirty years, I have this to say. Ours is an age when publishing houses are bought and sold like pig bellies. Names long hallowed are abolished overnight. Barely literate bosses ride herd over staff members who have given their lives to the service of books and their readers. But at Abrams, there is nothing of that.

I have been a friend of Paul Gottlieb, Abrams' President and Publisher, since 1980, and of Robert Morton, its Director of Special Projects, since 1965. With Ruth A. Peltason, Senior Editor, I have worked closely and happily since 1987 on Abrams books that are dear to me. Never did a cross word pass between us, though I have often tried their patience.

In the case of *London*, I have also been lucky in working with Catherine Ruello, who proved herself a dab hand with pictures and permissions, worldwide. Nor do I forget the Irish good nature with which Cathy Cain fielded my numberless telephone calls over a ten-year period. These were complete professionals, and I bless them, one and all.

Introduction

I N THE MATTER of the great and peculiar city of London, I have one or two qualifications. I was brought there in babyhood and lived there, on and off, for more than fifty years. I was sent to a school there, called St. Paul's, which had no equal when it came to putting a high gloss upon callow young minds and readying them for competitive examinations.

While in school, I spent all my lunch money in antiquarian bookshops on or near the Charing Cross Road. In adolescence, I spent every minute of my free time in a public library that Sir John Soane, architect and aesthete, had refashioned as his own house in 1803. I began my working life in London, as an unpaid novice in a great museum, the Tate Gallery. Later, and throughout much of World War II, I served in a great department of state, the Admiralty.

I was married in London (more than once). For twenty-seven years after leaving the Admiralty I worked for a great London newspaper, the *Sunday Times*, as had been my ambition ever since I sat on a beach in Picardy at the age of eight and watched out for the packet boat that was bringing the London Sunday papers across the English Channel.

I worked for several years as a drama critic, and for a quarter of a century as the art critic of the *Sunday Times*. My duties took me, day after day and in all seasons, into many parts of London. I lived at ten successive postal addresses, the designations of which (in no particular order) were SW10 (twice), SW3 (twice), W8, W1 (twice), NW8, NW3, and N6. These changes of address had it in common that they were all north of the river, but each one of them involved a course in readaptation. Necessarily, therefore, I came to know London rather well.

In boyhood I lived in Strawberry Hill, a Thames-side suburb best known for the sojourn nearby in the eighteenth century of Horace Walpole, the antiquarian

John Carter. *The Holbein Chamber at Strawberry Hill*. 1788. Watercolor, 8⅞ × 7⅛″ (22.5 × 18.2 cm). Courtesy of the Lewis Walpole Library, Farmington, Connecticut

John Giles Eccardt. *Horace Walpole (1717–1797), 4th Earl of Orford*. 1754. Oil on canvas, 15½ × 12½″ (39.4 × 31.8 cm). The National Portrait Gallery, London

and picture fancier who was one of the best correspondents in the English language. Needless to say, I knew nothing of Walpole at the time, and his wonderfully eccentric house was both out of bounds and much misused. But for anyone who aspired to live by the printed word and was to become interested in painting, the name of Horace Walpole can only seem, in retrospect, to have been auspicious.

For what is the lesson of Horace Walpole, if not that clever people make the best company in the world, and that it is possible to know a very great deal and yet never say a dull thing? Quite apart from that, I owe to the public gardens by the Thames in Strawberry Hill the earliest of my recollections and the idea—still valid, as I see it— of the unhurrying movement of fresh water in sunlight as a foretaste of paradise.

I also monitored the summer boating parties. Even in infancy, it seemed to me that something was lacking from them. Surely there was more to being on the water than splashing and larking? There was, of course, but it took me a very long to time to find it in its ideal form.

I did not find it in life, either, but in a painting called *The Sharpe Family* by Johann Zoffany. Sighted on the Thames near Fulham, in a boat none too large for them and their impedimenta, the Sharpe family were good looking, brainy, and versatile. They thought original thoughts, they could make music together, and they enjoyed each other's company unfailingly and without stint. If they had descendants, I never saw them on the river. But now I can slot the original group into my memories of the public gardens in Strawberry Hill, the way Humphrey Repton could slot a reimagined landscape into the view from the country house of one of his clients.

Meanwhile, the promise inherent in the name of Strawberry Hill was not fulfilled. Strawberries were hard to find, except in the shops. A hill there never was, in a landscape flat enough for the All-England croquet championships. Strawberry Hill was a backwater, somewhere between Twickenham and Richmond. But, a little way upstream, it had Eel Pie Island as the equivalent in London of the waterside resorts just outside Paris that were dear to Guy de Maupassant and Emile

Alfred Sisley. *Molesey Weir, Morning*. 1874. Oil on canvas, 19⅝ × 29½″ (50 × 75 cm). National Gallery of Scotland, Edinburgh

Among the French Impressionist painters who visited London, it was Alfred Sisley who loved the look of the river Thames as it poured through the weir at Molesey, just a few miles upstream from Strawberry Hill.

Johann Zoffany. *The Sharpe Family*. 1779–81. Oil on canvas, 45½ × 49½" (115.5 × 125.7 cm). The National Portrait Gallery, London

Zola, among storytellers, and to Claude Monet, Auguste Renoir, and Georges Seurat, among painters. Eel Pie Island has no place either in art or literature, and I was never allowed to go anywhere near it, but from what I overheard about it at the age of five or six I pictured it as the very heartland of debauch.

Even then, and even in Strawberry Hill, I became aware at the age of six or seven that ours was shaping up to be a terrible century. London has welcomed—"received" might be a better word—its share of the many millions of people to whom the twentieth century has said "Move on, no matter where!" One of the earliest of them was the former King Manoel II of Portugal, who in 1910 chose to live out his exile in Strawberry Hill.

He did not exactly have to beg for his bread, but in the England of the 1920s the loss of a European throne seemed contrary to the natural order of things. And

when echoes reached us of how he dawdled his days away, it was brought home to the back rows of the local schoolrooms that, at no matter what level, adult life in the twentieth century might not be a party of pleasure.

Other elements in my formation as a Londoner should perhaps be spelled out. In boyhood I haunted the London railway terminals, which at that time were remarkable for the beauty and variety of the steam locomotives and the distinctive colors (chocolate, royal blue, leaf green, oxblood red) that marked off one company from another. Possessed by a craving to read off, and to note down in a black book, the name of every steam locomotive of importance, I jumped for joy at the sight of an unfamiliar name picked out in shining brass.

Though rightly regarded by my classmates as too effete for contact sports, I saw the Arsenal football team in action at a time when it was the terror of the English earth. I was at Lord's Cricket Ground when Don Bradman, the greatest of Australian batsmen, put the English bowlers to rout, and I once rode a London bus for seven miles past my destination because I recognized in the old gentleman at my side the venerated figure of Jack Hobbs, Bradman's English counterpart.

I was at Wimbledon when four men in long white flannels—Jean Borotra, René Lacoste, Henri Cochet, and Jean Brugnon—set an ideal standard of elegance and sportsmanship in tennis. I watched the Hannibal biplane lift off at London's only commercial airport. (At that time, air traffic control was rudimentary and an incoming pilot had to find his way (so it was said) by the name—CROYDON—painted in big white letters on the tarmac.) I remember how silver airships felt their way like blind beggars around the London skies, and I remember the evening when the last double-decker tram slipped down out of sight into Kingsway tunnel.

Individual people are clear to me, too. I remember Winston Churchill slithering down a stone staircase to his underground war room in 1943, Bertrand Russell speaking against nuclear arms in Trafalgar Square, Evelyn Waugh, ear trumpet in hand, at the St. James's Club, Jawaharlal Nehru disdaining his toadies in India House, and T. S. Eliot in his large and lugubrious apartment in Cheyne Walk.

From prewar days in the Royal Albert Hall I remember an aged redhead called Ignace Jan Paderewski playing the piano, and a contemporary of mine called Yehudi Menuhin playing the violin in shorts. I remember Sadler's Wells Theatre on the evening on which, for the first time ever, Margot Fonteyn danced the polka in *Façade*. From the irreplaceable Queen's Hall, destroyed by bombing in World War II, I remember the first English concert performance, in 1934, of Alban Berg's opera *Wozzeck*—an occasion only fleetingly marred for me by the fact that so many of those present mistook me for a program seller.

I remember a later Sunday afternoon in Queen's Hall at which Richard Strauss on the podium did nothing whatever, in the way of waving and wagging, and yet seemed the very spirit of music. In the theater I remember Charles Laughton as Lopakhin in *The Cherry Orchard*, the young John Gielgud as Hamlet, Laurence Olivier as Romeo to Peggy Ashcroft's Juliet, and Alec Guinness as the Fool in *King Lear*. I also remember the Royal Opera House when Lotte Lehmann was on the stage and Sir Thomas Beecham was in the pit.

Through no virtue of my own, I lived at one time or another in James McNeill Whistler's house on Cheyne Walk; in the birthplace of Mrs. Gaskell, the Victorian novelist, two or three doors up the same street; in the house of John Constable, the great English landscape painter, on Charlotte Street; and in the house of Coventry Patmore, the Victorian poet and author of *An Angel in the House,* on Percy Street.

None of these installations can be classed as a personal achievement, and in every case my status, no matter how politely disguised, was that of a lodger, a house sitter or a stopgap. But in combination they gave me a heightened sense of London, just as in the 1970s it gave me a heightened sense of London to walk, day by day, past the house in Highgate in which Samuel Taylor Coleridge had lived. Who could pass that house on a clear day in early summer, when the windows are wide open, and not think of the "inexhaustible flow of undulating speech" that could once be heard, night and day, within its walls?

Thanks to this fifty years' backlog of wonderment, something of the great city was always with me, and when faced in youth with the question, "Where were you educated?" I would say with perfect truth, "On the streets of London." There is no better school of life than the streets of a great city, with the to-and-fro of people of every kind on the sidewalk and the ever suggestive march past of the buildings on either side of the road.

In that matter I stand side by side with that lifelong and fearless traveler Freya Stark, who wrote of London in 1950 that a walk on the pavements of the City of London was "one of the most romantic things in the world; the austere and unpretentious doors—the River Plate Company, or Burma Oil, or affairs in Argentine or Ecuador or Hudson's Bay—they jostle each other and lead away to strange places, and create a feeling of being all over the world at once among the messenger boys and the top hats which were then still visible in Moorgate." Companies have come and gone since then, and the doors of the latest arrivals may be neither austere nor unpretentious, but even in a City changed almost beyond belief we know what Freya Stark meant.

When it was pointed out to me that the words I had used—"on the streets of London"—were a form of professional suicide, I thought hard and long. Then as now, I felt strongly about the streets of the City of London, and about the (to me) arcane traffic that was carried on there. But I was preoccupied above all with the private life of London, and it did not occur to me that a private life could be led in the City.

The City of London is not, of course, the whole of London. It is a specific and quite a small area, a city within the city, barely more than a mile across at any point, that is given over almost entirely to banking, insurance, the practice of law, investment, imports and exports, and multifarious trading. Every morning, hundreds of thousands of people come into the City to make a living. Every evening, they get out of it as fast as they decently can, unless they are going to a play or a concert or an exhibition at that ambitious newcomer, the Barbican Centre.

It was to be a long time before I learned from John Betjeman, face to face, and from Leonard Woolf on the printed page, that the City could be a magical place to live in. In Woolf's exact words, "no one who has not lived east of Chancery Lane really knows what the essence of London is." Not until some time after World War II was there a concerted effort to get people to live in the City, and it remains to be seen how many of them will think it worthwhile.

Meanwhile, I stopped talking about the streets of London. Next time round, I said that I had been "educated in other people's houses." That, too, came from the heart. But it, too, went down very badly. Mooning about the streets was the fast track to perdition, they said. Peeking about in other people's houses was just as bad. But I did not agree. As I saw it, and as I still see it, a great city is theater. Knowing how grown-up people present themselves to one another is fundamental to education. So I went ahead. I mooned, and I peeked, and I do not regret it.

London was different then, of course. Every man wore a hat. Women dressed according to their station in life, with a degree of social calibration that has long since vanished. Accent and intonation were fundamental to advancement. People

Margot Fonteyn in *Façade*. 1935. By courtesy of the Board of Trustees of the Victoria and Albert Museum, London. Theatre Museum, London

who were not wholly and unmistakably "white" were regarded as curiosities with whom even a handshake had its hazards.

Huge areas of London were off limits. (People talk to this day of streets in the East End of London where in the 1930s no policeman dared show his face.) Elsewhere in London, there were houses that had a real upstairs, with well-dressed people of all ages ringing for service at every hour of the day, and a real downstairs, with people in mandatory uniforms ready to pound up the stairs at the first sound of the bell. There were also houses by the hundred thousand in which life was irremediably dismal.

To the life of privilege as it was led shortly before World War II, the photographer Bill Brandt will forever be our best guide. But this was a time at which, even from the street, good eyesight and sharp ears could yield a great deal. Air conditioning had never been heard of, and toward nightfall in high summer every window was flung open in hopes of a breeze.

Walking around after school, we got to know residential London, inch by inch. We found out which house had family portraits, which one had a dining room modeled after Amalienburg, near Munich, which one was done over every year by the decorators of the day, and which one was falling ever deeper into decay.

We came to covet the rounded corners of no. 29 Victoria Square. Ambling along the discreet red-bricked row houses of Lord North Street, we listened for the bells that told Members of Parliament to get up from the dinner table and cast their votes in the nearby House of Commons. At the top of Hampstead Heath, we monitored the wind-blown, white-faced houses that John Constable had loved to paint.

In Christmas week, we climbed the steep slopes of Campden Hill Square, and counted the candles that by tradition burned in every window. In those more trustful days we could walk along Downing Street with no one to stop us as we marveled at no. 10, the simple, straight-up-and-down house from which the greatest empire the world had ever seen was run.

We liked to look into the sexy little houses in Yeoman's Row, where the white-painted windowsills looked as if they would cut like heavy cream, and we headed for Bedford Gardens, week after week, at the time when one of the last pupils of Leschetizky, that legend among piano teachers, could be overheard at work on Brahms's opus 116. Walking down from Primrose Hill toward the zoo, we wondered what New Age pranks were being perpetrated in the nearby and resolutely modern apartment block by an English architect, Wells Coates.

Imagination was all, at such times, even if so-called reality sometimes fired us up. There was not a rectory, not a royal gardener's gatehouse, not a pair of rooms in the Inns of Court, nor a painter's south-facing studio in London that we did not fantasize about. Though too realistic to imagine myself as one of the great officers of state, I once or twice laid a covetous eye on the Keeper's House in the British Museum.

And then there was no. 25 Brook Street, in which George Frederick Handel had lived for thirty-five years. What had been good enough for him would be good enough for me. At other times, a disused boathouse downstream from Hammersmith seemed worth looking into. In moments of euphoria I dreamed of doing over the diminutive arsenal that stands not far from the Serpentine.

Frivolous from the cradle onward, I loved the hospitable house in Chelsea Park Gardens in which there was a room, without precedent in my experience, that had been decorated in the 1930s by the designer of the Ritz Bar in Paris. London, for us, was a school of the possible, and one from which we were in no hurry to graduate.

R. B. Kitaj. *Cecil Court WC2 (The Refugees)*. 1983–84. Oil on canvas, 72 × 72″ (182.9 × 182.9 cm). The Tate Gallery, London

In R. B. Kitaj's own words, Cecil Court, just off Charing Cross Road, is "a book alley I've prowled all my life in London." This painting is both a portrait of the alley, complete with its shop fronts and shop signs, and a compound echo of its role in Kitaj's life. In the foreground, he himself lies full-length in the Le Corbusier chair in the foreground, wearing the clothes he had lately worn at his wedding. Standing on the left, flowers in hand, is a refugee bookseller, Mr. Seligman, whose head is lifted from a painting by Tintoretto. Memories of Kitaj's own family, and of other people long known to him (in particular, refugees from the Germans), take on a strong new life in the context of what the artist calls "some of the strange syntactical strategies and mysteries and lunacies" of the Yiddish theater. The painting is, in short, an elegy both for a lost way of life and for a specific sensibility that survived in Cecil Court during and after World War II.

Lucian Freud. *Two Irishmen in W11*. 1984–85. Oil on canvas, 68 × 55¾″ (172.8 × 141.7 cm). Courtesy James Kirkman Limited, London

As a painter of the run-down area of London that is part Bayswater, part Paddington, Lucian Freud has no equal. In those huge, tumbledown houses, human entanglements of a potentially violent kind had been waiting for him to portray them.

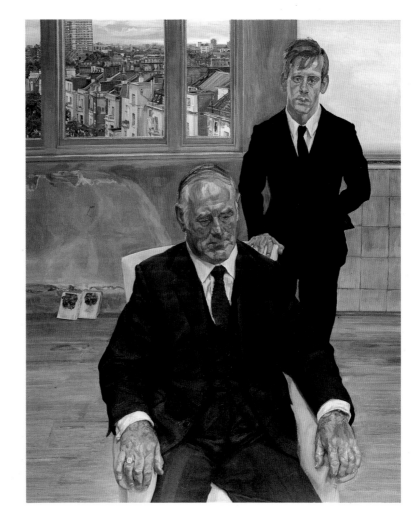

South of the river, we gazed in envy at the town palaces of Camberwell Row. Trinity Church Square in Southwark and Kennington Road in Lambeth gave us an exalted idea of areas not then rated as distinguished. We did not, in general, seek out the houses in which famous people had lived, preferring to fantasize freely.

But I remember the start of recognition with which we realized that the stout housefront before which we were standing was no. 2 The Pines, the former home of Algernon Charles Swinburne, as to which Max Beerbohm had given us so vivid an account. Nor could we hurry past the house in Howland Street, off the Tottenham Court Road, in which Paul Verlaine and Arthur Rimbaud had lived together in 1873.

Though absurdly sure of ourselves in many another context, we did not aspire to give high or low marks to this building or that. We were not there to give marks, but to find ourselves. Fantasy was our meat. Walking along Ebury Street, we remembered how fashionable it had been for men to have "rooms" there—a floor through, or two floors perhaps—with a "treasure" in attendance to prepare delicious meals and wait on table as if nothing could have been more fun. Trevor Square on a fine spring morning seemed to us to offer the very perfection of civilized life for young married couples who were not rich but would never quite know penury.

The circular icehouse in the grounds of Holland House seemed to us a suitable case for adaptation. And we long remembered the apparition in Canonbury of some of the most magnificent town houses in London—palazzi almost beyond compare, with rooms that cried out for Venetian painted furniture and Punchinello drawings by Giandomenico Tiepolo. To this day, the spirit of the costume ball inhabits those great houses.

Fantasies of this sort correspond to psychic realities. Whether or not it is true that "we are what we eat," it is certainly true that where we live is what we are, and vice versa. Every time we buy a new teapot, hang a new picture, or recover a sofa, we add a line or two to a wordless autobiography that is there for all to read. It is the role of London to prompt us, provoke us, and set our standards of comparison.

It has something to say to us, too, whenever we settle into a new address. "So this is where you will live?" it says. "And what will you do with it?" London leaves the question open. In this matter, as in so many others, it has lately settled for charm and amenity, tolerance and good nature.

A hundred years ago, and even fifty years ago, the foreign visitor had to deal with a class system that was coded and nuanced to such a degree that No stranger could master it. Strangers who did not look right, dress right, speak right, and act right were made to feel it—not directly, but by a subtle process of exclusion. They came. They saw. They admired. And then, at their approach, every shoulder was turned away.

Many were the foreign visitors who took it amiss. Even as a young man, Henry Adams was not nobody. He was the great-grandson of the second President of the United States and the grandson of the sixth President. His father would shortly be named Minister to the Court of St. James. He had the entrée to many of the great houses of London. But even at that level a stylish wariness prevailed, and Henry Adams did not feel at home in London.

This is what he wrote in 1905 of the London that he had known half a century earlier.

London was still London. A certain style dignified its grime; heavy, clumsy, arrogant, purse-proud, but not cheap; insular but large; barely tolerant of an outside world, and absolutely self-confident. . . . No strang-

Bill Brandt. *Airing the Downstairs Rooms.* © J. P. Kernot

er had rights even in the Strand. The eighteenth century held its own. History muttered down Fleet Street, like Dr. Johnson, in Adams's ear; Vanity Fair was alive on Piccadilly in yellow chariots, with coachmen in wigs, on hammer-cloths; footmen with canes, on the foot-board, and a shriveled old woman inside; half the great houses, black with London smoke, bore large funereal hatchments; everyone seemed insolent, and the most insolent structure in the world was the Royal Exchange and the Bank of England. In November 1858, London was still vast, but it was the London of the eighteenth century that an American felt and hated.

When Henry Adams heard from his fellow American the historian John Lothrop Motley that "the London dinner and the English country house were the perfection of human society," he thought that Motley had gone out of his mind. The food in London was dreadful, he said. And "the manners of English society were notorious, and the taste was worse. Without exception, every American woman rose in rebellion against English manners."

Where were these favorite houses, in which "the tone was easy, the talk was good, and the standard of scholarship was high?" Henry Adams had never been anywhere like that. Pickings had been thin, in his experience. "Sydney Smith, who had amused, was dead; so was Macaulay, who had instructed, if he did not amuse; Thackeray died at Christmas, 1863; Dickens never felt at home, and never appeared, in society; Bulwer Lytton was not sprightly; Tennyson detested strangers; Carlyle was most detested by them; Darwin never came to town. . . ."

Decidedly, Henry Adams never cracked the codes of London. "Society had no unity," he went on. "One wandered about it like a maggot in a cheese; it was not a hansom cab, to be got into, or out of, at dinner-time."

Others were more easily pleased. But the visiting foreigner of genius who had not yet been acclaimed sometimes found that his lot was rude indeed. Read the letters of Vincent van Gogh, isolated in London as a novice-evangelist. Read what Paul Verlaine, and what Stéphane Mallarmé, had to say when they were in London as poets with their reputations still to make. Listen to the cawing of the woodwind in Claude Debussy's *Gigues,* and you will hear the very distillation of central London on a Victorian Sunday afternoon, when the juices of human feeling had curdled and never a convivial face could be seen.

Fundamental to the now-vanished imperial London was not simply power, and the wealth that comes with power, but the self-confidence of which Adams wrote. London saw no reason to adapt to the rest of the world. The rest of the world was thought of as curious (certainly), fascinating (possibly), but by definition subordinate. How could that not be so, when half the world was subject to London's whims? British was best, in every department of life, and even the unprivileged Londoner felt that with a hat made in Luton, a suit cut from good Yorkshire cloth, a

François Xavier Vispré. *Portrait of John Farr.* c. 1765–70. Pastel, 17½ × 23⅞″ (44.5 × 60.5 cm). Ashmolean Museum, Oxford

Rarely has a painting told us so clearly what it is like to stretch out in first youth with a favorite book, a long free day ahead, and not a care in the world.

Canaletto. *The Old Horse Guards, London, from St. James's Park.* c. 1749. Oil on canvas, 48 × 98″ (122 × 249 cm). Collection Sir Andrew Lloyd Webber

The subject matter of *The Old Horse Guards* is part governmental, part military, uncluttered, and still almost countrified. It suited Canaletto to perfection.

pair of boots made in Leicester, a knife and a fork from Sheffield, and a bicycle made in Birmingham he could travel the world and stare the foreigners down.

London at that time had in its more well-to-do quarters a sense of perfection. Labor was cheap. Labor relations were nonexistent. It was taken for granted that a great city would look its best. Even in our own century, T. S. Eliot could write about "the damp souls of housemaids sprouting despondently at area steps," and get away with it. Even people who were starving tried to look their best, and in that distant London everyone—and I mean everyone—knew his place.

This was the tight, vigilant, hierarchical world of John Galsworthy's *Forsyte Saga,* in which eyes were narrowed and lips pursed at any uncovenanted show of feeling. St. John's Wood was exile, in those days, for the question of where one could live, and how one could live, had been settled long before and was not subject to amendments.

Standards and conventions had been set once and for all. Fifty years ago, any man who spoke on the radio after 7:30 in the evening was expected to turn up in a dinner jacket. ("The listeners like it," was the four-word answer to those who demurred.) And when Charles Morgan, the novelist, was drama critic of the *Times,* he wore white tie, tails, and a flowing cape to the theater, and to the office afterward.

Even after World War II, the foreign visitor did not always find London a treat. French visitors in the late 1940s were disconcerted to find that bread was rationed, and that if they wanted to have some beside their plate in even the best restaurants it was a good idea to bring it with them in a brown paper bag. There were winters that killed, in those first winters after the war, and hotels that had had no heat since 1939.

It was in the 1960s that all began to change for the better. London for the foreign visitor became a place where you can be warm and snug, dress as you like, do as you please, and see only smiling faces around you. The visitor was treated to a dance of seduction that would have been exceptional even thirty years earlier and quite unthinkable in the nineteenth century. It worked, moreover. Short of staying home all day, unhooking the telephone, and hiding under the sofa, it would have been difficult not to know in the 1960s and 70s that foreign visitors almost without exception were crazy about London.

The charm was instantaneous. After two or three days, and in some cases after a single hour, the foreign visitor looked up at the Great Shopkeeper in the sky and said, "Wrap it up for me, will you? I'll take it."

The London that they cherished was an old London. Defoe was still right there in London, just as something of Virginia Woolf was still right there, and something of Anthony Powell and Elizabeth Bowen and the young Graham Greene. What is deeply felt and memorably put will always endure, even if the London that it describes may seem as distant from us as Alexandria in its heyday.

Besides, what is lost can come back to us, and past and present can be made one. Walking to the theater, or to the opera house, on a fine summer's evening in London, I remember what Edward FitzGerald, the translator of *The Rubaiyat of Omar Khayyam*, wrote in June 1877: "You must be hot enough in London: yet I always remember the shady side of the long well-watered streets, and the smell of mignonette and roses in the balconies, in the days when *Medea in Corinto* with Giuditta Pasta, was on at the dear old King's Theatre, and Edmund Kean could yet totter on to the stage in *Othello* — never to be forgotten in his last decay." As much as anything in Defoe, that speaks for an unchanging London.

But there was also a new London. It was a yearlong resort town that needed visitors from abroad and would do everything in its power to keep them amused. No longer the impressive but daunting capital of a great empire, London had settled for charm and amenity, tolerance and good nature.

In temper and in tempo — and also, alas, in its skyline — London since World War II had changed more radically than at any time since the Great Fire of 1666. This is true on the most elementary level, and it is also true in ways that take some time to disentangle. You do not have to be an architectural scholar to notice that the view of London from the top of Primrose Hill has changed almost beyond recognition. Tall buildings — each one more hideous than the last — are conspicuous all the way along the horizon.

Nor do you have to be either a sociologist or a demographer to notice that in the little shops that give London so much of its character the tone is now set by shopkeepers who began their lives in Asia, in Africa, or in the Caribbean. They have an animation, a readiness to please, and a speed of wit that did not always distinguish their Anglo-Saxon predecessors.

As for the formal manners and the *phlegme britannique* that once impressed the foreign visitor, they survive — where they survive at all — as a triumph of self-parody or camp. If your appointment is with someone not yet forty who is making several hundred thousand pounds a year in a business that he founded himself, he may look as if he had never owned a necktie, let alone worn one. Tatterdemalion hordes loll the day away in hotels that would once have locked the doors against them. And if after a long night in an airplane you feel too shabby to face the man in the bank, you don't need to worry, for he is likely to look worse than you do.

But it would be quite wrong to think that the city has "let itself go," as older English people say, even if there are streets in central London where every other shop is either a money changer or a souvenir store. The changes in London are not all for the worse, by any means, and one of the good things about them is that they are tailored to the individual. London has had to think small, in a geopolitical sense, but it has chosen to think small in other ways, too, for which the visitor is likely to be grateful.

It still has its huge hotels, its once famous restaurants on the scale of General Motors, its monster dance halls, and its department stores in which almost every imaginable wish can be fulfilled. It has town houses that once employed a staff of thirty-one, and parish churches larger than many a cathedral, and a natural history museum that looms above us like the *diplodocus carnegii* that is one of its more disquieting exhibits.

But the trend today is toward the small hotel that aims at a Swiss perfection, the restaurant with fourteen tables that refuses to get any bigger, and the pretty little house that gives no trouble. The pretty little house is not only in Mayfair, either. Since World War II it has got through to the Londoner that you can live perfectly well without leasing your house from the Grosvenor Estate in Mayfair, the Cadogan Estate in Chelsea, the Eyre Estate in St. John's Wood, or the Bedford Estate in Bloomsbury. You can go where "nobody" went before. Fulham, Pimlico, Kentish Town, Islington, the huge and till lately dilapidated crescents north of the Bayswater Road—all have found a new identity.

Nor are they the only parts of London to which a new charm attaches. The whole of London south of the Thames is there for exploration. In the dockland area to the east of Tower Bridge, where it was thought to be unsafe to walk by night, there are town houses of potential splendor, with original paneling still intact. "I have bought the house in which I shall be murdered," said the English painter Francis Bacon, one of the first people to see the point of those houses. But within a year Her Majesty's Secretary of State for Foreign Affairs had bought the house next door, with the result that theirs became one of the best-protected streets in London.

The changes talked about here owe nothing to Authority. No government planned them, foresaw them, or sanctioned them. They are owed to the experimental, liberated, and sardonic temper of the individual Londoner as it has evolved since the end of World War II. No mass movement had a part in them. They were unsystematic in the extreme. Men and women in ones and twos brought them about.

Someone showed that you could have nice furniture, and someone else that you could have nice clothes, without spending a fortune. Someone showed that there could be neighborhood restaurants where you didn't have to eat swill, and someone else that your kitchen could be a place of pleasure, as much as of drudgery. It also got about that the theater need not be a place where you had to dress up, buy your date a box of chocolates, and sit through some ghastly middlebrow play.

In these and many other ways, Londoners were set free to be the people they actually were, and they have never got over it. Like every other big city in the western world, London was built for a society that no longer exists. But whereas many a big American city has deserted areas that are almost beyond redemption, Londoners have known how to adapt to the loss of industry, the loss of a thriving port, and the loss of a dominant position in world affairs.

Other people in other big cities might have grieved and grumped about those losses, but Londoners simply turned the page and "made it new." And if today's visitors fall in love with London, it is partly because individual Londoners woke up to the fact that patterns of gentility can be patterns of servitude.

To much of this I was a witness. When the time came to leave town and live several thousand miles away, I did not by any means know "everything" about London. But I knew one or two little somethings about it, and I hope to pass them on here.

Getting Acquainted

WHEN THEY WALK out of Heathrow Airport after an eight or nine hours' journey, first-time visitors to London may well decide that the two most beautiful words in the English language are "Taxi, sir?"

Those visitors are not wrong, either. If there were freshman orientation for the foreign visitor to London, it is with those two words that it would start.

The London taxi is democracy made visible. One size fits all. Duke and dustman are treated alike. As a living space—even if our lease is for no more than a few minutes—the London taxi is ample, almost luxurious. Once inside the bulky, boxy, entirely hospitable interior, passengers sit back and sit high. Long legs are at home. The diesel engine minds its own business. The meter ticks away as if it were there simply to measure our thoughts and keep them steady.

Passengers can see out, of course. But if they crave eyeball contact with their companions, the London taxi has a fabled potential for intimacy. Should they talk of this and that with the driver, they will be warmed by the sunshine of good manners. For the cab driver is the archetypal Londoner.

He knows his city from Adam and Eve Mansions, W8, to Zoar Street, SE1. He talks just enough, in an idiom as juicy as a classic steak-and-kidney pudding. It is of him, as much as of anyone else, that Osbert Sitwell in 1943 said, "How is it possible not to love Londoners, with their understanding of life, their want of envy?"

Londoners are crazy about their taxis. Not so long ago, connoisseurs would argue by the hour as to which brand of taxi had been the more seductive. Was it that paragon of the 1890s, the electric-driven Bersey cab, with its maximum speed of nine miles an hour and its maximum range of thirty miles? Or was it its rival, the French-built Sorex, which as late as 1907 was still committed to the solid tire?

James-Jacques-Joseph Tissot. *London Visitors.* c. 1874. Oil on canvas, 63 × 45″ (160 × 114.2 cm). The Toledo Museum of Art, Purchased with Funds from the Libbey Endowment. Gift of Edward Drummond Libbey

Tissot's well-dressed, well-to-do, and slightly hesitant visitors to London have never gone out of style. They are standing at the top of the National Gallery steps, with the church of St. Martin-in-the-Fields just behind them. In their ears is the wing-beat of the pigeons in Trafalgar Square. They share the scene with two self-possessed scholarship boys from Christ's Hospital. Tissot missed nothing of all this.

Joseph De Nittis. *The National Gallery and Saint Martin-in-the-Fields.* c. 1878. Oil on canvas, 27½ × 41½″ (69.9 × 105.4 cm). Collection of the Musée du Petit Palais, Paris

Still today, the visitor can stand on the north side of Trafalgar Square and have on every side something to look at and something to think about. Whitehall, the Strand, the Admiralty Arch, St. James's Park, the Houses of Parliament, and The Mall are right there at hand. So is Trafalgar Square itself, with its sky-high statue of Admiral Lord Nelson and its long history as a bastion of free speech and peaceful assembly.

Lewis Cubitt. *King's Cross Railway Station*. 1851–52. Watercolor, 20 × 50″ (71 × 127 cm). By permission of the Keeper of the National Railway Museum, York

There were those in 1905 who vaunted the well-named Rational cab, with its 10/12 horsepower two-cylinder engine, its two-speed epicyclic gearbox, and its Palmer pneumatic tires. And nostalgia clung like a burr to the 1905 Vauxhall motor hansom, with its driver lofted high above his passengers.

Then there was the Scottish-built Argyll cab, where the driver sat on top of the engine. There were contenders from Italy (Fiat) and from France (Citroen). There were cabs that ran on propane gas, and cabs with sliding doors, and cabs that had an exposed platform with a protective strap for steamer trunks.

In time, all of the above went out of service. In their place was, and is still, a uniform, long-lasting, universally acceptable cab. For close on forty years now, the London taxi has been one of the rare ingredients in everyday life that is immune to fashion. The basic model and its derivatives have been around since 1958 and nobody—but nobody—has ever said, "It's time for a change." A better mousetrap is always possible, but a better cab? And a better cab driver? Someone would have to be joking.

Somewhere on the road into London, a sense of well-being comes over most visitors. It may have been as disoriented beings that they step into their first London cab. But by the time they step out of it, half an hour or more later, they simply can't wait to be at home in London.

As to that, I have strong opinions. London is above all an indoor city. Spectacular as it may be here and there, and capable of the grandest formality on state occasions, it is not a city in which people normally while away the day out of doors. It is scaled not merely to the individual human being, but to those who feel themselves most completely realized within four walls.

And who are those people? In no particular order, and without distinction of gender, they are the merchant, the doctor, the parliamentarian, the philosopher, and the scientist. They are the lawyer, the bishop, the composer, and the chief executive officer. They are the actor and the actress on stage, the inspired teacher and the novelist.

They are the painter, the clubman, the publisher, and the banker. They are the cooks, whether private or professional, who have given a whole new spin to the potential of hospitality in London. And they are the bookseller, the tailor, the auctioneer, the editor, the connoisseur, the daylong dreamer, and—not least—the lover and the loved one.

London suits them all. In other cities that I could name, interior spaces gang up on us and conspire to break down our morale. They make us feel stressed-out,

Sir George Gilbert Scott. *Design for St. Pancras Railway Station and Midland Grand Hotel, Euston Road, London.* c. 1865. Pen with sepia pen and wash, 29⅛ × 53⅜″ (74 × 135.5 cm). The British Architectural Library, RIBA, London

talked-out, idea-less, and alienated. But London's interior spaces urge us to find ourselves, once and for all.

For young women visitors, that urging is under august patronage. I would lay money that in 1929, when Virginia Woolf argued that "a room of one's own" should be among the inalienable human pleasures, she was thinking of a room somewhere in London. With luck and determination, that room can be a part of the birthright not only of every Londoner, but of every long-term visitor to London.

In the last sixty and some years, visitors beyond counting have got the message. Somewhere in London they have found an indoor space, a potentially paradisal interior, that might have been made expressly for them. No sooner are they within those four walls than London says to them, "Be your entire selves, forthwith!" And London will not settle for less.

Rare, however, is the visitor who can, as it were, carve out his own cave from London's granite. A ready-made cave makes for a more comfortable beginning. All things considered, therefore, it is just as well that so many first-time visitors to London pull up at a well-recommended hotel. In the course of a long life I have crossed the threshold of more London hotels than I can remember the names of. But, whether from good fortune or from lack of initiative, I can count on the fingers of one hand the hotels in which I have passed the night.

My acquaintance is incomplete, therefore. I can neither praise nor Fault the service in this hotel or that. An admired colleague of mine on the London *Sunday Times* was once assigned to check into the best hotels in London after midnight, without luggage. Once inside her room, her mandate on every occasion was to call housekeeping for a nightdress and room service for a chocolate soufflé. Her report made wonderful reading, but I was never asked to rival it.

Nor can I speak for that new speciality: the confidential hotel, which gives nothing away and may not even have its name over the door. Some of the best and most personal of London's hotels are now confidential, in that sense. (I do not, however, know of a London hotel that—like one of its equivalents in New York—has refused to be listed in the telephone directory.)

Where new hotels are concerned, space is money. No matter how well they look in the design magazines, the rooms may turn out to be tiny. But the confidential hotel has nothing of the raucous, unrespectable, rough-and-tumble quality of the old-style coaching hotel. It has been thought through to the last centimeter. It is small, quiet, very comfortable, and has all the advantages of modern technology. The work force, where visible, can rarely be faulted.

Philip Charles Hardwick. *Design for the Coffee Room, Great Western Hotel, Praed Street, Paddington, London.* c. 1852. Sepia pen and watercolor, 18½ × 26¾" (46 × 68 cm). The British Architectural Library, RIBA, London

All this I know by hearsay. If it is true, it may mean that it was wrong to assume, as foreigners have often done, that the English would never know how to run a good hotel. If they came on as welcoming, in former days, the bonhomie was clearly faked. If they turned away or glazed over when asked a question, they were acting out a lifelong grudge of some kind.

Service in those days was confused with servility, and eagerness not always mated with competence. Rarest of all was the kind of impersonal brilliance, the infrastructure of 360-degree awareness and the understated psychological insight that characterize the European professional in the field. To make the clients feel at one with themselves is the mark of the true hotelier.

Whether that mark is now widespread in London is not for me to say. But in the matter of some of the older London hotels I have a certain historical perspective. When faced with a new hotel, large or small, I remember that hotel standards in London were set forever, as it then seemed, in the 1850s and 1860s. At that time, the great new railroad terminals of London were vying with one another as to which should have the most truly palatial hotel. This was in part vainglory, but flattery also entered into it.

Arriving passengers were meant to feel that a palace was theirs for the asking. In their hometown they may have been nobody. But with a shilling or two to spare, they could be Somebodies in London, even if it was only for the half an hour during which they tackled the father and mother of all cooked breakfasts.

Interiors spacious and inventive beyond all their previous experience were waiting for them. Servants in livery would jump to their every command. Above all, they would have a sense of ordered space that they might never have had before.

It was happening all over the town. The St. Pancras Hotel (1868–76) has now been turned into offices, but it is still one of the most arresting buildings in London. The Grosvenor Hotel at Victoria Station (1860) has echoes of the Second Empire in France. When the fashionable way to go from London to Paris was to take the Golden Arrow express from Victoria, the Grosvenor Hotel gave us a Gallic send-off.

Way above the bustle of the station courtyard, the Charing Cross Hotel (1863–64) conveyed a sense of privilege. The Langham Hotel, designed in 1863 and lately raised from the dead, was large enough to have a wing for gentlemen only, an ambassadors' reception room, and more than six hundred other rooms, thirty of which were private suites with their own bathrooms and separate water closets.

Anonymous. *A London Coffee House.* 1668. Watercolor, size unknown. By permission of the Trustees of the British Museum, Department of Prints and Drawings

(Nikolaus Pevsner and Bridget Cherry point out in their encyclopedic *Buildings of England* that, with its thirty-six bathrooms, the Langham was way ahead of the Charing Cross Hotel, which made do with exactly six.)

But the real winner in this contest was the pioneer—the Great Western Hotel at Paddington Station. Designed by P. C. Hardwick and built in 1851–54, it persuaded passengers lately arrived from what was later called the Cornish Riviera Express that a new life, and an expansive one, lay before them.

The spirit of the age ran in Hardwick's veins. Stuccoed figures of Peace, Plenty, Industry, and Science looked down on Praed Street from the pediment of the hotel, but they were supererogatory. Hardwick had already made the point that this was an age, and a country, in which everything was possible and nothing was going to go wrong.

Nowhere was this more evident than in his more-than-ducal Coffee Room. Given the current status of the coffeeshop, and the status in Victorian times of the coffeestall, it is nothing short of amazing that Hardwick should have been allowed to produce this glorious High Renaissance pastiche simply in order to say, in effect, "If you want a cup of coffee, just come in and ring for a servant."

His Coffee Room was the apotheosis of the High Victorian interior in London, in which space went on forever and nobody ever said, "That's enough." It was addressed to the new men of High Victorian times, who saw no reason why they should not live very well and have things made easy for them. It was also addressed to their wives, who seconded the motion. London hotels that are specifically of our own time may not look like the Great Western Hotel in its heyday, but fundamentally they have that same ambition.

Visitors who have had enough of hotels (or perhaps do not think the money well spent) have an alternative ready to hand. To be in lodgings of one kind or another in London is a classic metropolitan adventure.

At its best, the London bed-sitter can be the instrument of liberty and a bastion of independence and self-exploration. It can be a continual party of pleasure with like-minded people who also live in the house. Those people are fun to be with, but they also know when to leave one alone.

The bed-sitter can also have a very agreeable location—on the blowy heights of Highgate, for instance, or in Chelsea overlooking the Thames, or in the streets parallel to Tottenham Court Road, which have been home to artists from John Constable and Richard Wilson to Walter Sickert and Augustus John.

In conditions such as these, affectionate attentions may abound, and idiosyncratic wishes be fulfilled. Friendships made then and there can last for a lifetime. London at such times is irresistible, just as it was for Henry James when in 1869 his long search for an endurable landlady ended in the discovery in Half Moon Street, off Piccadilly, of a more than endurable landlord.

Lazarus Fox was his memorable name, and in no time at all he served the twenty-six-year-old Henry James as "butler, landlord, valet, guide, philosopher and friend." Even to take breakfast with his fellow lodgers was something to look forward to, passed as it was in the company of highly conversible young Englishmen who had time to linger over fried sole and Oxford marmalade before strolling down to their governmental duties.

Not everyone who sets up in a rented room is so lucky. Worst of all, in this context, is the fate of the visitor who knows no one in London, has not the knack of making friends and has to sit alone, evening after evening.

On that lowest point in metropolitan experience, the poet George Darley (1795–1856) is unbeatable:

At this sweet hour, all things beside
In amorous pairs to covert creep;
The swans that brush the evening tide
Homeward in snowy couples keep.

In his green den the murmuring seal
Close by his sleek companion lies;
While singly we to bedward steal
In a London lodging lit by gas,
And close in fruitless sleep our eyes.

That was quite a while ago, of course, and George Darley was distinctly one of nature's downers. But alas! A long spell in a London bed-sitting room can still be a rite of penurious passage that leaves an ineradicable scar. The house may be a place of degradation and abasement. The room can be dingy, noisy, smelly, and small. Bathroom and telephone may be way down the hall. A gas fire eight inches square may have to be fed with coins of the realm every hour on the hour. Dehumanizing rules may be in force. Even attempts at a curfew cannot be excluded.

Worse still, fellow lodgers may prove at best incompatible and, at worst, intrusive and manipulative. Harassment of one kind or another may occur. Like every other big city, London has its quota of men and women who are best avoided.

Even a house with hallowed associations can turn out badly for the lodger. A case that, even today, has its cautionary side is that of Mary Anne Evans, later to be known as George Eliot. In January 1851 she arrived in London and lodged with Mr. and Mrs. John Chapman at no. 142 Strand. For a woman of thirty-two who wanted to earn her living by writing, it seemed an ideal arrangement.

John Chapman was young, dynamic, and vastly good looking. A publisher and bookseller, he was shortly to own and edit the *Westminster Review*. Previous lodgers at no. 142 included Ralph Waldo Emerson, who had stayed for nearly three months and regarded Chapman as "a phoenix of a publisher, and a man of integrity." Chapman's was a huge house, with his offices at street level and no lack of rooms for lodgers.

Unknown to Miss Evans at the time of her arrival was the fact that Chapman did not only have Mrs. Chapman at his beck and call in the house. He also had his mistress, Elisabeth Tilley, whose menstrual periods were carefully noted down in his diary. Nor was he averse either to playing one off against the other, or to recruiting Miss Evans as a possible new partner in his pleasures.

Anguished notes to him from one or another of the parties concerned were leaked to the others. Of the future George Eliot he wrote in his diary that "I feel her to be a living torment to the soul." It cannot surprise us, therefore, that both Mrs. Chapman and Miss Tilley were disquieted by the arrival of Miss Evans.

Initially she was known, where known at all, as the anonymous translator of David Friedrich Strauss's *Life of Jesus*. But Miss Evans soon showed herself to be both a brilliant book reviewer and a born strategist in all matters pertaining to the *Westminster Review*. Before long, she was one of its assistant editors. At the Friday evening receptions that John Chapman gave at no. 142, she met the coming men of Victorian England, together with many of the men who had already arrived.

Though anything but a conventional beauty, she had a gentle, sweet-spoken presence and an intelligence that was the equal of any man's. (The philosopher Herbert Spencer considered her "the most admirable woman, mentally, that I have ever met." He sought her company continually, walked with her by the hour on the riverside terrace of Somerset House, but was careful never to declare himself.)

Chapman in reality was not so much a satyr as a trousered coquette who finally thought of nothing but his own face in the mirror. After close on two years as an intermittent lodger at no. 142 Strand Miss Evans was so depressed that, as she wrote to a friend, she imagined that the "four walls are contracting and going to crush one." In October 1853 she at last left the house.

Was this the very archetype of the bad bed-sitter? Should we snort when we read that in 1852 Mrs. Chapman had advertised the house as offering "the Advantages of an Hotel with the Quiet and Economy of a Private Residence"?

Snort we may. But it remains true that in more ways than one George Eliot's life was shaped for the better by her sojourn at no. 142 Strand. Her biographer, Gordon S. Haight, is right to say that Chapman maintained "in the heart of mid-Victorian London a household no novelist would have dared to describe." But it was in that same house that George Eliot met the intellectual elite of London on easy terms and found herself to be their equal. It was there that she learned to write readily and with conspicuous intellectual command on subjects that ranged from the latest thing in evangelism to "Silly Novels by Lady Novelists."

Above all, it was through Chapman that she met and came to love G. H. Lewes, the many-sided man of letters with whom, in March 1855, she formed a union that was to last twenty-five years.

Even in the 1990s, women visitors to London may have to cope with the John Chapmans of our day. (The Mrs. Chapmans may also be on the prowl.) But if they feel that a Chapman-style household would be too taxing, they can easily arrange to be—let us say—not so much in the center of things.

A satisfactory bed-sitting room need not be fancy, either. The room portrayed by Harold Gilman just before 1914 in his *Tea in the Bedsitter* may look like nothing much. But we should need not be sorry for those two young women. One of them could even be Katherine Mansfield, newly arrived in London and shaping up to add new luster to the English short story.

Once the visitor is settled, the idea of casing the shops is hard to resist. Buying

is best, but looking around runs it a close second. As with the hotel and the lodging house, the London shop has a long history, and one that is still relevant today.

In Ackermann's *Repository of the Arts,* published in 1809–28, many shops are shown, and some of them are large. But they are large in a reticent, almost scholarly way. Lackington's Temple of the Muses in Finsbury Square was the biggest bookstore in town, for instance. But it was large for one reason only — because nothing smaller would do. Marketing played no role.

In 1809 there was in Catherine Street, off the Strand, an innovative furniture store called Morgan & Sanders. It featured such novelties as the Metamorphic Library Chair and Merlin's Mechanical Chair. It, too, was light and large and roomy, but hustling was unknown.

After close on two hundred years, there are still big shops in London — and little ones, too — that have that same civilized and unintrusive attitude to the potential customer. There are others, admittedly, in which the sales staff have been trained to try everything short of a mouth-to-mouth resuscitation to shift the merchandise. But in the classic London stores old-style ways still prevail. Even in a thunderstorm, the staff of Swaine, Adeney & Brigg do not stand at the door in hopes of selling out of their incomparable umbrellas.

When that great scholar the late James Byam Shaw was in charge of prints and drawings at P. and D. Colnaghi's in New Bond Street, he treated even the novice as an equal. "Just come in any time and go through the boxes," he would say. "Treat the place as a club." At Sotheby & Co., up the road, the late Peter Wilson was the acknowledged architect of the firm's postwar success. But if he came ambling through the sale rooms, it was with the air of an undergraduate who has decided to

Harold Gilman. *Tea in the Bedsitter.* 1916. Oil on canvas, 28 × 36⅜″ (71 × 92.5 cm). Huddersfield Art Gallery, Kirklees Metropolitan Council, Huddersfield cut a lecture. And if he were on the rostrum when a price at auction were to break all records and the room buzzed with applause, he would simply say, "Well now, ladies and gentlemen, we really must get on with the sale."

At Heywood Hill's, the bookshop in Curzon Street, Nancy Mitford was for a time during World War II a salesperson whose comments on the customers have passed into legend. Unchanged in fifty years, the atmosphere of the shop is that of an English country house in which covetable books have spilled out all over (not least on the floor).

In shops such as these, the old unhurrying one-on-one ways still flourish. But by the 1850s an alternative approach was making headway. It had become the architect's job to waylay the passerby. "Do drop in!" the shop was meant to say. "You won't be sorry."

And they weren't sorry, either. The new-style shops were wonderland, in

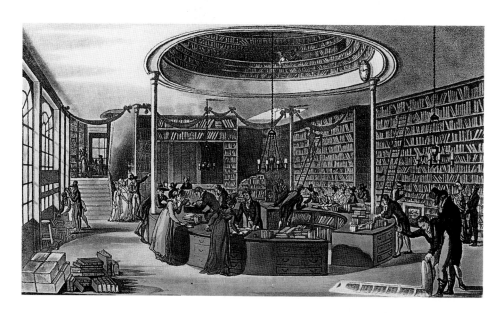

Lackington's Temple of the Muses, Finsbury Square. Aquatint from Rudolph Ackermann's *Repository of Arts*, 1809. The Museum of London

Robert Lewis Roumieu. *Design for the Interior of Mr. Breidenbach's Shop, 157 New Bond Street, London.* 1853. Pen and watercolor, 20½ × 27" (52 × 68.5 cm). The British Architectural Library, RIBA, London

which nothing was quite what it seemed but everything held out the promise of a richer, happier, more voluptuous existence.

A master deceiver, in that context, was an architect called Robert Louis Roumieu (1814–1877). He was an early example of the architect as couturier—a man who could dress a given space the way Paul Poiret or Jacques Doucet could dress a pretty woman in Paris in the first quarter of our century.

Roumieu in every context was a wild card. Among architectural historians he ranks very low. "Utterly undisciplined and crazy," said Pevsner. At the mention of Roumieu, Henry-Russell Hitchcock blew his stack. But Roumieu redefined the London shop, just as surely as Hardwick redefined the London hotel.

One of his great successes was an exact contemporary of Hardwick's Great Western Hotel. At no. 157 New Bond Street there was a perfumier and distiller of eau de cologne called Breidenbach. A big man in his field, he was an appointed purveyor to Queen Victoria. Roumieu made sure that people who walked into the shop would recognize it as a special place, and their visit as a special occasion.

Trade was transacted, but there was also time and room for the sweeteners of London life. Fresh flowers were in place every day above a circular settee. Mirrors doubled and quadrupled the apparent space. A stately lamp hung from the ornamented ceiling. Carpets were deep and spotless. Round-topped arches soared high above the customers' heads. Height, width, and distance—all were counterfeited. Thanks to Roumieu, Breidenbach's was a world of make-believe in which everyone played a part.

Roumieu, like Hardwick, got the current priorities exactly right. Who has improved on the Great Western Hotel, in terms of spatial amenity? Nobody. Who has confected a more fanciful, dream-laden shop than Roumieu? Nobody.

But the shops now most in vogue are in full reaction against Roumieu. His idea of seduction, though often still practiced, now looks almost absurdly genteel. A demonic alliance now binds the avant-garde architect to the shopkeeper who presses gently on the nerve of the times. They do not look backward, as Roumieu did, for ways to tease the customer. They look sometimes sideways, and sometimes forward. In this regard, Norman Foster Associates did the work of pioneers in 1978 with a store called Joseph in Sloane Street. With its clip-on lighting, its huge undressed windows onto the street, its bolted frames, its immediately helpful but free and easy staff, and its refusal to encourage any distraction whatever from the business of selling clothes, Joseph marked the end of an era.

Everything there is up front and out front, within touching distance. Seduction is immediate and wordless, with none of the leisurely courtship that was mandatory in the big stores that have by now gone out of business. You come, you look, and you buy. That's the way it is. In hotel and store alike, the upmarket formula is now the same: a gold-plated playpen with big money somewhere at the exit.

Not every shop in London comes gold-plated, however. Within a less intimidating price range, a tenacious survivor dear to me is called the High Street. All over London, there are High Streets. Time was when they existed primarily for their immediate neighbors. People shopped where they lived, as a matter of course. Only on special occasions—during the January sales in the mammoth department stores, for instance—did they shop anywhere else. Not to use the High Street shops was regarded by the neighbors rather as a failing of character than a sign of superior judgment.

The High Street had a bank, a butcher, a baker, a grocer, a haberdasher, a dairy, a hardware store, a home furnishing store, a post office, a shoe shop, a tea shop, a milliner, a laundry-cum-dry cleaner, a jobbing tailor, and a tobacconist who

THE STRAND FROM THE CORNER OF VILLIERS ST

George Scharf. *The Strand from the Corner of Villiers Street.* 1824. Watercolor, 8⅝ × 14⅝″ (21.8 × 37.2 cm). By permission of the Trustees of the British Museum, London

doubled as a candy store and had newspapers on the side. Many of these were family-owned and family-run and had been there forever. "Their ways are our ways," the locals said to one another.

Common to almost every High Street until the 1930s were two great rivals in the food line. One was the Home & Colonial. The other was the Co-Op. To shop at the Home & Colonial was the act of a patriot. For what was the Home & Colonial, if not a living reassurance that the British Empire was still very much alive and a source of plenty beyond the reach of lesser nations? Over the legs of New Zealand lamb, the Kenya coffee beans, the spices and the pineapples from India, and the coconuts from the Caribbean, the Union Jack had flown.

The Co-Op, by contrast, struck at the very heart of private ownership and private profit. In the world of the small shopkeeper, to cross the threshold of the Co-Op in the 1920s was tantamount to raising the Red Flag. In reality, the pork pies on sale in the Home & Colonial were much like the pork pies on sale in the Co-Op. They may even have come from the same factory. But that was not the point. "It's the principle of the thing," people would say as they marched along with noses high in the air.

After World War II, that rivalry disappeared. So did the British colonies, one by one. Even the word *colonial* was sometimes a deterrent. Meanwhile, to the consumer society, the high moral tone of the Co-Op was ridiculous. As for the one-family shops, they were swamped by the paperwork, by the difficulty of maneuvering on a small scale in markets that had become both exacting and volatile, and by the competition of chain stores that bought in bulk, kept their prices way down, and offered a far wider range of attractions.

So the intimacy of the High Street was lost. So was the continuity of human contact. The video stores, the money changers, the launderettes, the packaged travel agents, and the realtors who did so well in the 1980s—all have eased out the little shops in which a penny was routinely subdivided into four farthings and even a single-figure purchase was treated as cause for celebration.

Just occasionally there is a relatively out-of-the-way shop that maintains intact the tradition of the High Street as the equal, in its field, of any shop in the center of London. One of these is W. Martyn's in Muswell Hill. Four generations of Martyns have kept this beautiful store in pristine condition. Unaltered since it was first opened in 1897, it still has great sacks of coffee beans on the floor, each clearly marked with its country of origin.

It also has its noble and numbered jars of China tea, its jams and preserves by the score, its cookies from all over, its chutneys, its mustards and its sauces, its crystallized fruits, and its high-rise heapings of canned fruit and rare vegetables and nuts. It shows, in short, what can still be done in a High Street by love and care and a sense of dignity.

Shopping and looking at shops make hungry work. Besides, and no matter how pleased we may be with our hotel, or with our lodgings, we may prefer to go out to eat. Restaurants are theater, after all, and many are the Londoners who realize themselves completely in the favorite restaurants of the day. In those restaurants, the companionable tumult has hardly varied in essence since it was portrayed close on three hundred years ago in a famous watercolor, now in the British Museum. It is in restaurants that Londoners now take on a kind of generic bounce that foreign visitors do not always expect of them.

In some restaurants, the bounce is in-built. The champagne-bar table at Corney & Barrow's in Moorgate, in the City of London, was by its very nature convivial. It was as if tailored by a master cutter to the euphoria of money management in the 1980s, and even in leaner times there were many who were sad to see it go in 1992.

But there is still plenty of bounce, even in restaurants where a glass of brackish "house white" is more often seen than a glass of champagne. The near-universality of that bounce is something new. Many thousands of Londoners now eat out all the time, as a matter of course, who before World War II would have eaten out perhaps once or twice a year. But the good restaurant today does double duty.

It is a place to eat, self-evidently. But it is also an arena stage in which every customer is a potential performer. This does not apply only to the restaurants that get reviewed in the magazines. It applies to every place in which people flock to eat.

It was true even of the classic *Eating House* that was marvelously portrayed by Harold Gilman in 1914. This was not a place where anyone went to show off, but it was not a place where anyone was ever put down, either. High wooden partitions stood for privacy. An unvarying menu stood for habits formed long ago and not yet ready for adjustment. If challenged, waiter or waitress could have a well-turned riposte ready to hand, but otherwise went about their business with hardly a word spoken. Run-down relationships died a natural death between those wooden walls, and new ones were negotiated. This, too, was London, and it has not yet gone away.

At the other extreme was the handful of restaurants that were universally and quite rightly ranked as "amusing." Up till the outbreak of World War II there was, for instance, a conversational exchange that could be heard over the telephone, day after day, in stylish houses all over central London. "Supper at the Savoy?" someone would say, and someone else would say that nothing could be nicer. There would be an early dinner at home, an 8:30 curtain at the theater, and supper at the Savoy.

Among those who thought themselves more adventurous, there was talk of Madame Prunier and Monsieur Boulestin, both of whom had nurtured restaurants of the first order, the one in St. James's Street and the other in Covent Garden. There was (and happily there still is) the Etoile in Charlotte Street. There was the Ivy — much in favor with theater people, and now more than reinstated in that regard — and there was the Café Royal, on Regent Street and just a few doors from Piccadilly Circus. The grill room in the Café Royal dates from around 1860 and is still the prettiest and most voluptuous restaurant interior in London.

In the 1930s, Londoners kept to long-standing patterns of what, and what not, to eat. Oysters were not yet a luxury, for instance, and there was known to be a great private house in which the staff had stipulated that oysters were not to be served more than twice a week in the servants' hall. That finest of all fish, the Dover sole, was still affordable. Beef and lamb, though much massacred in the kitchen, could be of superb quality. The great international tradition of the Jewish delicatessen was still intact. As for the London fish and chip shop, once much in demand among visiting Parisians, it had some of the best cheap food in Europe. (Though not in favor with strict dietarians, and much eroded since World War II by the pizza parlor and the creperie, the London fish and chip shop at its best still has its devotees standing in line.)

Other forms of food indigenous to London have survived, rare as is the foreign visitor who forms a taste for them. If you are interested to sample a classic London menu that specializes in jellied eels, meat pies, and mashed potatoes served with a green sauce that is high on parsley, it will be worth your while to take a taxi to F. Cooke & Sons on Kingsland High Street in Dalston, E8.

Not only is the food indisputably authentic — and so it should be, given that the Cookes are said to have two tons of live eels on the premises at any given time — but the eating room has an austere and delicate elegance (dated around 1910). With its touches of stained glass, its unemphatic and linear decoration, its marble-topped wooden tables and its high-backed wooden benches, it could go straight into any serious museum of the decorative arts.

Soho for much of this century had no rival in London as an enclave of good or nearly good restaurants that maintained a certain style and did not overcharge. Almost without exception, those restaurants were owned and run by foreigners — Frenchmen, Italians, Swiss, Hungarians, Spaniards, Poles, Chinese, Turks, and Greeks. When he called one of his novels *Casanova's Chinese Restaurant*, Anthony Powell caught exactly the flavor of those multicultured streets at a time when the scheduled aircraft and the package tour had never been heard of and an evening in Soho was almost as good as an evening abroad.

This amiable cosmopolis can still be found in Soho. But in recent years the restaurant industry has fanned out to north, south, west, and east. Anyone who rides on the top of a bus through almost any part of London will soon see that the roster of London restaurateurs now includes not only those listed above but Indians, Pakistanis, Japanese, Moroccans, Caribbean islanders, Portuguese, Austrians, Swiss, Koreans, Vietnamese, and North Americans.

It took a long time to bring this about. Not so long ago, there were huge areas of London in which eating out was a furtive and rather dingy activity. Sadness was built into it. Hopes were best kept low, and the word *gastronomy* lay in the dictionary, forgotten. It was inconceivable that there would one day be a restaurant cuisine designated in admiration as "modern British."

Progress was slow. It was a firm called J. Lyons & Co. that first brought about in the 1920s an upward shift in mass-market comfort and amenity. In the Lyons

Harold Gilman. *An Eating House.* c. 1914. Oil on canvas, 22½ × 29½″ (57.2 × 74.9 cm). Sheffield City Art Gallery

Opposite:
Sir William Orpen. *The Café Royal.* 1912. Oil on canvas, 54⅛ × 53⅛″ (137.5 × 135 cm). Musée d'Orsay, Paris

The Café Royal was until World War I the preferred habitat of an upper Bohemia in which writers and painters and amateurs of the arts liked to pass an unhurried hour or two in search of the mot juste—or, better still, a promising flirtation.

Thomas Sandby. *The Piazza, Covent Garden.* c. 1760. Watercolor with pen and ink, 20⅛ × 26⅝″ (51 × 67.5 cm). By permission of the Trustees of the British Museum, London

Though much mutilated over the years, the Covent Garden Piazza (first promoted in 1630) was a model of high-style architectural planning, with its arcaded blocks of noble houses and its church of St. Paul by Inigo Jones. Plainness here can touch perfection.

Corner House, here and there in central London, a live orchestra played in the evening, the cigarette-girl did a roaring trade all through the meal, and there were fourteen different kinds of ice cream sundae on the dessert menu.

Meanwhile, the art of gastronomy was practiced above all in a small number of private houses. The very notion of the "foodie"—the person who eats out habitually—had never been formulated. The magazine of the Wine and Food Society, founded by André L. Simon, was very agreeable to read, but it was not in business to tout this restaurant or that. The memorable meals described therein took place in someone's house, for four or six guests, each one of whom were named.

All is now changed. In recent years the potential of eating out in London has been transformed in ways that could not have been predicted. In the immediate postwar period, people who could at last get out of England came back from Europe with a craving for surprise and delight at the table.

Before long, they had plenty to read. Elizabeth David did for the 1950s what Mrs. Beeton's *Household Management* had done for the 1860s. Newspapers and magazines carried regular columns about food and wine and where to find them at their best. English chefs began to have the status of movie stars. Not to have been to the new restaurants was to be left out of the conversation.

Last, and by no means least influential, was the arrival in London of ethnic groups who wanted to eat the way they had eaten at home. Crowded together into this or that neighborhood—Brixton, Kilburn, Spitalfields, West Ealing—those groups often felt themselves lost, unwelcome, and exploited. (They weren't always wrong, by the way.) What better consolation than to be able to eat their own food in their own company?

Long-time Londoners got around to the fact that the food in question could be both palatable and cheap. When the talk turned to eating out, amateurs of good and unfamiliar food began to swap stories of memorable meals eaten in Dalston, Sydenham, Wandsworth, New Cross, and Muswell Hill. Words like *ocakbasi* (Turkish), *nam prik* (Thai), and *dhansak* (Indian) came out of the glossary and into everyday use.

It was a transformation that operated at every level. I have before me, as I write, a publication that lists "over 1,500 of London's best restaurants, cafes and bars" and makes a pitch for just about all of them.

It is, of course, possible to be disappointed. In London, as in Tallinn or Singapore, Ahmedabad or Port-au-Prince, back-street food can have its hazards. Guidebooks and newsletters can go way over the top in their recommendations. The long-running restaurant, like the long-running play, can become a caricature of itself. But, all this notwithstanding, eating out in London today is at every level more innovative than at any previous time. As for the restaurant itself, it is a department of the Great Indoors, and one that has a whole new status in London life.

However good a dinner may be, visitors often feel that it leaves the evening incomplete. Forty and some years ago I was deputed to take Mr. and Mrs. James Thurber back to their hotel after as good a dinner as London could provide. Though stone blind and not in rampageous health, the great draftsman-cum-storyteller clearly did not regard the evening as over. "Where's the place?" he said, more than once. "Where is it—the place where people go? There's always a place."

A catastrophe! Never had anyone put so much trust in my adequacy as a guide to London. As a nighthawk, I had no credentials then and have even fewer today. I have a horror of gambling. I can't dance. I have never set foot in a nightclub. I never

Thomas Rowlandson. *A Gaming Table at Devonshire House.* 1791. Pen and watercolor on paper, 12⅛ × 17⅛″ (30.8 × 43.5 cm). The Metropolitan Museum of Art, New York. Harris Brisbane Dick Fund, 1941

drink after dinner. "But there must be a place," said Mr. Thurber, undeterred. "Ask the driver to take us to the place!"

He was, of course, quite right. There had always been, and there doubtless is still, "a place" in which informed visitors to London finish the evening. Every good concierge knows where they are. From a safe distance, I even rather enjoy thinking about them.

I cherish, for instance, the memory of the gambling table at Devonshire House as it was immortalized just two hundred years ago by Thomas Rowlandson. Glorious alike in looks, in bearing, and in costume, two beautiful women are on heat for gain. The stakes are way up in the thousands. One of the women— reputedly Georgiana, Duchess of Devonshire—raises the dice high above her head, in hopes of a decisive throw, and directs at her rival a terrible, money-crazed glare.

This was Devonshire House in 1791. There are doubtless gaming rooms in central London today at which stakes are routinely just as high, but they are under professional management. It is fundamental to the charm (and to the sense of terror) that what Rowlandson recorded was a private, not to say a confidential, encounter. Fire and flame raced back and forth across the round table. As the great ladies battled on, giving no quarter, every man present was as if stunned and castrated.

Gambling is not the only context in which enthusiasts for the inner life of London sometimes feel, as Mr. Thurber felt on that evening long ago, that they are missing out on something. If they want to gamble, every taxi driver can tell them where to go. But there are those would rather hear some good talk. "Where are the salons?" they ask.

A difficult question. The salon, like the calling card, has largely gone out of London life. There are people who for business reasons give big parties that get into the papers. There is a diplomatic corps that gives big parties as a matter of professional duty. There are learned societies that from time to time give what is still called a "conversazione," at which men and women of high professional standing murmur to one another in small groups. None of these quite count as salons.

And then there are Londoners who like one another's company so much that they cannot get enough of it. In the heyday of the Bloomsbury group, laughter ran round Gordon Square like quicksilver and nobody was ever dull. But this was in its way a secret society, rather than a salon, and never more so than when its core members met of an evening and read aloud from memoirs that were very much for their ears only.

And, then again, there are houses in London to which ambitious people go in search of advancement. If they want to get on in politics, in banking, in the law, in the theater, in newspapers or television, on the stock exchange, in the museum world, in the literary world, and in academia, there are houses that they would die to go to. Yet these houses are not salons. They are way stations on the road to success. They come and go, moreover, whereas the true salon is about continuity. Once launched, it will go on until a new generation decides to live in another way.

To have a salon, you need a nice house, but not necessarily one that is either big or grand. You need a little money, and you need a hostess who can get the best out of everyone and knows how to listen as well as to lead. (In a true salon, even the bears get to dance). In a salon, a sense of leisure is all important. Ideas must run their natural length. Busy people must be relieved of their busyness. Slow-burning guests must be brought to the point of combustion. Friendship must be coaxed along. If love strikes, it should not singe the air, but be savored with discretion, eye-to-eye. There are rules in every true salon, and it is assumed that if visitors do not know them they would not be there in the first place.

Other vital components must be mentioned. In every true salon there is on hand a man friend of the house whose even-tempered and ever-dependable presence brings ease and comfort. He never shows off, never interrupts, never upstages the timid. But he is always and consummately there, and when something goes wrong he gets the conversation back on the rails without seeming to do anything at all.

It is also desirable to have a faithful, long-running servant who knows all the secrets but would never dream of betraying them. Such people are now rare? Yes, but so are the employers who know how to treat them.

A salon that fulfilled all the stipulations listed above was maintained in London, at Holland House from 1797 till 1840. If I shall linger over it, it is because it established certain modalities that still flourish in London. The Holland House era has long vanished, like Holland House itself, but here and there in London there are houses where life goes on in something like the same way.

When Henry, the 3rd Lord Holland, married a divorced woman in 1797, it was widely taken for granted that a lifetime of social ostracism lay before her. But they were young (he was twenty-four, and she twenty-six) and Elizabeth, Lady Holland, was not put off even by the fact that some of those who went gladly to see her at Holland House were embarrassed to find themselves in the same box with her at the circus.

Important things were in the Hollands' favor. Lord Holland was both the nephew and protégé of Charles James Fox, one of the great Englishmen of all time. He was clever, studious, good-natured, high-principled, and not at all puffed up. His wife was directly descended from the owner of the *Mayflower,* and had inherited a large fortune based on property and the slave trade in Jamaica and Barbados.

She had shown herself able to form the most amusing salon in Florence when she and Lord Holland were living there together but not yet married. Once in London, as a strikingly beautiful young woman, still in her middle twenties and newly embarked on an ideally happy second marriage, she lost no time.

This is how her biographer, Sonia Keppel, summed it up.

Charles Robert Leslie. *Lord and Lady Holland, Dr. Allen and William Doggett in the Library at Holland House*. 1839. Oil on canvas, 22¾ × 29″ (57.8 × 73.7 cm). Private collection

The ingredients of her salon in London were the same as they had been in Florence, but used with a superior sense of application, sugaring the opinions of some guests, peppering others. Above all, on a basis of tolerance, allowing all shades of opinion to be expressed. Beside her, her husband contributed his inexhaustible good humour, charming all comers with his wit and erudition. Such a combination was irresistible.

The amenity of the salon was further enhanced in 1802 by the arrival in Holland House of Dr. John Allen as resident physician and librarian. Dr. Allen was not an upper servant, but a learned and companionable man who became indispensable to both the Hollands and remained with them until he died in the house, of dropsy, in 1843.

The salon thus constituted lasted for forty years. Unlike other salons, which remain tied to one particular generation, it had prodigious powers of self-renewal. The Hollands did not think of Europe as alien territory, but as a source of vitality and potential enlightenment on which they were always happy to draw.

The dinner lists so meticulously kept by Dr. Allen make it clear that people went to Holland House because it had the best conversation in London. An

American traveler, George Ticknor, said early on that in Holland House he had encountered "a literary society not to be equalled in Europe." Charles Greville the diarist had heard a lot of good talk in his time, but he described Holland House as the epitome of all that was most covetable. As for Thomas Creevey, a diarist of the second or third rank, he was appalled by his own inadequacy at Holland House and felt himself (quite rightly) "a listener on a lower plane."

Lady Holland also had some of the best food in London, with a French chef and a French pâtissier. From her landowning guests, she had continual supplies of Irish salmon, live eels, turtles, and game birds. And if her diplomat friends sent her half a sheep from the Ardennes, some wild boar ham from Denmark, and a consignment of truffles from Périgord, she made the best use of them.

There were drawbacks, undoubtedly, to an evening in Holland House. As she grew older, Lady Holland saw herself almost as royalty. When Thomas Babington Macaulay first met her, in 1831, she struck him as "a large bold-looking woman, with the remains of a fine person and the air of Queen Elizabeth."

A day or two later, the young Macaulay came to dinner at Holland House for the first time. Promptly at seven o'clock his glass coach came bowling along the avenue of elm trees. Shown into the library, he admired the "little cabinets for study, warmly and snugly fitted out," that branched out of the library. Of the books he said that they "contained almost everything that one has ever wished to read."

Macaulay stood out even among the great talkers that Lady Holland collected. Yet when he was in full flood she could be rough with him. "We have had enough of this, Macaulay. Give us something else," she was heard to say.

But when Macaulay came back in 1839 after his years in India, with a solid reputation and the concept of his great *History of England* firmly present in his mind, it was to Lady Holland that he confided his ambition.

But sometimes she really went too far. Eminent men who are no longer quite young do not like to be shifted around in the middle of dinner. Lord Palmerston, though a master of self-control in public life, walked out of Holland House after being asked to change his place at table once too often.

As for Count d'Orsay, that most worldly of men was delighted to pick up his hostess's napkin when she dropped it under the table. But after he had been asked to retrieve in rapid succession a fan, a fork, a spoon, and a wineglass, he asked the waiter if the rest of his dinner could be served to him on the floor. "It would be so much more convenient for Milady," he said.

And if a cabinet minister was rash enough to have confidential papers brought to him in Holland House for immediate perusal, she was not above saying, "Oh, what's that one about? Do let me see!"

But, all this notwithstanding, her old friends kept coming back, sometimes in tears of joy at the reunion. When Talleyrand was French Ambassador in London — and, by any criterion, the most fascinating man in Europe — he enjoyed himself hugely at Holland House. "Talleyrand generally comes at ten or eleven o'clock and stays as long as they will let him," Charles Greville said in his diary, and we cannot imagine them pushing him out.

To the end of their days, moreover, the Hollands were fascinated by the coming young people, and the coming young people (not least, the just-enthroned Queen Victoria) were fascinated by them. People loved Lord Holland, without exception, and although Lady Holland at times treated them abominably they almost all came back for more, as if knowing that they would never again know someone so spontaneous, so discerning, so deeply affectionate, and yet on occasion so monstrously rude.

In 1839, the fortieth year of the salon, C. R. Leslie painted Lord and Lady Holland, Dr. Allen, and William Doggett (a page long in favor and lately promoted) in the long library that was, with the dining room, the natural focus of the house.

To a remarkable degree Leslie captured both the look and the feel of the house and the relationships between the four people portrayed. As Macaulay had at once noticed, the library was a real library, not a book-lined sham. Portraits (family, mostly) peered down in long rows above the topmost shelves. Omnipresent beneath them were the well-worn reds and the soft, weathered browns, touched here and there with gold, of the hundreds of books. Other subdued reds, not too recently renewed, were the mark both of the curtains and of the leather upholstery of Lady Holland's favorite armchair.

A large portrait in a gilt frame stood on the floor, at an angle to the red-and-white striped silks of a little sofa. Ormolu gleamed on a French clock and a French writing table, and through the big window that looked out onto the park the London light was on its best behavior.

When C. R. Leslie was at his easel no guests were on hand, and none of the four people portrayed was doing much of anything. There might never have been a salon in Holland House. Lord Holland at sixty-six looked exactly what he was—an old gentleman, grown plump, who had only a year to live. Himself pushing seventy, Dr. Allen was also not getting any younger but he was, as ever, both an impeccable lieutenant and a lifelong student, ever with a book in his hand.

Perhaps it was with a little help from the painter that Lady Holland looked twenty years younger than her age. (She held a very pretty fan toward the light, to keep her still flawless complexion in the shade.) The faithful Doggett stood by and waited for his instructions.

What Leslie recorded for posterity was a group of people who for half a lifetime had been completely content with one another. The Hollands had enjoyed having their friends around—there were often dinners for sixteen or eighteen people, six nights a week, with other guests coming in afterward—but Leslie caught them on a quiet morning.

We might even feel that, exceptionally, they didn't need to talk. Companionship was all. Leslie made the most of his opportunities, and it is thanks to him that we see, intact and forever vivid, a key moment in the sociabilities of London.

Holland House itself was destroyed by enemy action during World War II. Not a stone of it now remains. Should we grieve? Would the Hollands' salon be more vivid to us if we could pay to get into the house and walk round it on a plastic drugget, gaping at roped-off books and a table laid for sixteen people who would never sit down for dinner?

I doubt it. A salon is certainly the better for handsome surroundings and good food and good service. But it depends primarily on the wit and the initiative of host and hostess, on winged words heard and overheard, and on eye contacts that will be remembered forever but cannot be replicated. Imagination is all, in this context, just as companionship was all when C. R. Leslie went to work with his brushes.

And is the London salon extinct? Absolutely not. No sooner are favorite front doors shut for the last time than others open up elsewhere. If the private room in one restaurant drops out of favor, there will be no lack of successors. In every generation, there are Londoners who can't imagine being out of touch with one another. What they set up is, in effect, a free-form, unnamed salon. As much as Holland House, it has its own ways, its own passwords, its own core members, its probationers, and its honored guests from overseas. To be a part of it is to learn, all over again and in the happiest possible way, the importance of a room in which one is completely at home.

In the House of Commons

IT IS WITHIN four walls, as much as anywhere outside them, that a great city declares itself. Four walls in London are not like four walls in Paris, or New York, or Rome, or Berlin, or Jerusalem. They have a different feel, a different fit, a different intimation, and a different echo.

Nowhere is this difference more apparent than in the layout and the procedures of the House of Commons. That layout and those procedures have been much imitated, but it is only in London that they seem quintessentially right. On great occasions, that rightness is instantly apparent. On lesser ones, the long narrow room seems to stand a little apart, as if waiting for things to improve.

It is in the House of Commons, on great or traumatic occasions, that London within four walls reaches apotheosis. The British House of Commons has its ups and downs, like every other elected assembly, but from time to time it touches the heights in ways that are peculiar to itself. An important role in this is played by the layout.

The House of Commons is neither large nor overbearing. It is the legislators, not the architecture, who on momentous occasions can give it dignity. It does not have the circular or semicircular shape that invites political fragmentation. Unlike its new-begotten counterpart in Moscow, it does not have raked rows of seats that give a distant view of the rulers of the day. The Members of Parliament sit on one side or the other, with no hedging as to their allegiance. Only in the House of Lords does tradition foster the phenomenon of the cross-bencher who has opted for neutrality.

Nor does the House of Commons go in for the apparatus of modern technology. Members do not sit at desks. The octavo-sized computer is never seen in the chamber. Nor is the cordless telephone. Members cannot vote by pressing a button, but must personally leave the chamber and be recognized. Nor can they reach for a microphone to make themselves heard.

The House of Commons in general is not luxurious. The office accommodation allotted to its members would be grounds for mutiny in the headquarters of even quite a small American corporation. The food is not famous. (The best thing about it may well be tea on the terrace, overlooking the Thames, in summer.)

The layout of the House itself looks back—doubtless coincidentally—to a civilized place of assembly that was built in the open air in the fourth century B.C. at Priene. Priene at that time was a thriving port on the coast of Turkey. The plan of its Senate was ideally suited to civilized exchange. Like the House of Commons, it was small and built along a narrow rectangle, with tiered benches that rose just high enough for everyone to see, to hear, and to be heard. Never did those benches rise so high as to allow any one citizen to glare down at all the others.

The same is true of the House of Commons as it was rebuilt after being destroyed by enemy action in 1941. Power does not reside with men and women who sit high above the others. On the contrary, the men and women who debate the future of Great Britain sit low. Ministers are even allowed to put their feet up on the table (though no woman member of the Cabinet has hitherto attempted it).

A posture of ease, and almost of nonchalance, is traditional on the front bench.

Joseph Mallord William Turner. *The Burning of the Houses of Parliament*. 1834. Oil on canvas, 36¼ × 48½" (92.7 × 123.2 cm). The Cleveland Museum of Art. Bequest of John L. Severance

The destruction by fire of the Houses of Parliament in October 1834 was a great and sinister spectacle. Luckily, J. M. W. Turner was on hand to record it. No less luckily, the time was exactly right for new and flamboyant buildings that would speak for an England that with the passing of the Reform Bill had just taken a turn for the better.

After the mandatory bow to the Speaker, members can stroll in and out, hands in pockets (if they so wish). It is desirable to look to be perfectly at home even if, among intending speakers, knees may be weak and hands close to shaking.

The extremes of traditional posture have never been better recorded than in a picture painted in the circa 1890s by Sydney Prior Hall, a graphic artist who had more than thirty years' experience of sketching the Commons scene.

On the left he emphasized the stiff, upright, and slightly thick-headed concentration of Joseph Chamberlain, the Colonial Secretary. Here, if ever, was a man convinced of his importance. On Chamberlain's left was quite another character. Arthur Balfour, Leader of the House, sat low, stretched out his long legs, put his hands in his pockets, and looked as if he could think of more amusing places to be.

And which of the two was the more likely to attain the highest office in the land? A good question. There are no certainties in the House of Commons. It is always rash to say that this one "will go straight to the top" while that one is "not Prime Ministerial timber."

In that context, it is a good idea to remember what was said not long ago by William Rees-Mogg, formerly editor of the London *Times* and a lifelong observer of the parliamentary scene. "Men of the finest intellect do not necessarily make the best political leaders," he said. "The best Prime Minister in history, as a political professional, was probably Robert Walpole. He was a strong man of business, rather than a profound philosopher. Crude vigor and brazen self-confidence are useful in the sweaty cockpit of the House of Commons."

Now that debates in that same sweaty cockpit can regularly be seen on British television, it is known to every viewer that ours is not one of the great ages of Parliamentary debate. It is sometimes sad, and at other times comical, to watch members addressing a three-quarters empty House, or one whose numbers dwindle as sentence follows sentence.

Certain ancient courtesies are still observed, but we are unlikely to hear it said in the House today, as it was said by Sir Robert Peel in 1832, that the previous speaker had inspired "a not ungenerous envy," thanks to "his wonderful flow of

Karl Anton Hickel. *William Pitt (1759–1806) Addressing the House of Commons, 1793.* 1793. Oil on canvas, 127 × 177″ (322.9 × 449.8 cm). The National Portrait Gallery, London

At twenty-four, in 1783, William Pitt the Younger was already Prime Minister of England. He was remarkable for his tall slender figure, his commanding good looks, and his initially dexterous command of the House of Commons. But by 1793, the year here evoked by Karl Anton Hickel, the war with France overseas and radical agitation at home put him in a very unpleasant situation.

natural and beautiful language, and his utterance which, rapid as it is, seems scarcely able to convey its rich freight of thought and fancy."

Nor do we have a politician today who could rival the oratorical powers of William Ewart Gladstone (1809–1898), who was four times Prime Minister. When close on seventy years old, on a bitterly cold winter afternoon, Gladstone made his way across London to Blackheath Common, where an infuriated crowd of more than six thousand people was waiting to shout him down. In the open air, and without benefit of loud hailer or amplification, he addressed them on the subject of the Bulgarian atrocities that were the hot topic of the day. He spoke for an hour and a half, without notes, while those who had come to insult him stayed to applaud.

If the public at large no longer craves to read every word of what is said in

Sydney Prior Hall. *Arthur James Balfour (1848–1930) and Joseph Chamberlain (1836–1914) in the House of Commons.* c. 1890s. Oil on canvas, 24 × 36⅛″ (61 × 91.8 cm). The National Portrait Gallery, London

Parliament, it is not simply because they have shorter and faster ways of finding out about it. It is because the day is long past when the House of Commons was a place set apart both for the poet of the spoken word and for the speaker who could master a great and complicated subject and present it lucidly and with an irresistible force. (Gladstone could quote Lucretius in the original and get away with it.)

Both for men and for ideas, the House was the proving ground on which careers were made or marred. Readers of the parliamentary novels of Anthony Trollope will remember how earnestly Phineas Finn, as a young Member of Parliament, was urged to make his mark in the House. When he hesitated, the voice of a devoted female admirer would haunt him. "But you will speak, Mr. Finn, won't you?" she had said. "You will speak?" It was if the fate of the nation hung upon it.

It is difficult for the novice member of today to feel that same way. Across the entire spectrum of political conviction, from Aneurin Bevan on the left to Enoch Powell on the right, no more than a handful of speakers since World War II have had an absolute command of the House. Irrespective of whether one loved or loathed what they stood for, their speeches have gone down in history. As for the farewell of Margaret Thatcher on her retirement from the Commons, it was as spectacular in its way as the immolation of Brünhilde at the end of Wagner's *Götterdämmerung*.

But for the rank and file of new entrants, Julian Critchley set the general tone when he wrote from long experience about the House in his book, *Palace of Varieties*. Thin were the pickings, he said, and "the best time for a backbencher to speak is immediately after the front bench, ministers having usually gabbled through a civil servant's brief, pausing only to scratch their private parts."

Even if he catches the Speaker's eye, the novice has to contend with conditions that are far from advantageous. Ministers can read their speeches in comfort, bending over the dispatch box on which the text has been laid out. But, as Mr. Critchley says, the backbencher "hovers precariously over the bench in front, his seat catching him behind his knees, his notes clutched in his right hand. If he attempts to read, the House will resound with cries of *Reading!*, a facility which convention denies to backbenchers."

In fact, the best that can be said about the novice's lot in the House is that, no matter what he says, he will be spared the ribaldry that used to greet a member who had become known for his lucrative appearances on a television commercial for a dog food. No sooner did he rise from his seat than simulated barking broke out from every corner of the House.

Times were very different, and so was the House, when the epochal Reform Bill was introduced in March 1831. This was a key moment in the history of Britain. Inequities that had prevailed since the reign of Queen Elizabeth I were to be remedied. The right to vote in parliamentary elections was to be extended to many thousands of gifted, hard-working, and prosperous people who had had to stand by, unrepresented, while the business of government was carried on without regard for their views.

Until that time, the composition of the House of Commons had never been democratic. Of the first half of the eighteenth century, the English historian J. H. Plumb once said that "it is doubtful if any member of the ruling classes, no matter how odd or eccentric his political views, was ever kept out of Parliament, if he really wanted to get in." In that same century, the right to nominate a Member of Parliament could be bought for £1,500. There were Members of Parliament at that time who could gaze round the House and count up to fifty of their own relatives among those present.

Major industrial cities like Birmingham and Manchester had no representative in the Commons, whereas a borough in Surrey that mustered only six houses and exactly one voter had a member all of its own. In the middle of the eighteenth century, the country was run, in effect, by an inner cabinet of not more than half a dozen men. As Plumb put it, this inner cabinet "kept few minutes, rarely recorded its decisions, and met wherever suited itself best, and often this was at dinner." This happened to work very well when Sir Robert Walpole was at the head of the table, but it was not the best way to ensure that ministers were answerable to Parliament.

On these and other matters, feeling rose in the end to white heat. By 1832 the choice before Parliament, and before the country, was between reform, on the one hand, and revolution on the other. In the clubs of central London, men would almost come to blows for possession of the morning paper. This was the great age of the London newspaper, when readers wanted the news in full. They would have been horrified by the current importance of the sound bite, and by the amiable blather of the talk shows.

The major speech in those days could sway the temper of the House from moment to moment. It could also enter into the folk-memory of the nation and be prized by many thousands of people who had not heard it at the time and might never set eyes on the speaker. Nothing was more exciting than an idea perfectly formulated and delivered to an audience that was hungry for it.

In that regard, the passing of the Reform Bill was one of the great hinge-points in British history. (Sir George Hayter's huge group portrait of the House of Commons gives us a very good idea both of the soon-to-be-burned-down chamber and of the mien and bearing of its members). This was a moment at which a crowded House would sit through long speeches and wish them even longer. The House of Commons was the forge in which democracy would be beaten out anew. Both parties knew it, and they looked at one another across a symbolic, as well as a physical, divide.

At such times, not only was every vote counted, but every word also. When a Member caught the Speaker's eye and got up on his feet, he heard in his very bones a cry of "Tell it how it is!" that seemed to come from all over the country. It was as if Britain could be remade in a long day's work in the House of Commons, with a long night's work tacked on to it.

When the Commons today is going nowhere in particular, as is often the case, and when the charismatic speaker is almost as rare as the proven statesman, I often think back to the tumultuous days and nights of the struggle for reform, as they were portrayed in Macaulay's letters to his sister.

Macaulay was the unsurpassed narrator of those memorable nights, even when he himself had mistaken the temper of the government and gone home at three A.M. For this reason he once missed a famous scene, toward eight in the morning. The Speaker was almost fainting from the night's work. It might be another day, and perhaps another night, before the vote was called. Emergency measures were taken. "Old Sir Thomas Baring had sent for his razor," Macaulay told his sister, "and Benett, the member for Wiltshire, for his night-cap. They were both resolved to spend the whole day in the House rather than give way."

And then there was the night in March 1831 when the progress of the Reform Bill through the Commons seemed likely to be halted. When the time came to take the decisive vote, and all strangers had been turned out of the gallery, and the doors had been locked, "we had six hundred and eight members present—more by fifty-five than were in a division before."

In those days, first one side and then the other cast its votes. The Reformers

were counted in an atmosphere of anxiety and excitement that was almost unendurable. Macaulay wrote that as the tally crept toward the three-hundred mark, "we were all standing up and stretching forth, telling with the tellers." In the end, it was three hundred and two.

And on the other side? No one could be sure. There were those who hazarded as high as three hundred and ten. But the figures inched downward, one by one, until suddenly someone who was near the door jumped up onto a bench and said "They are only three hundred and one!"

At that, "we set up a shout that you could have heard at Charing Cross, waving our hats, stamping against the floor and clapping our hands." When the numbers were formally announced, "again the shouts rang out, and many of us shed tears. I could scarcely refrain. And the jaw of Peel fell; and the face of Twiss was as a damned soul; and Herries looked like Judas taking the necktie off for the last operation."

Nor was that the end of it. When the doors were opened, "Another shout answered that within the House. All the passages, and the stairs into the waiting rooms, were thronged by people who had waited till four in the morning to know the issue. We passed through a narrow lane between two thick masses of them; and all the way down they were shouting and waving their hats, till we got out into the open air. I called a cabriolet, and the first thing the driver asked was 'Is the Bill carried?' 'Yes, by one.' 'Thank God for it, Sir.'"

Things are quieter now, and speeches more gaseous. Many a member can empty the House. Few can fill it. Rare is the debate that catches fire. Where there is cut and thrust, most often the swords are of cardboard.

There are speakers who watch the clock, fearing to miss the chance of being quoted on the television news. Others grind a local ax, having a favor to repay to their supporters. The member who is on his feet may suddenly realize that nobody—nobody—is actually listening to what he is saying. At such a moment he

Above:
Sir George Hayter. *The House of Commons*. 1833. Oil on canvas, 118½ × 196″ (300 × 497.8 cm). The National Portrait Gallery, London

In 1833, Sir George Hayter became the first painter to attempt a collective portrait of the House of Commons since the passing in the previous year of the climactic Reform Bill.

Opposite:
Libero Prosperi. *The Lobby of the House of Commons*. 1886. Oil on canvas, 13 × 19¼″ (33 × 49 cm). The National Portrait Gallery, London

Professionally known as "Lib," Prosperi was best known as a racing cartoonist. In this painting, the central group consists of (from left to right) Joseph Chamberlain, Charles Stewart Parnell, the Irish political leader, W. E. Gladstone, four times prime minister of En-

gland, Lord Randolph Churchill (the father of Winston Churchill), and the 8th Duke of Devonshire.

The other men portrayed cover a wide social and political swath. At the extreme left is Inspector Denning of the Metropolitan Police, and at the extreme right is Mr. Hansard (the Hansards had been printing the day's proceedings in the Commons for more than 100 years).

The company also includes Charles Bradlaugh, the champion of votes for women, birth control, and atheism, Henry Labouchere, anti-imperialist and editor of *Truth* magazine, and John Bright, proponent of free trade and laissez-faire.

In this delirious little painting, parody got the better of documentation. But Prosperi conveys the full range of English attitudes as they were represented in the House of Commons.

will envy those others who, having failed to catch the Speaker's eye, have thought better of the whole thing and gone off to dinner.

It is not a galvanic scene. Some members who are gifted and delightful human beings in private just happen to be dull when on their feet. Occasionally there is an outsize human being who is said to be "too good to be Prime Minister." But the Chamber itself is there, and when the great issue and the great orator come along, it will be worthy of them, just as it was worthy of Winston Churchill in the summer of 1940.

Meanwhile, the House of Commons and its purlieux are still indispensable to the student of English mores. It is, for instance, indicative of something important that the Speaker's House is quite as grand, in its way, as no. 10 Downing Street. The Speaker does not govern. But he (or, as at the moment of this writing, she) is there to see that government is carried on in a correct and orderly manner and without interruption from anyone who is not a Member of the House. These are heavy duties, and it should not surprise us that it is traditional for the newly appointed Speaker to feign reluctance to take up the office.

There is also the matter of the lobbies. There are the Lords' Lobby, the Central Lobby, and the Commons Lobby. They are fundamental to the circulation of those who have to get from one part of the Palace of Westminster to another. They offer, quite literally, a breathing space in times of crisis. And it is in the Commons Lobby that a private citizen may hope to have a word with Members of the House as they come and go. It is a long shot, admittedly, and the novice is unlikely to succeed in it.

But "lobbying" is now a universally recognized activity, and a "lobbyist" is a member of an influential and sometimes massively rewarded profession. The words would seem to have first emerged in the 1850s and 60s in the United States, but it is to what went on, and to what still goes on, in the House of Commons Lobby that they owe their beginnings.

The Palace of Westminster is a characteristically English construction. The

Thomas Shotter Boys. *The Club Houses etc., Pall Mall.* 1842. Color-tinted lithograph, 12³/₁₆ × 17⁵/₈″ (31.4 × 44.7 cm). Guildhall Library, Corporation of London

On the south side of Pall Mall, at the foot of Lower Regent Street, there is a group of clubhouses—the Athenaeum, the Travellers', and the Reform—which for generations have played a role in the London life of diplomacy, politics, and literature.

existing Houses of Parliament had long been wretchedly insufficient, and after they burned down in October 1834 no time was lost in the matter of their replacement.

In June 1835 a competition, open to all, was announced, with the proviso that all designs had to be either in the Gothic or the Elizabethan style. Ninety-one Gothic designs were submitted, as against six in the Elizabethan.

The winner was Charles Barry. He was the complete professional. For him, as for Philip Johnson in our own day, "Get the job!" was the first rule of architecture. Privately, he favored what he called the "Anglo-Italian" style of architecture that he had practiced with great success in the Travellers' Club (1830–32). He was to use it with even greater success both in the Travellers' next-door neighbor, the Reform Club (1839–41), and in the great mansion called Bridgewater House, off St. James's Street, in 1847–54.

But the "Anglo-Italian" style would not have done at all for the new Palace of Westminster, of which the Houses of Parliament are a part. Perpendicular Gothic had primacy, and Charles Barry went along with it to triumphant and spectacular effect.

To cope with the workload that would be entailed in so enormous a building, Barry virtually invented the modern profession of architecture. To quote from the architectural historians Elain Harwood and Andrew Saint, his methods "introduced the concept of the building team, established the profession of the quantity surveyor, and led to a new kind of architectural partnership."

He also perfected an art—that of dealing with the client—that had always been fundamental to his profession. Politicians are licensed to interfere, directly or indirectly, in every department of life, and nowhere more so than when their own working conditions are at stake. In the case of the new Palace of Westminster, everybody had an opinion, and everybody wanted his opinion to prevail.

In this way, Barry had to put up with several hundred self-appointed clients. Suggestions, requests, second thoughts were piled high on his desk every morning. Quite apart from aesthetic considerations, two more general complaints could be counted upon. "You're too slow!" was the substance of one of them. "You're too expensive!" was the substance of the other.

Barry fought his corner in magisterial style. It was all very well for the Lords and the Commons to run the country, but he was not going to have them running his office.

Himself forty years old in 1835, Barry lost no time in taking on board Augustus Welby Pugin, who at the age of only twenty-three was both a rapid and immaculate draftsman and a one-man encyclopedia of historical Gothic, and a master of its adaptation to every last detail of life.

No two men could have been more unalike. Nikolaus Pevsner brought them both to life when he said that whereas Barry's working methods were staid and reliable, "Pugin drew amidst a continuous rattle of marvelous stories, slashing criticism and shouts of laughter." (He added that whereas Barry was knighted and died at the age of sixty-five, Pugin went insane and died at forty.)

Barry and Pugin exactly complemented one another. Barry was all for regularity and symmetry, order and lucidity. It was he who thought out the grand design, with its long straight axes running from north to south and from east to west. How simple and natural that design looked on the drawing board, and how richly and complicatedly it was ornamented by Pugin!

Barry had in mind the orderly and dignified transaction of the nation's business. Pugin was more interested in the intricate poetry that could reside in the asymmetrical and the picturesque. Moreover, he did not see the Gothic style in terms of mere convenience. He saw it as a sacred trust and a first cousin to holiness.

There was really nothing that Pugin could not do. He could do ceilings. He could do stained glass. He could do tiled floors. He could do furniture. He could do flocked wallpaper. He could bind books as they had never been bound before. He could do inkwells, ashtrays, keys, hinges, lamps, and coal buckets. He would seem never to have been tired, and quite clearly he knew how to bend the work force to his will.

It was as if he were out to give a whole new spin to the notion of London between four walls. New painting and new sculpture played a big role in the new Palace, also, thanks to the enthusiasm of Queen Victoria's consort, Prince Albert. The paintings did not wear well, in physical terms, and the sculptures were mostly journeyman work. But the ambition to bring high art into the Palace of Westminster was not an ignoble one.

Meanwhile, Pugin made full use not only of the patriotic overtones of Perpendicular Gothic, but also of the can-do ethos that somehow permeated the making of the great and brand-new building. It was in the House of Lords—still happily almost unchanged—that his genius found apotheosis. To while away much of the day in that great chamber—and to get paid for doing it—is one of the more agreeable destinies.

Barry also had his share of that can-do ethos. The Palace of Westminster may have been the last of the great English romantic buildings, but in its inner construction it was also the first and the largest of England's great modern buildings.

Such, moreover, was Barry's mastery of exterior silhouette that he took the disadvantages of the given site and made them work for him. In the 336-foot-high Victoria Tower and in the Clock Tower that houses Big Ben, he introduced at either end of the Palace an element of high drama. Nobody could have foreseen them. Asymmetry for once was Barry's henchman.

The two towers are set down in places where most great government buildings peter out. Without them, we should have lost the romance that comes with the Palace of Westminster, no matter how repetitive the exterior may be at a lower level. Barry and Pugin, between them, set fancy free. Nowhere in London has a busy and productive life between four walls been more vividly imagined.

The Spirit of Place

THE NINETEENTH CENTURY spawned huge areas of London that opted for uniformity. In those areas, house after house, mile after mile, is virtually identical. In almost every approach to London there is a stretch of that sort. Coming in by train to Waterloo, or Victoria, or Paddington, we feel as if the life of the English imagination had been snuffed out.

And then, suddenly, a building turns up that is a nonpareil. To get a sense of that, we have to graduate from a school of differentiation. But that school has no staff, holds no classes, and offers no degrees. We have to invent it for ourselves. In doing that, we sharpen our senses and become aware of ignorance as something that can be put to rout.

For the native Londoner, not to have graduated from the school of differentiation is to have missed out on an important part of growing up, and to be by that much the less alive. In this matter, I started way behind. To put it plainly, I could not tell good from bad, or true from false, in my surroundings.

A prototypical bookworm and obsessional student of the weekly reviews, I rarely raised my eyes from the printed page. All the beauty of the world was mustered for me in the standard iron book stacks to which every reader at the local public library had access.

Elsewhere, I was as if anesthetized. Unseeing, I walked. Unseeing, I sat. Unseeing, I woke up in the morning and reached for the new French books. (Thanks to a far-sighted schoolteacher, those novels and those plays reached me on publication day.)

As near as was possible, I ignored my surroundings. And then, one day in the summer of that year of foreboding, 1939, I turned away in revulsion from the European news as it was spread out in the reading room of Pitzhanger Manor, which at that time served as the Ealing Public Library. Looking at that room closely and for the first time, I managed to divest it in my mind of its municipal trappings.

Little by little, I found consolation and reassurance in the order, the proportion, the finesse, and the wit with which someone, sometime, had endowed that room. As it happened, that someone was one of the most original of English architects, Sir John Soane, who had bought the house in 1800 and added a new central block over the next three years.

In essence, the house then became a duet for Soane and for its original architect, George Dance the Younger. (As it happened, Soane had begun his career in Dance's office in 1768, at the age of fifteen, and he was sensitive to the subdued elegance of what Dance had done.)

The house as completed by Soane was still quite small, but it was one in which he could on occasion entertain two hundred people to that convivial novelty, the fork-luncheon. In 1939, there was nothing fancy about that little house, and yet it

George Pyne. *The Circular Dining Room at Carlton House.* 1819. Watercolor and gouache heightened with white, 18 × 15″ (47.7 × 38.1 cm). Private collection made poetry out of day-to-day life in a way that I had never experienced before.

In whatever he did, Sir John Soane made magic. The entrance to Pitzhanger Manor was by way of one or two steep steps and a hallway barely big enough to turn around in. Soane endowed that straitened staircase and the tiny square of level ground above it with high drama.

Taking breakfast in the little room immediately to the right, Soane did not want to look at bare walls and standard embellishments. He wanted a room with a personality all its own.

A flat and low ceiling was not to his taste. So he designed a ceiling that was floated above what looked like (but were not) structural pendentives. The coved look for which he sought was accentuated by neo-Classical motifs that made the pendentives look as if at any moment they would start to revolve.

Marble would have suited his intentions. So would porphyry. Bronze would not have come amiss. But it seemed to him that pots of the right paint would do the job equally well and amuse him even more as he sat over his breakfast and reviewed the business of the forthcoming day.

In this way, simulated marble and painted porphyry did away with the bother of shipping the real thing from overseas. As for the "bronze" of the caryatids on either side of the fireplace, that too was owed to brushes and paint. Add to all that a geometrical structure that still has a look of the avant-garde, and we realize why Soane so detested the monotony and the unsound construction that threatened, in his view, to "finally root out every vestige of good architecture" in London.

Since 1986, Pitzhanger Manor has been re-created as a museum. Much could still be done, but already it emerges as one of the most remarkable small town houses in England. It was fundamental to Soane's character that he had no sense of the incongruous. Whatever he wanted to do in his own house, he did. Much was owed to what one of his pupils called his "acute sensitivity and a fearful irritability." If anyone had ventured to say that his house was really too small for the grand and detached Ionic order of Portland stone that he had used for his new facade, Soane would have thrown him out.

Not only is that Ionic order very imposing, and derived eventually from the Arch of Constantine in Rome, but it carries four standing statues, based on those that stood in front of the Temple of Pandrosus in Athens. The anthologist in Soane prompted him to rack up other references to former times in two roundels, each with a Medici lion and a panel with a putto.

Beneath the windows, wreathed and paneled eagles had been copied from antique sculptures on the church of Santi Apostoli in Rome. With its forthright verticals and horizontals and its well-assorted echoes of the distant past, this facade makes an arresting effect. The notion of bric-a-brac has not often been so ennobled.

For quite some days after I got the point of Pitzhanger Manor, I did not let Soane out of my sight. Arm in arm with him (in thought, at any rate), I took myself off to no. 13 Lincoln's Inn Fields, where he lived from 1813 until his death in 1837. Nowhere in London is there a more curious interior. Magic is multiplied. Bric-a-brac becomes a way of life. The "fanciful effects" which in Soane's view constituted "the poetry of architecture" are there in superabundance.

Archaeology lives beneath the same roof as major paintings by Hogarth. Tall slender pillars of metal alternate with the classic mahogany of English bookcases. Concave and convex mirrors give a sense of make-believe just where it is needed. Vistas come to life on the instant as we monitor the results of a lifetime of benign and harmless rooting among fragments of ancient Rome. Every inch of the interior is freighted with fancy.

After that, I went to the Dulwich Picture Gallery, which Soane built in 1811–14. During the fifty and some years that have passed since my first visit, more museums have been built (or enlarged) in more places than at any other time in history. Since World War II, a city that does not have a big new museum is regarded the world over as lacking in civic virility.

Architects have knocked themselves out in the search for a perfected museum. Many a competition has been held, in that context, and colossal sums of money have been forthcoming. International interest is such that the opening of a new museum now takes precedence over almost any other metropolitan or municipal adventure. None of them has made Soane look out of date.

The Dulwich Picture Gallery predates this frenetic activity by almost 150 years. Soane designed it as a monument to a close friend of his, Sir Francis Bourgeois, and as a home for the many paintings that Bourgeois had left to Dulwich. So far from making a killing by its construction, Soane waived his fees and even offered to dig deep into his own pocket when money ran short. (The museum was, by the way, completed well under Soane's estimated costs.)

The gallery consisted initially of a mausoleum for Bourgeois himself and a series of five unornamented and top-lit galleries. Round-headed arches led the eye from one gallery into the next. Overhead, the light came down from high clear panes of glass, and the high coved ceiling was tipped forward and downward in such a way as to encourage a subliminal concentration on the paintings, rather than on the architecture.

When working for himself alone, Soane could be the master of an almost insane complication. But, when it came to lighting pictures, his was indeed "the art that conceals art." Lecturing at the Royal Academy in 1815, he said that "in galleries, light is often introduced very advantageously above the cornice, so that the window is not seen from below. By this contrivance a pleasing kind of demi-tint is thrown over the whole surface of the ceiling."

Someone who took note of Soane's views about lighting was a great painter, J. M. W. Turner. When he built his own picture gallery at 46 Queen Anne Street West in 1819–21, he settled for a long narrow room, top-lit with octagonal

Camille Pissarro.
*Dulwich College,
London.* 1871. Oil
on canvas, 19¾ ×
24″ (50 × 61 cm).
Private collection

Opposite above:
Sir John Soane. *Design for the
Front Entrance of Pitzhanger
Manor.* 1800–1803. Water-
color, 23⅜ × 36″ (59.5 ×
91.5 cm). By courtesy of the
Trustees of Sir John Soane's
Museum, London

Opposite below:
John Scarlett Davis. *The Library at Tottenham, the Seat of
B. G. Windus, Esq.* 1835. Watercolor, 11¾ × 21⅞″ (29.9 ×
55.7 cm). By permission of the
Trustees of the British Museum, London

B. G. Windus was a dedicated
collector of J. M. W. Turner,
and his library exemplifies the
small-scale and relatively informal surroundings that many a
true collector has favored in
London.

skylights. Turner had his walls covered with the damson-red fabric that was almost mandatory at the time and still looks just right in the upper gallery at Thomas Agnew & Sons at no. 43 Old Bond Street.

What Soane produced in Dulwich cannot be called "clever." As architecture, it could almost be said to absent itself. It has, in fact, the quality most to be desired in what Shakespeare's Hamlet calls "enterprizes of great pith and moment"—a moral dead-centeredness. That quality cannot be faked. Soane had it in Dulwich, just as he had had it in the Bank of England, which he built, off and on, between 1788 and 1833. Soane's Bank was destroyed in the 1930s, but Dulwich survives, with some tactful enlargements by others. Those bald, self-echoing interiors have rarely been rivaled in museum design.

When Camille Pissarro, the white knight of French Impressionism, was in London in 1871, he went mainly to South London for his subject matter. When in Dulwich, he did not paint the art gallery—perhaps because it stood for an aesthetic of monumental sobriety with which he had never had to come to terms. He preferred to paint the steep-pitched, ornamented, and apple-red facade of the newly built Dulwich College. It was one of his most glorious paintings, and Dulwich village is still worthy of it. But it is the art gallery, not the college, that goes deeper than the picturesque.

Those summer days in 1939 were for me what people now call "an epiphany," and I have never forgotten them. Once I had recognized that, my life took a new turn. So did my feeling for London. I had learned, however late, that the perfected interior was at home in London. And I went on to look for it—in daydream, in documents, face to face, everywhere.

Many a perfected interior no longer existed. Until the outbreak of World War I, there was in the center of London a congeries of private houses in which power, wealth, authority, and high living were concentrated. There were the great patrician mansions of the eighteenth century—Spencer House at the bottom of St. James's Street, Devonshire House in Piccadilly, and Chesterfield House with its initially uncluttered view of Hyde Park. As for Apsley House in Piccadilly, the home of the great Duke of Wellington, it had an association that dwarfed all the others.

These were family houses. In some of them—contrary to what is often supposed—ideas held court. There have always been such houses in London. Sometimes they were small and unpretentious, but nonetheless effective for that. Sometimes they were enormous, blocking the horizon and blocking the sky. Either way, they contributed to the prevailing idea of civilization.

Finest of all, in that company, was Carlton House, the residence of the Prince Regent. Later to become George IV, he lived for building, and he was not at all afraid of the new. First with Henry Holland and later, after Holland had died in 1806, with John Nash, the Prince Regent got himself one of the most splendid houses in all Europe.

Nowhere in London, before or since, was a town house put together with such a resourceful, unerring, and spendthrift taste. Nowhere was hospitality more lavish. As for the arts of decoration, they were indulged and reindulged according to whims that changed, almost, every hour on the hour.

Visitors to London who would have liked to call at Carlton House in 1821 can go right ahead and picture themselves as privileged to do it. Imagination will have to work hard, admittedly, for Carlton House was pulled down in 1827. But in its brief heyday it was something to see. Built in 1709 as a plain brick house, Carlton House was given to the Prince Regent as his official residence on his coming of age in August 1783. He moved in forthwith, and for the next thirty and more years he was involved, to the point of obsession, with the enlargement, the re-enlargement, the decoration, and the furnishing of Carlton House.

Given his youth, his natural extravagance, and the volatility of his tastes, all this was bound to cost money. But it turned out to be expensive beyond all expectation. Sometimes the money was well spent. Much of the English and French furniture is in Buckingham Palace today. Posterity cannot scold the Prince Regent for having bought great paintings that are still in the royal collection—Rembrandt's *Shipbuilder and his Wife,* Rubens's *Self-Portrait* and *Landscape with St. George and the Dragon,* the eighteen paintings by George Stubbs, Gainsborough's *Diana and Actaeon,* and the portrait of David Garrick and his wife by William Hogarth. Carlton House in its heyday was one of the greatest houses in all Europe.

If today's visitors like to imagine for themselves, instead, a call on the Marquess of Westminster in Park Lane in the year 1831, there is a painting that tells them exactly what they would have seen when they walked into the picture gallery of Grosvenor House. (This is not, by the way, the hotel that now bears the name, but the great mansion that stood on the same site in Park Lane until it was pulled down in the late 1920s.)

The painting is by the American-born artist C. R. Leslie. As in Holland House, he did a capital job of telling us what size and shape the room was, what was hanging on the wall, what the family looked like, and how they were spending the late afternoon. (As fourteen people in all are portrayed in the picture, Leslie may be said to have earned the money.)

Three generations were present in the gallery, which had been added to Grosvenor House in 1805. No expense had been spared, and when the family acquired four enormous tapestry designs by Rubens in 1818 they went ahead and made the gallery even bigger to fit them.

It is this enlargement that forms the rearground of Leslie's painting, with two of the tapestry designs deftly brushed in. Leslie also made a stab at portraying (aslant, on the right) the Velázquez that shows Prince Baltasar Carlos learning to ride a royal horse outside the Buen Retiro palace in Madrid.

These images within the picture bring light and animation to what is distinctly a pre-Victorian family scene. Though he is head of the family, the Marquess of Westminster does not come on as a tyrant. His grandson (later, in 1874, to become the first Duke) nestles against his knee. His wife is playing the piano, his daughter-in-law is playing the harp, and two of his granddaughters pick up their skirts and dance away to general admiration.

His third son, Lord Robert Grosvenor, bursts in from the right as if in impatience to see his new bride, who is the niece of the great Duke of Wellington. The other men are dressed informally, but Lord Robert wears the uniform of Comptroller to the royal household.

Everyone in Grosvenor House would seem to be pleased with everyone else. No one shows off, and no one sulks. Even the parrot stands free. With a little help from C. R. Leslie, this looks like a very happy family. We are entitled to believe that our daydreaming visitor would be made welcome, even if this was clearly a close-knit family circle.

Many, many years later I set foot in the largest and the grandest survivor among these private houses. A year or two before World War II, I read of a forthcoming piano recital by Louis Kentner, a Hungarian lately arrived on the London scene and much praised by Sacheverell Sitwell for his way with Franz Liszt. With every seat on sale at a shilling, how could I fail to go?

I was in two minds about it, even so. The concert was not in a concert hall at all, but in Lancaster House, in Stable Yard, off Pall Mall. I had never heard of Lancaster House. Ambling down St. James's Street, and turning right along Cleveland Row, I thought that it was a house of modest size in which amateurish "musicales" were given from time to time. Knowing nothing, I expected little.

I could not have been more wrong. Lancaster House, in this context, was anything but an unknown quantity. It was the house in which, in 1846, Frédéric Chopin had played before an audience that included Queen Victoria, her consort, Prince Albert, and the Duke of Wellington. Lancaster House was a stupendous mansion, which under its previous name of Stafford House had been one of the all-time great domestic interiors of London.

Walking into the amazing interior, with its underplayed entrance hall, its marble-lined double staircase, and its imposing though clearly inauthentic paintings after Veronese, I gazed in awe at the cast-iron stair balustrade. Though it doubled at the time as the London Museum, and for that reason was shorn of almost all its former éclat, this was clearly no ordinary town house. Had I come to the wrong address?

Apparently not. My shilling went all the way, and I found myself in what had been, in the 1830s, 1840s, and 1850s, the preeminent private house in all London. As had happened with Pitzhanger Manor, the first bloom of the house had long before been rubbed off.

But it was possible to see that it was a house in which hundreds of people could be entertained in the evening and none of them would feel overlooked, unwelcome, or underprivileged. As Lady Eastlake, the wife of the director of the National Gallery, said in her diary, there could never be a "crowd" in Stafford House. "The size is such that the stairs alone would accommodate hundreds, the galleries the same, the hall below thousands."

When the German connoisseur Dr. Waagen was touring England in the 1850s, he said of Stafford House (as it was then called) that "in extent, grandeur of proportions, solidity of materials, and beauty of situation, it excels every other mansion in London."

It may sound as if Stafford House was the very heartland of English privilege. Behind its construction and completion lay virtually unlimited money. It had been commissioned by the Duke of York, brother and heir presumptive to King George IV. Benjamin Wyatt, who had worked for (and fallen out with) the Duke of Wellington on Apsley House, was its first and main architect. The house was to be in every way (and not least in its location) "fit for a king."

But when the Duke of York died in 1827, the house was nowhere near finished. The Duke's debts were enormous. Work stopped. The future of the huge building seemed problematic. It is not everyone who wants to take on an embryonic palace, carry it through to a glorious conclusion without counting the cost, and live in it in

Charles Robert Leslie. *The Grosvenor Family*. 1831. Oil on canvas, 40 × 57″ (101.6 × 144.7 cm). By kind permission of His Grace The Duke of Westminster

Joseph Nash. *Stafford House (Lancaster House) Grand Staircase.* c. 1850. Pencil and gouache, 14¾ × 19⅝″ (37.5 × 50 cm). The Museum of London

quasi-royal style for close on fifty years. But Lord Stafford, who in 1833 became the 1st Duke of Sutherland, was delighted to take the house off the government's hands.

The Sutherlands could afford it. For the 2nd Duke, to have forty-eight servants in the house and ten in the stables did not give him pause for a moment. He adored spending money on beautiful (and sometimes not so beautiful) things. And he had married in 1823 a wife who was, if possible, even richer than he was.

No less important was that she was the ideal hostess for a great town house. According to John Cornforth, the ranking authority on the house, she was "built, mind and body, on a huge scale, and overflowing with joie de vivre." Winterhalter's portrait of her bears this out.

Even so, these might have been two class-bound millionaires, living in terror of the mob that had broken even the Duke of Wellington's windows after the rejection of the Reform Bill in 1831. They might, alternatively, have thought of the house primarily as an aesthetic experience.

One family member, Lord Ronald Gower, spoke of the great hall as being "like some grand poem turned into solid masonry, imperishable and immutable to time, and age, and human changes." But even he had to say that by some strange alchemy that same room could double as a sitting room in which a dozen people could sit comfortably and not feel lost.

More important still was that the Duke and Duchess of Sutherland were paragons of social awareness. It was in this very house that William Lloyd Garrison was invited to put the case for the abolition of slavery in the United States. The Sutherlands were equally sensitive to the realities of life in England. Harriet, Duchess of Sutherland, worked hard for prison reform, for the improvement of the miners' lot, and for a new degree of humanity in the workhouses to which the poor were consigned.

It was there that in 1864 the 3rd Duke of Sutherland welcomed Garibaldi, the savior of Italy, while half London stood outside to cheer him. And it was there, as much as anywhere, that Lord Shaftesbury campaigned against the ill treatment of children in English factories and did much of the groundwork for the Factories Act of 1874.

Standing on that great staircase today, and remembering Stafford House as Eugène Lami portrayed it, we can imagine ourselves back there in the years when, as Virginia Woolf put it, "an aged Prime Minister would sit on the sofa and recount to Lady So-and-So with the curls and the emeralds the true history of some great crisis in the affairs of the land." In many of those crises, Stafford House in the nineteenth century had its part to play.

George Scharf. *The Staircase of the Old British Museum.* 1845. Watercolor over pencil, 14⅛ × 11″ (36 × 27.9 cm). By permission of the Trustees of the British Museum, London

Toward the end of the century the life of the house underwent a subtle change. Ideas had been at home there for many years, but under the influence of the group of friends known to the public as "the Souls" a new lightness of tone came over the great mansion.

The Souls were a group of well-born and well-favored young people. They could have been completely vacuous, but they weren't. Disdaining the pleasures of shooting, riding to hounds, drinking heavily at the end of the day, and gambling all night at the card table, they kept themselves apart. They thought higher thoughts, they dreamed, they wrote (not least to one another), and they were open to new ideas of every kind. Where romancing was concerned, they were not at all backward. They were, in fact, the absolute reverse of what might have been expected.

One of them was Arthur James Balfour, a regular at Stafford House. In his manner, he was wonderfully, archetypally languid. Such was his mastery of this tactic that it was widely believed that he was too frail for the rigors of high office. But when he became Prime Minister in 1902, it turned out that he had all the intellectual energy, and more, that was required of him.

It still amused him to address himself to frivolous subjects—the role of baccarat in social life, for instance—but then it had never been good form, among the Souls, to be too serious. But in spite of what was once called his "air of lackadaisical lucidity," Balfour was capable of taking part at a moment's notice in a four-hour discussion about the Dutch influence on Roman law. What posterity remembers primarily about Balfour is that his name, as Foreign Minister of Great Britain, was on the Balfour Declaration of 1917 that led in time to the establishment in Palestine of a national home for the Jewish people.

Lancaster House today is still a great house, but it is also a lost house. Nobody now lives in it, and no one human being owns it. Inevitable as that may be, it banishes the excitement that, as Stafford House, it had generated in the nineteenth century.

It is now a "Government entertainment center," open to the public from two to six P.M. on weekends in summer but subject at all times to official preemption. Though no foe of governmental hospitality, I grieve to think of the bureaucratic anonymity and, on those hospitable occasions, the temporary nature of host and hostess.

Governmental ownership is better than destruction. It may or may not be better than corporate ownership. Still, nothing can bring back the days when it was run as a private house like any other, but bigger and grander and, at the same time, more convivial.

But, even if it is now, in effect, the social bivouac of the government of the day, who is to say that it is not still dealing with crises, and playing a part in their resolution?

To get the feel of ambitious interior spaces in London that were accessible at any time, its museums are a good place to begin. For years, the Natural History Museum on Cromwell Road had inspired me with terror, unalloyed. Why was it so horribly big? Would the dinosaur and the diplodocus come back to life, stumble down the steps, and eat us all up?

I might have been reassured by the fact that the architect of the Natural History Museum, Alfred Waterhouse, was also the architect of my school, St. Paul's, barely more than a mile away. Vast ensembles came naturally to him. Even so, at 170 feet long, 97 feet wide, and 72 feet high, the central hall of the Natural History Museum stood high in the scale of intimidation.

George William Joy. *The Bays-water Omnibus*. 1895. Oil on canvas, 48¼ × 69″ (120.6 × 172.5 cm). The Museum of London

William Roberts. *The Cinema*. 1920. Oil on canvas, 72 × 72″ (183 × 183 cm). The Tate Gallery, London

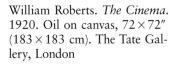

John Henry Henshall. *Behind the Bar*. 1882. Watercolor, 15¾ × 28⅜″ (40.2 × 72 cm). The Museum of London

A diplodocus needs house room, admittedly, and the 1880s were not a time at which the bijou museum—or, indeed, the bijou anything—had clout. Whether skeletal or stuffed, it was the bigger animals that people wanted to see. Who ever forgot the stuffed giraffes that had stood at the top of the stairs in what later evolved into the British Museum?

Later, when I started to look all over London for the spirit of place, I found that it seemed to sprout, unbidden and unforeseen, all over town. I found it in the Wigmore Hall on Wigmore Street. Built in 1900, it originally bore the name of Bechstein, the piano manufacturer. Reached from the street by way of a long narrow paneled corridor, it is small. It is also a model of period design. As for the gilded decorations by Gerald Moira above the stage, in which the Spirit of Music basks in the golden rays of the Genius of Harmony, I hold them in affectionate regard.

From Ferruccio Busoni onward, many a great visiting pianist had loved the Wigmore Hall. Even when he was a veteran who had long had his pick of halls the world over, Arthur Rubinstein was happy to return to the Wigmore Hall. During and immediately after World War II, it was in effect the only true concert hall in London that was still in service.

Survivors of that period will never forget the afternoons when John McCormack sang songs by Hugo Wolf in their orchestral versions, when Benjamin Britten's *Serenade* for tenor, horn, and orchestra had its first performance, and when Francis Poulenc and Pierre Bernac returned to London after the liberation of Paris.

Those occasions were unique. The sound was perfect (even if it was a neat trick

to keep the orchestra down in the Hugo Wolf). There was not a dull or an unresponsive face in the audience. This was an interior space that truly deserved well of London. Happily, and at the time of this writing, the Wigmore Hall is newly restored and in very good hands.

Drawing rooms that looked out onto plane trees and locked gardens could also do the trick—in Bedford Square, especially, where Vaslav Nijinsky watched a game of tennis in 1912 and got from it the idea of a ballet that, with some help from Debussy, later turned into *Jeux*.

I also found the spirit of place in that sanctuary of sweet silent study, the former Reading Room of the British Museum, in the years when Angus Wilson, later to become famous as a novelist, was never too busy or too grand to jump down from his chair of office and help the novice reader.

And then there was the box in the Royal Opera House in which I was allowed to crouch unseen at the back, during orchestra rehearsals, and the off-hours drinking club, upstairs in Soho, that was presided over with an uproarious freedom of speech by Muriel Belcher, the inspiration of more than one of Francis Bacon's best paintings.

Publishers' parties I enjoyed very much, and not least at John Murray's on Albemarle Street, in the very room where Lord Byron and Sir Walter Scott had met and talked. The headquarters of learned societies had their magic, too. Long lodged in central London, they were as if permeated by centuries of the banked-up will to learn. Foreign embassies, whether stately or way under budget, could yield many a revelatory moment, though there are times when we wait for them in vain.

There were barristers' chambers in the Inns of Court where professional banter could be counted upon till late in the evening, and tailors' anterooms in which the London *Times* of the day was folded for our pleasure with regimental precision. I also remember a rented room not far from Holloway Prison that the best English painter of his generation, Lucian Freud, had turned into a hallucinatory likeness of a room in a French provincial hotel.

Among less secret spaces, auction houses have had a role in London for three hundred and more years. Some of them began small, in bookshops or private houses. Others were held in Somerset House, no less, or in Inigo Jones's Banqueting House in Whitehall. Some were substantial even by the standards of today.

After the death in 1680 of the portrait painter Sir Peter Lely, a favorite of King Charles II, the sale of his collection of Old Master paintings drew connoisseurs from all over England. (The sale of his prints and drawings in 1682 went on for eight days). The auction room as proving ground between man and man has never changed. Once we have a firm grasp of the fundamentals, to hang out in Christie's or Sotheby's is "as good as the play," and not seldom better.

In the lean days after World War II, the audience at auction sales in London sometimes barely made it into double figures. But even today, when going to "black-tie auctions" is to a fashionable audience in New York or London what going to the bullfight is to the cognoscenti in Seville or Madrid, the number of serious bidders may not be much larger.

The difference is that in the late 1940s the auction houses were subject to governmental restrictions that hobbled the import and export of works of art in London. Their function was fundamentally to redistribute what was already in Britain. Prices were low, the atmosphere was Rowlandsonian, and catalogues were skeletal and unillustrated.

Forty years later, the auction market was a subdepartment, and not an insignificant one, of the market in general. In the attitude of those who crowded in to

John Loughborough Pearson. *Design for the Church of St. Augustine, Kilburn, London.* c. 1874. Sepia pen and watercolor, 37¼ × 21⅜″ (94.5 × 55.5 cm). The British Architectural Library, RIBA, London

watch the proceedings, there was something of vicarious greed and envy, something of the casino, and something of the prize ring. There are prettier sights.

Among the resources of London are places in which Londoners unknown to the visitor can be studied at close quarters.

One of them is the London omnibus. Ten minutes with a map of London's bus routes will show that many of them snake their way across the length and breadth of the city. On long journeys, and if the visitor comes on as an innocent abroad, the London bus can take on the aspect of a free-form salon on wheels.

Unlike a journey by stagecoach, where travelers might have had to sign up for days on end, the bus ride may be a matter of minutes only. But they can be memorable minutes. The novelist Wilkie Collins got that right once and for all when he wrote in his *Basil* in 1852 that the London omnibus was "a perambulatory exhibition-room of the eccentricities of human nature.

"I know of no other sphere," he went on, "in which persons of all classes and all temperaments are so oddly collected together, and so immediately contrasted and confronted with one another." In that sense, the bus still has no rival in London. Nor is London anywhere better seen than from the top of a bus.

The London movie houses also had a special character until they were cut up into separate self-sufficing bits. Before radio, and before television, the movie house

had a monopoly of day-long, come-when-you-please entertainment. We can see from a painting by William Roberts in 1920 how people came in off the street, tumbled down the narrow stairs, and scrambled for a seat as if their lives depended on it. Meanwhile, the pianist stuck to her eight-hour stint with one eye on the screen, the other one on the audience, and both hands racing up and down the keys.

There is also that often overrated feature of London life, the public house, as to which every kind of opinion can be held and just about all of them can be sustained. The London public house is a chancy and a fallible affair, in which the men and the women behind the bar set the tone, and the pace, on which all else depends.

No sooner are we inside the door than they can persuade us that our arrival has made their day. In their "regulars" they have a repertory company in which even bit players and supers are made to feel their contribution is of value. It is in the pub, not at home, that they have an audience. If they are lucky, their host and hostess will be nature's diplomats, and know from long experience when strangers would like to be coaxed along and when they would rather be left alone.

A pub of that sort is a club that has no admissions committee, no initiation fee, and no dues. An almost naval brilliance can be the mark of the brasswork. Even the name of a pub can have a special ring. ("Meet me at the Bishop's Finger" was an invitation not likely to be forgotten.)

In a good pub, the housekeeping is without fault. The cut-glass partitions between one bar and another give off a sparkle that is infectious. The drink is well served, and the food may be better than we expect. This is a stage on which all can hope to shine, and it is addictive. The pub is, or was, a place for trysting, deal-making and un-making, local news, local gossip, celebration, and sad remembrance.

But the London pub can also be slovenly and cheerless. It may reek of stale beer. The archetypal greasy spoon lies on every plate. The bar is the resort of bad characters who do not keep themselves to themselves. Ethnic slurs and racist anecdote can be heard all too clearly.

There may even be a sense of terminal social decay that will remind us of the bar in *The Iceman Cometh* by Eugene O'Neill. The pub may bring happiness, but it may also be the place of last resort for the defeated, the dismal, and the dispossessed. In this matter, a verbal poll of one or two experienced Londoners may be advisable.

The enquiring visitor should also keep in mind the ancient institution of the London parish church. When it comes to pulling in a crowd, these are not the glory days of the Church of England. Many a parish church is simply too big for its current needs. Some are locked. Some have been put to other uses. Some have been pulled down. Sometimes the language of the Anglican service has been modernized to hideous effect.

But in spite of all this there is much to admire in the soaring ambition of many a Victorian church in London. That ambition was not necessarily powered by a rich community or a fashionable location. Kilburn, for instance, was not grand then, and it is not grand now, but in 1871 work was begun on the church of St. Augustine, for which John Loughborough Pearson was the architect.

It took nine years to complete, and it did not get its steeple till 1898, but Pearson achieved the Victorians' aim of bringing Heaven down to earth in structures that both astound and embrace, dazzle and console. Pearson's perspective drawing shows how elaborate was his ornamentation, how delicate the soaring arches, and how massive the galleries. In that drawing, Pearson may have somewhat upgraded the social standing of the local congregation, but we sense how proud he was of the vertiginous and multicolored interior. And rightly so: Pevsner called this

Walter Richard Sickert. *Ennui.*
c. 1917–18. Oil on canvas,
29⅞ × 22″ (76 × 56 cm). Ashmolean Museum, Oxford.
Bequest of Mr. F. Hindley
Smith, 1939

"one of the best churches of its date in the whole of England: a proud, honest, upright achievement."

In a way that was pictured to perfection by Thomas Hardy in a diary entry in 1878, the London parish church is the locus classicus of the London daydream. It is a place in which the Londoner is never interrupted and never intruded upon. Devotions play their part in it, but the Church of England service is a well-mannered affair. If thoughts wander, remorse and shame do not follow upon it. People stand up, sit down, and kneel down according to standard practice, but their inner life proceeds unhampered.

Skirts were longer and more sumptuous in 1878, and the congregation in the lately completed church of St. Mary Abbots in Kensington High Street was well dressed and well-to-do. Sitting there, Hardy noted how, "When the congregation rises, there is a rustling of silks like that of the Devil's wings in *Paradise Lost*. Every woman there, even if she had forgotten it before, has a single thought to the folds of

her clothes. They pray in the litany as if under enchantment. Their real life is spinning along beneath this apparent one of calm, like the District Railway trains underground just below—throbbing, rushing, hot, concerned with last week, next week . . ."

"Could those true scenes in which this congregation is living be brought into church bodily with the personages, there would be a churchful of jostling phantasmagoria, crowded like a heap of soap bubbles, infinitely intersecting, but each seeing only his own."

"That bald-headed man is surrounded by the interior of the Stock Exchange; that girl, by the jeweler's shop in which she purchased yesterday. Through this bizarre world of thought circulates the recitative of the parson—a thin solitary note without cadence or change of intensity—and getting lost like a bee in the clerestory." Though possibly unfair to the diction of today's parsons, this passage captures something that will last as long as the Church of England itself.

In any of the places thus far described, daydreaming may lead to a craving for a house, or for an apartment, in which we would find our very own four walls and live in them happily forever. London is quick to oblige in that respect. Even a walk past the estate agents after office hours can fire that particular craving.

But . . . "men were deceivers ever." There are tens of thousands of rooms in London, as in every other big city, that do not augur well for a long, happy, and peaceful home life. In those rooms, life has come to a standstill. In his paintings, Walter Sickert more than once got them to perfection. In the several versions of his *Ennui,* there is a dead-end sadness. Over some of his other, darker imaginings it is possible to feel that the debt collector, if not eventually the hangman, stands watch.

Henry Treffry Dunn. *Dante Gabriel Rossetti with Theodore Watts Dunton.* 1882. Watercolor, 21¼ × 32¼" (54 × 81.9 cm). The National Portrait Gallery, London

When he lived on Cheyne Walk, the poet and painter D. G. Rossetti had a famously odd and original interior, of which a small zoo (not visible here) was at one time a feature.

Yet London within four walls can also have, even today, a healing silence and a healing stillness. The uncluttered quiet of the room in Hampstead portrayed by William Rothenstein has not gone out of style. Somewhere in that room, there is epitomized the notion set out in more than one of Anita Brookner's novels—that there need be nothing second-rate about living by oneself.

One thing remains to be decided: the kind of house in which we should most like to live. My own inclinations in this matter are really quite modest. A low profile would do. What I should most like is a small house in the London of the 1820s and 1830s. It would not be the work of a major architect, though I think highly of whoever built Peel Street, off Kensington High Street, in 1824, and I would gladly look out, every day, on the elegant round dance of the linked little houses in Lloyd Square, just across the river from the Houses of Parliament.

My house would have no claims to novelty. Trim, plain, and unpretentious, it minds its own business in the general scene. In the heyday of Constable among painters, of Hazlitt, Coleridge, Charles Lamb, and Leigh Hunt among writers, and of many a first-rate actor and actress on the London stage, houses of this sort were just what they wanted. One could live in London like a turtle in its shell—though perhaps a little faster on one's feet—and find all the world within a mile or two.

William Blake, the poet, painter, printer, publisher, and visionary, was an example of that. He was the complete Londoner. Born just off Golden Square, the son of a hosier, he went to a drawing school in the Strand, studied at the Royal Academy School in London, and was married in Battersea Church by the Thames.

Anna Alma-Tadema. *Sir Lawrence Alma-Tadema's Library in Townshend House, London.* 1884. Pen and ink and watercolor, 13 × 17¾″ (33 × 45 cm). Private collection

The 1880s were the heyday of the "artist's interior" in London. The interiors were often offset by gardens, small but lush, in which the outdoors was brought indoors and the big city was told to go away and come back another time.

He set up house near Leicester Square and sang songs of his own composition at a friend's home on Rathbone Place, a still-extant little street, just off the Tottenham Court Road, in which Constable and Hazlitt had also lived. He started a business of his own on Poland Street, lived for much of the 1790s in Hercules Buildings in Lambeth, and died on Fountain Court, off the Strand.

Blake lived in London as if it were an extension of his own skin. Plain and simple in his ways, though occasionally he liked to drink wine by the tumblerful, he could make the tiniest big-city garden stand in for the Garden of Eden.

In their little summerhouse in Lambeth, he and his wife—then in their thirties—liked to sit stark naked on a fine summer afternoon and read aloud from *Paradise Lost*. If a friend happened to pass by, Blake would call out and say, "Come right in! It's only Adam and Eve, you know!"

The little houses that I now covet were habitable in the highest degree. This, for instance, is what Charles Lamb wrote about Colebrooke Cottage in Islington not long after he took possession of it in the 1820s:

> It is a white house with six good rooms, the New Rover river (rather elderly by this time) runs (if a moderate walking pace can be so termed) close to the foot of the house. Behind is a spacious garden, with vines (I assure you), pears, strawberries, parsnips, leeks, carrots and cabbages to delight the heart of old Alcinous.
>
> You enter without passage into a cheerful dining room, all studded over and rough with old books, and above is a lightsome drawing room, three windows, full of choice prints. I feel like a great Lord, never having had a house before.

That's what I should have liked. This was a time at which almost all persons of good character would have settled for a small house—a cottage, some would call it—on the edges of Hampstead Heath. On a small scale, indoor London is nowhere more seductive. Houses on Well Walk, let us say, or on Keats Grove, are irresistible to this day. But in 1812, when Leigh Hunt and his family had just moved into one, they were paradise itself.

"Our cottage," Hunt wrote to a friend, "is really and bona fide a cottage, with most humble ceilings and unsophisticated staircases; but there is green about it, and a little garden of laurel; and I can put you in a room where there will be a little library of poets, and an original portrait of Milton to overlook us as we sit drinking our glass of wine."

With his sense of fun, his delight in the sweet and simple life, and his unremitting but largely ill-rewarded intellectual activity, Leigh Hunt (1784–1859) was in many ways an archetypal Hampstead resident. The son of an English father and an American mother, he was in 1812 the editor of *The Examiner,* an independent journal that was unusually disrespectful in its opinions. As a drama critic of near-genius, Leigh Hunt is one of the least well known and most generally underrated figures in English literature. If for no other reason, he would have his place in history as the man who introduced Keats to Shelley and stood up for both of them in print.

As the collaborator of Byron in a short-lived magazine called *The Liberal,* he published a poem by Byron called "A Vision of Judgment" and some translations by Shelley from *Faust* that were vital to the spirit of the age. As a critic, and as a translator, he had a magical ease and fluency. As a polemicist, he was brilliant but injudicious, and as a magazine editor and a champion of liberal causes, he had great opportunities and botched every one of them.

In the management of his life he made every possible mistake. Of his father it was once said that, although he took holy orders and became a popular preacher, "a want of steadiness, want of orthodoxy and want of interest conspired to prevent his obtaining any employment." Leigh Hunt himself was hardly ever out of trouble, of one sort or another, and in 1812 he made his most conspicuous mistake.

Widespread pleasure was given in 1812 when he attacked the Prince Regent. He called the Prince, among much else, a "fat Adonis." Nothing in the attack was strictly untrue, but it was too well put for human endurance. In December 1812 Leigh Hunt was prosecuted for libel and found guilty.

This could have been terrible news. In London, as most everywhere else, it is better not to be in jail. Prisons in Hogarth's day were hell on earth for almost everyone who was sent to them. I could name prisons in London today of which much the same is said.

But Leigh Hunt was not going to show fear. On February 3, 1813, he presented himself for sentence. He was dressed, as if for a festive occasion, in his best suit, with a new hat and a new pair of gloves. In his hand he had a book called *Comus* by the Dutch poet Erycius Puteanus. He was sentenced to two years in prison, and he served them without remission.

A catastrophe, one might think. A paradise lost. An inferno substituted. And what is prison doing in this chapter, where the notion of four walls has so often gone hand in hand with the notion of human fulfillment?

It is here because in the 1790s, in that same Southwark, an architect named George Gwilt built what was intended as a model prison. Its name was the Horsemonger Lane Gaol.

As it turned out, Leigh Hunt's life on Horsemonger Lane was a party of pleasure from morning till night. The former prison yard, outside the window, had been turned into a garden, with pansies and trellised scarlet runners for his guests to marvel at. He had two rooms, one of them wallpapered and distempered, with the ceiling "a Florentine Heaven, prepared and freshly painted."

His wife and children lived with him. He had a piano, a lute, some busts of the great poets, and bookcases full of Chaucer, Milton, Spenser, and Dryden. Visitors were sent away with scented bunches of flowers from his garden. In May, there was Persian lilac in full bloom, and rhododendrons, and broom with white blossom on its stems.

When Jeremy Bentham came to call, he and Leigh Hunt played with battledore and shuttlecock. Cowden Clarke, who had taught Keats in school, came by with fresh fruit, fresh vegetables, and new-laid eggs. When the painter Benjamin Robert Haydon had a large new canvas, *The Judgment of Solomon,* sent round for Leigh Hunt's opinion, the prison gates were opened to let it through.

Hunt was allowed to edit *The Examiner* from prison. Shelley asked if he could help with the cash flow. Byron first met Leigh Hunt in prison, thanks to the intermediacy of the Irish poet Thomas Moore. Early visitors could order breakfast, and Hunt's friends could stay until ten P.M., when the under-turnkey knocked on the door, lantern in hand, and bowed them out into the street.

And this was prison? We rub our eyes. Yet the Horsemonger Lane Gaol should have a place in any history of the domestic interior in London. The story of Leigh Hunt is exceptional? Yes, of course it is. But it is indicative of an endearing aspect of Londoners—their buoyancy, their loyalty to friends who are in trouble, and their ability to make the best of whatever four walls come their way.

The Thames, Back Then and Right Now

IKNEW THAT SOMETHING very curious had happened to London when I opened a book of aerial photographs a year or two ago and found that the Tower Bridge had been repainted in blue and white, like an Easter bonnet. The Tower Bridge! A working bridge, across a working river! What would this transformation have done to Sir John Wolfe-Barry and Sir Horace Jones, who had designed the Tower Bridge in 1886 and seen it opened in 1894 as one of the last authentic monuments of the late Victorian age? Would they have turned in their knighthoods and opted for emigration? Or would they have gone back to counting their debentures and receipting their dividends? And what would the City Corporation have said, who had spent £1.5 million in late Victorian money, when pounds came in solid gold sovereigns and one of them would buy a night in the best hotel in town?

The prettifying of the Tower Bridge is not altogether a libel. As far as the Thames is concerned, the great bridge today has nothing much to do but look nice and act as a backdrop to the Tower of London. Rare is the big ship that calls for the raising of its center span—always an awesome moment—and the momentary suspension of road traffic between the north and the south banks of the Thames. Watching that solemn raising in the 1920s and 30s, we said to ourselves, "It's being done for the Empire" and inwardly we saluted (or snarled, according to our political stance).

The Tower Bridge at that time was, as much as anywhere else, the true center of the British Empire. And it looked the part, with its near-Gothic towers, its cutwaters worthy of the great ships of the Royal Navy, and its graceful but oh! so powerful profile. There was nothing trivial or perfunctory about the Tower Bridge, and we felt that if Sir Edward Elgar had not written music in its honor, it was an oversight that he still had time to put right. What better subject for the old gentleman than the gateway to London—or, conversely, the last link between one shore and the next one that the mariner man would remember as he headed for the open sea? To look back on those towers as they diminished in the dusk was truly to see "the last of England."

We were quite right, too. London would not be London without the river Thames. For hundreds of years it was by courtesy of the Thames that people arrived in England, got rich in England, lived high off the hog in England, pursued a criminal career in England, or thought it best to leave England forever. Without the Thames, the great Palace of Whitehall would not have been where it was. Nor would the Houses of Parliament have looked right, or been right, had they not been on the north bank of the Thames and next to Westminster Bridge.

There had been a fortress on the site of the Tower of London since Roman times, and it was the Thames that made it mandatory. In the nineteenth century the Royal Docks, downstream from Tower Bridge, were the very symbol and epitome of Britain's mercantile prowess. There were great monasteries (now gone) on the Thames.

The primacy of the Thames has not quite been lost to London. Upstream from

Aerial view of Tower Bridge, the Thames, and St. Katharine's Dock. 1987

Den Tower van London

the Tower Bridge, the Thames today has a great hotel (the Savoy). It has a great art gallery (the Tate). It has the National Theatre, the Royal Festival Hall, and the National Film Theatre. In the heyday of travel by rail you could leave town from Cannon Street, Blackfriars, London Bridge, Charing Cross, and Victoria stations and almost dip your feet in the Thames on the way to Madrid—as it might be—or Constantinople, or St. Petersburg.

It was on Bankside, on the south bank of the Thames, that William Shakespeare trod the stage. At one time or another J. M. W. Turner, James McNeill Whistler, Henry James, and T. S. Eliot looked out every morning along the same short stretch of the Thames. It was in Chelsea, on the north bank, that Sir (later St.) Thomas More spent time, and in Battersea, on the south bank, that William Blake was married.

But the cosmopolitan element in the Thames came primarily from overseas. Foreigners of every kind and stripe came in from the sea, made an early landfall, went ashore, and settled down not too far from the river (just in case they wanted to get back out again). When the great Flemish painter Anthony van Dyck came to England in 1632, a house was immediately found for him at Blackfriars, the better for him to receive royal and other visitors. (Taking a boat was the best way to get around the center of the city.)

When the young Peter the Great roistered in London in 1698 it was the river, the shipyard, and the docks that made him feel completely at home. When Canaletto was in London in the 1740s and 1750s it was the Thames, above all things, that inspired him. When Claude Monet came over from Paris he did not go roving in search of motifs, like his friend and colleague Camille Pissarro. He took a room overlooking the Thames near Waterloo Bridge and worked from his window.

If foreigners were drawn to the Thames, it was because it offered them a world in continual flux. With the Thames at your back, you could meet anyone and do anything, with few or no questions asked. If you preferred to lose your identity and vanish like a mouse in a wheel of Brie, there were plenty of people beside the Thames, downstream from London Bridge, who would be happy to help you to do it.

When the great docks were built, from 1802 onward, that part of London had

Wenceslaus Hollar. *View of the Tower of London as seen from the Thames.* c. 1637–43. Pen and brown ink with watercolor over black lead, 4⅜ × 11⅛″ (11.1 × 28.3 cm). By permission of the Trustees of the British Museum, London

Though saddled since World War II with many a bruising and uncongenial new neighbor, the Tower of London has kept its place as a model of stylish officialdom and a treasure house of baubles beyond price.

more than ever the character of an open city. Money in one form or another was pouring into the London docks. With a little bit of mischief here, and another little bit of mischief there, men and women could live well, from day to day, and laugh at the law. Meanwhile, and thanks to the train, the bridge, and the tunnel, Londoners could live all their lives in London and never set foot on a boat in the Thames. As for the dockland, the very name of it made them shudder.

Until well into the lifetime of Charles Dickens, as readers of *Oliver Twist* well know, life on or near the Thames was compounded of stealth, violence, and illegality. The thief, the whore master, the hired killer, the man on the run—all saw the Thames as their accomplice. Even in the 1920s, folk-memory insisted that it was as much as one's life was worth to cross Hungerford Bridge alone at night, and only a few years ago an Italian banker was found hanging from a bridge in central London in circumstances that have never been explained.

This is not, of course, a phenomenon peculiar to London. There never was yet a great port that did not foster criminality. From New York to Odessa, and from Shanghai to Antwerp and Amsterdam, a great commercial harbor is quintessentially lawless. How could it be otherwise, given the continual turnover in the population, the opportunity for thieving and a quick getaway, and the presence of men and women who are adventurous and without scruple?

In the case of London, in the heyday of its enormous harbor, the situation was further enriched both by the configuration of central London and by the huge, stark, fortresslike character of the docks that in the nineteenth century were built one after another on cheerless and marshy land downstream from Tower Bridge on the north bank of the Thames.

There is to this day something implicitly sinister about the steep and narrow stairs that lead down from the Thames at point after point on the long serpentine journey from the Pool of London to the sea. A hundred years ago, it was just possible to see the view from those steps in purely pictorial terms. When Hippolyte Taine was in London, he stood at the corner of Shadwell Basin and

> gazed upon the slate-colored waters before me, shining and exhaling mist; the northern bank bounds the horizon with its blackish edges mottled with red; a few ships come down river with the supple and slow movement of a sea-bird; their somber hulls and brown sails balance themselves upon the shimmering water. The silence is all but complete; all that we hear are the sounds of distant hammering, the vague tinkling of a bell and the fluttering of birds in the trees. A Dutch painter—van der Heyden, Backhuysen—would delight in this plain of water, the distant tones of brick and tar, the uncertain horizon where stretch the drowsing clouds. I have seen nothing in London more picturesque.

As to that, both James McNeill Whistler and James Tissot agreed with Taine. But visitors to London also noticed the ferocious, hyperactive degradation that lay no more than a minute's walk from that picturesque river view. They wrote of the disreputable cellars—half drinking shop, half whorehouse—where jobbing violinists played for pennies and women of the street would fight one another almost to the death. ("I noticed blackened eyes, bandaged noses, bloody cheekbones," Taine wrote, "but most horrible of all are their shrill, high-pitched, cracked voices, like that of an ailing screech-owl.")

Ratcliff Highway, notorious from 1811 onward for some particularly gruesome murders, was the epicenter of dockland as it was known to the sailors of every race, color, creed, and size who went on the rampage twenty-four hours a day and 365 days a year. Oysters and baked potatoes—not a bad diet, by the way—were theirs for the asking as they stormed along the street. They could spend money, all the time and however they liked, and they could borrow money, too. (Sextant and boatswain's pipe were the staples of every pawnshop.)

According to one survivor of the late Victorian era, they were a sight to see:

> The black cook who was flush went in for adornments that no other sailor-man would have dreamed of: a white shirt, a flaming tie, a black coat with satin facings—even a white waistcoat and a top hat. There were Spaniards, swart, long-haired, bloodshot-looking fellows, whose entire shore outfit consisted commonly of a red shirt, blue trousers, ankle-jacks with the brown feet visible over them, a belt, a big knife and a pair of large gold ear-rings. Big, yellow-haired, blue-eyed Swedes, who were full pink with sea and sun, not brown or mahogany-colored like the rest; slight, wicked-looking Malays; lean, spitting Yankees, with stripes, and felt hats, and sing-song oaths; sometimes a Chinaman, petticoated, dignified, jeered at; a Lascar, a Greek, a Russian; and everywhere the English Jack, rolling of gait . . . .

W. R. Noble. *Portrait of a Royal Bargeman.* 1843. Oil on canvas, 13⅞ × 10″ (34.3 × 25 cm). The Museum of London

Put like that, it sounds like the march past of "Chinois, Hottentots, bohémiens, niais, hyènes, Molochs . . ." that Arthur Rimbaud evokes in his *Illuminations.* Rimbaud had been in London in 1872 and 1873. Given his taste for the lower depths of great nineteenth-century cities, there seems no reason why he should not have gone adventuring along Ratcliff Highway. And it is of Ratcliff Highway in its heyday that I, for one, think when Alban Berg's opera *Lulu* reaches its final scene. It is with a hand of genius that Alban Berg magics from the orchestra pit the ghost of a late Victorian barrel organ while we wait for Jack the Ripper to cut Lulu to pieces.

But it may be that what Nathaniel Hawthorne had to say was more to the point. Roaming the docklands of London, he wrote that it seemed as if "its heart had been cleft open for the mere purpose of showing how drearily mean and rotten it had become. The shore is lined with the shabbiest, blackest and ugliest buildings that can be imagined, decayed warehouses with blind windows, and wharves that look ruinous; and the muddy tide of the Thames, reflecting nothing, hiding a million of unclean streets with its breast—a sort of guilty conscience, as it were, unwholesome with the rivulets of sin that constantly flow into it—is just the dismal stream to glide by such a city."

Charles Dickens in 1861 put it more concisely when he said that "down by the Docks is a region I would choose as my point of embarkation if I were an emigrant. It would present my intention to me in such a sensible light; it would show me so many things to turn away from."

To live on, or by, the Thames took toughness. It could also call for professional skills of a high order. The deal porter, for one, deserved every penny of what he earned when he tackled the enormous loads of timber from Canada, Norway, and Russia that arrived by ship at the Surrey Commercial Docks in Rotherhithe. The timber was put down on the quays. It then had to be sorted, cut, and carried to warehouses by deal porters who could balance no matter how heavy a load upon their shoulders. In 1939 over a thousand deal porters were still at work in the Surrey Docks.

The coal whippers did a terrific job, too. Working in gangs of four, they raised heavy loads of coal from the decks of a newly arrived ship by bringing their own weight to bear on a rope and tipping the coal into a waiting lighter. It was nothing for a boatload of whippers to unload ninety-eight tons of coal in a day. (Mayhew in his *London Labour and the London Poor* said that "to whip one ton, these men jump up and down 144 feet."A day's work corresponded, he said, to the raising of a standard load to a height of four miles.)

When the television series "The London River" was made in the late 1980s there were still veteran dockers around who could testify to the unpleasantness of unloading sugar, talcum powder, iodine, or tea from Assam. Nor was it a party of pleasure to deal with horses' skins and cattle skins, or with the dog skins (up to a thousand a day) that arrived still wet with blood.

The Thames was not the place to go to in search of a secure and comfortable nine-to-five life, even if one or two gentrified pubs may suggest otherwise today. The very names of the points at which watermen plied their trade are eloquent: Gallions Reach, Cuckold's Point, Limehouse Hole, Pickle Herring Stairs, Bugsby Reach, Dock-and-Duck Stairs. As for the watermen themselves, their command of foul language was without equal in the eighteenth century, and one historian tells us that even Dr. Samuel Johnson, when on the river, caught the contagion and "exercized his powers of objurgation to overwhelm some astonished Londoner on a passing boat."

The watermen were members of, or at any rate witnesses to, a largely anarchical society. Ships came upriver and had nowhere to dock. Cargoes were unloaded, put down on the quayside, and left there. Sometimes they sat there for weeks, for lack of warehouse space. At nightfall, if not before, bad characters moved in. (Among those who worked in the area, one in three was reckoned to be either a thief or a receiver of stolen goods.)

The London of docks and dockers impinged hardly at all on the rest of London

William John Huggins. *The Opening of St. Katharine Dock, October 25, 1828.* 1828. Oil on canvas, 12 × 18¾″ (30.5 × 47.6 cm). The Museum of London

but did a great deal to make London prosperous. Until just a few years ago, water generated wealth. In the 1930s it was very pleasant to stand on Tower Bridge and watch the big ships nosing their way into the Pool of London and hear the big cranes loading and unloading. The noise—uninterrupted, loud, and inescapable—was that of an immense cauldron. One felt oneself at the very center of the largest empire that the world had ever seen. The Pool of London was a paradigm of frenetic activity, but in those days it also seemed to stand for something stable, continuous, and—why not?—eternal.

Even forty years ago, the Pool of London and its nearby docklands could still impress a much-traveled visitor as Cosmopolis itself. Someone who toured them in 1956 in a yacht lent for the purpose was Mario Praz, the Italian connoisseur, collector, polymath, historian of the decorative arts, and autobiographer.

"Entering the Royal Docks," he said, "was like entering vast cathedrals, vast houses full of ships drawn up one behind the other like precious plants with exotic names, or like privileged altars, like confessionals for all the languages of the world."

One of the port officials explained to him that "the *Malabar* was bound for Karachi, Bombay, and Calcutta; the *Sunda* was en route for Padang and Singapore; the *North Star,* a beautiful white ship, very modern, green below the waterline, was going to Brazil. At that moment the *Malabar* was taking on board two big packages of a fine indigo color. Other ships were carrying rubber; yet others, timber and grain; from New Zealand, pears and apples were arriving."

"Here," Praz went on, "the extremes of the earth came together, and the world seemed like a heart where the blood of the whole world flowed in and out. Elsewhere, the history of England revealed itself in this or that aspect of solemn pageantry, of customs full of charm, but here was life itself, and the feeling of an empire unfolding before one's eyes."

Even as Praz wrote, that state of affairs was unraveling. But in her guide to the docklands Stephanie Williams reminds us that as late as the 1950s the Royal Albert Dock, opened in 1870, was handling ships from Jamaica that arrived with cargoes of up to 160,000 stems of bananas. There were cold stores in that same dock that could handle more than 300,000 carcasses of beef, lamb, and mutton.

Yet we can date almost to the very day the moment at which the Pool of London lost out and what had seemed the eternal became the temporary. On the day of Winston Churchill's funeral in 1965 an unwonted silence enveloped the whole city of London. In that silence, ears were sharpened. In a paradoxical way, they found plenty to listen to. The English have a genius for the state funeral, and this particular one had been planned with a sense of poetry that astonished many a foreign visitor.

It had been decided that the "Former Naval Person," as he liked to style himself, should make part of his last journey by water. As the coffin passed under Tower Bridge on its roundabout route to Paddington Station, there could be heard an unprecedented salute—a perfectly concerted clanking and rattling that came from Hays Wharf on the south bank of the Thames, where giant cranes were lowered in unison to the equivalent of half-mast.

In later years, that sound seemed more and more to have been a salute not only to a great warrior but to an idea, and an actuality, whose time had passed. It was for the Pool of London, and for the London Docks, as much as for Winston Churchill, that that metallic requiem had sounded. For one reason or another, the Thames as the instrument of power, wealth, and protection had given in without a struggle after World War II.

John Thomson. *Workers on the "Silent Highway."* c. 1876–77. Gelatin silver print. Collection of the George Eastman House, Rochester, New York

The great nineteenth-century forts—Cliffe Fort, Coalhouse Fort, and Shornmead Fort—would never again fire their guns. The great docks closed, one by one. The big ships went elsewhere. There was no longer an empire to pump rum and hardwood into the West India Dock, sugar, wool, and rubber into St. Katharine's Dock, grain into Millwall Dock, softwood into the Surrey Dock, and coffee, cocoa, ivory, and spices into the London Docks.

As to the impact of those docks, I cannot better the brief account in Weinreb and Hibbert's *London Encyclopedia:*

> The splendid warehouses of brick, with stone plinths and rustications, carved with ammonites and sea patterns, were mostly four stories high. They stood above remarkable, brick-vaulted wine cellars of vast extent, joined beneath the roads by tunnels and skilfully ventilated. Surrounded by the obligatory high walls, the works had a Roman dignity, thanks to the designer, Daniel Asher Alexander.

James McNeill Whistler. *Rotherhithe.* 1860. Etching, 10¹³⁄₁₆ × 7⅞" (27.5 × 19.9 cm). The New York Public Library Astor, Lenox and Tilden Foundations

To those who grew up in London in the 1920s and 1930s, the docks were omnipresent, even if we never saw them. We imagined the big ships slithering in and out of the narrow deep-water channels. We dreamed of that terrifying novelty, the refrigerated carcass of meat, which was said to lie in the hundreds of thousands, if not in the millions, somewhere in the docks. We knew that the docks were continually being improved and enlarged and perfected. London without the docks would die, we thought, or starve, or at any rate be disgraced.

Did they not have the stamp of royalty? The King George V Dock had been opened as recently as 1921. Without the docks, King George V could not count on his Darjeeling tea for breakfast, his Patna rice at luncheon, or his naval tot of Jamaica rum in times of stress. Without the docks, England would come to a standstill and shrink to the status of Jersey or Guernsey.

Quite apart from that, there was still something irresistibly and irreplaceably raffish about the Thames as it moved in its sluggish, broody way toward the sea. Elsewhere, the edges of London petered out in gentility. But the Thames was not bourgeois, and never would be. We remembered how Samuel Pepys—at that time an exemplary officer of state, who could calculate the Navy's accounts and bring them in correct to the last penny—would lie on his bunk in an outgoing naval ship and train his telescope on the pretty women on board the East Indiaman that sailed conveniently close.

We also remembered the pirates who had been hanged on the narrow foreshore of the Thames. After being cut down, they were left to lie on that same foreshore until three tides had washed over them and declared them truly dead. At the foot of Wapping Old Stairs there can still be seen at low tide a post to which condemned pirates were chained and left to drown in the rising tide.

In the 1930s, the tone of those now-distant trips from Charing Cross pier to Greenwich was not at all nostalgic. As the excursion boat puttered past Woolwich, the loud speakers retold the story of the Royal Dockyard, and of the Royal Arsenal, next door to it, as if their great days would never come to an end. No one was told that the dockyard, in which great men-of-war were built in the sixteenth and seventeenth centuries, had later fallen into decline and been closed in 1869. As for the Arsenal, it was to serve us well during World War II, but it too is now closed and best known to Londoners as the name of a great football team.

What mattered then was the present, the here and now, just as it had mattered to James McNeill Whistler when he lived near the river and the docks in the late

James McNeill Whistler. *Eagle Wharf*. 1859. Etching, 5⁷⁄₁₆ × 8⁷⁄₁₆″ (13.8 × 21.4 cm). The New York Public Library Astor, Lenox and Tilden Foundations

James McNeill Whistler. *Black Lion Wharf*. 1859. Etching, 5⁷⁄₈ × 8⁵⁄₈″ (14.9 × 22 cm). The Metropolitan Museum of Art, New York. Harris Brisbane Dick Fund, 1917

1850s and early 1860s. Both in the painting called *Wapping* of 1861 and in the series of etchings called *The Thames Set,* he caught the dockland of his day to perfection.

There were inns by the water, where sea captains took a day or two on shore with their mistresses. Sitting on the balcony of one of those charming, practical, and discreetly unrespectable inns, they could count the big ships at anchor, and the little ships beating upstream, and the oarsmen making their best speed in and out of the traffic, and the busy, Venetian look of the houses on the north bank.

The new factories blew their smoke high in the air, the ancient sails were the very devil to mend, and the sturdy little steamships came puffing by as if they couldn't wait to put the brigs and the schooners out of business. One could lunch off Dutch eels that had been shipped in Dutch bottoms from the Zuyder Zee to the Pool of London since the reign of Queen Elizabeth I. (A glass of Dutch gin was not lacking, either, and it made them taste all the better.)

Whistler monitored all that activity from an inn called the Angel, which stood on the south bank of the river in Rotherhithe and looked across the water to Wapping. Working on a painting of just that scene, and changing it over and over again, he handed down to us the look, the color, the texture, and the animation of that part of the Thames at that time. If the painting has an emotional vibration that we can none of us miss, it may be because Whistler suggested that the thing most worth looking at in the tumultuous scene was the red hair of his Irish mistress, Joanne Hifferman—a red that Whistler described to the French painter Fantin-Latour as "not a gilded red, but a brazen red—the red Venetian hair that we have always dreamed of!"

More than any other painter, Whistler at that time disentangled the life of the docks in terms not of transients and outcasts and criminals, but of men and women who made an avowable living there. Incomparable as he was at the depiction of vast, vague spaces from which the night had withdrawn every last semblance of the particular, he was just as good at portraying the ship's chandler, the jobbing boatman, the lime-burner, the sail maker and mender, and the longshoreman.

He knew how the everyday people of dockland lived, what they wore, how they carried themselves. His friends were amazed, in fact, at his mastery of detail, given that he could not even see whether his shoes were properly polished without reaching for his eyeglass.

Secretive by nature, he did not care to let anyone know what he was doing, or how he was doing it, though he did occasionally allow his friends to come down and spend a convivial evening. Some of them—Fantin-Latour, for one—did not much care for it. On the way, there were just too many places in which, as Dickens said in *Our Mutual Friend*, "the accumulated scum of humanity seemed to be washed from higher grounds, like so much moral sewage, until its own weight forced it over the bank and sunk it into the river." But, on balance, there were others who found the adventure worthwhile.

One or two things remain to be said about the Thames between the Pool of London and the sea as it existed until a generation ago. One is that it was once the most abundant of rivers. Rather more than four hundred years ago, it was said in Holinshed's *Chronicle* that for fat and sweet salmon, readily available in large numbers, no river in Europe could rival the Thames. As for shrimp, flounder, gudgeon, dace, roach, bream, perch, barbel, trout, and cub, there were enough even for the avarice of those who fished them and made a good living out of it. "Oh that this river might be spared but even one year from nets, etc.!" Holinshed wrote. "But alas," he added, "then should many a poor man be undone."

Myself neither fisherman, birder, nor botanist, I cannot speak from experience of the Thames estuary in any of those contexts. I do, however, take counsel from those better equipped. In particular, Nicholson's *Guide to the Thames* is a treasure house of indications as to what the estuary may still have to offer. Whether the Stanhope Café in Stanhope le Hope, on the north bank of the Thames, is still remarkable for that English delicacy the sultana roll is not for me to say, but I raise my hat to the vagabond who first spread the good news. As for the boat store in Sheerness, I salute its designer, G. T. Greene, who in 1858–60 built the huge and elegant structure that is believed to be the world's first multistory iron-framed building. ("Until fairly recently," our guide tells us, "it was thought to be a 20th century structure.")

On a more intimate level, I treasure from that same guidebook the information that "at Bromley by Bow gasworks there is a colony of rabbits, paler than normal rabbits and with a slightly darker back." From the fast-vanishing Erith Marshes I mourn—perhaps prematurely—the thousands of wild daffodils that flourished in

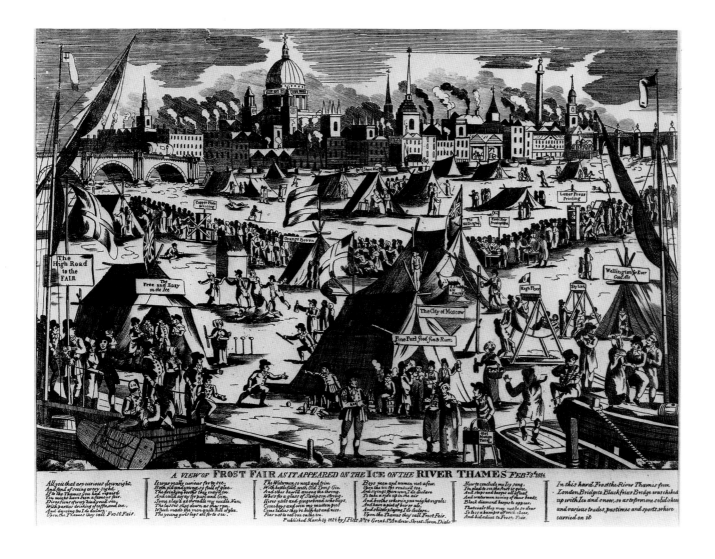

A VIEW OF FROST FAIR AS IT APPEARED ON THE ICE ON THE RIVER THAMES FEB.³ᵈ 1814.

Anonymous. *A View of Frost Fair on the River Thames.* 1814. Woodcut, 15 × 20¼″ (38.2 × 51.3 cm). The Museum of London

Abbey Wood, the skylarks that sang around Beckton Gasworks, and the *A. absinthium,* from which absinthe was made.

Farther downriver there is an echo of a bygone cosmopolitanism in the presence of *Rumex cristatus,* a giant weed from Asia Minor, and of *Verbascum phlomoides,* a wooly mullein from western Asia. Whether wild horses still roam around Tilbury Fort is another matter as to which I cannot pronounce. But I should grieve to think that asparagus and *Foeniculum vulgare* (fennel) no longer grow near Tilbury, or that the walker along the seawall of the Thames estuary can no longer count on seeing the "shelduck, mallard, widgeon, garganey, gadwell and shoveler" that once fed there. It is in survivals such as these that the ancient particularity of the Thames estuary so long resided.

If any one thing can be said with assurance about the placid, much-put-upon Thames of today it is that it is no longer dangerous. In former days it froze. It burst its banks. It gave city life a whole new slew of possibilities. At the Frost Fairs of the seventeenth and eighteenth centuries, bears were baited on the ice, a coach drawn by six horses was driven across the river for a bet, and you could go skating, sledging, and debauching by day and by night.

But, more often, the Thames was trouble. In 1762, and again in 1791, Westminster Hall was flooded. In 1881, Woolwich Pier was washed away. As lately as January 1928, the North Sea played false—4,350 families in London lost their

William Marlow. *The London Riverfront from Westminster to the Adelphi.* c. 1771–72. Oil on canvas, 53⅜ × 74¾" (135.3 × 190 cm). The Museum of London

homes and the moat in the Tower of London was filled for the first time in hundreds of years. In 1953, 309 people were drowned by flooding.

At the time of the flooding in 1953, the understated heroics of wartime once again came into play. Canvey Island, on the Thames estuary, could be reached only through a manual telephone exchange, which at night had only one operator. A key witness said of him that "he sat literally in the rising water until the telephone system went out of operation."

Floods arose almost without warning, in those years, and defenses were few and paltry. In 1971, another flood made the point clearer than ever. The Thames might no longer be indispensable to the prosperity of London, but it still had its full potential for damage.

That is why, between 1974 and 1982, the Thames Barrier was erected across Woolwich Reach. When raised from the riverbed in times of possible emergency, it is an arresting and even a rather romantic object, suggestive of a row of stalwart ships that are ready to set forth at a moment's notice in defense of London. In reality it is a sevenfold concrete obstacle that can turn itself at short notice into a steel barrier that, if need be, can turn back the Thames. Hardly had it been built, at a cost of £450 million, than in February 1983 it was put to the test and came through triumphantly. From the fear of flood, London was delivered.

That was a happy turn of events for London as a whole, but the future of the docklands remained undecided. One by one, the great docks had closed. That great

André Derain. *London Bridge.* 1906. Oil on canvas, 26 × 39" (66 × 99.1 cm). Collection, The Museum of Modern Art, New York. Gift of Mr. and Mrs. Charles Zadok

Working with big slabs of pure and bright color, André Derain in 1906 disassembled the traditional idiom of European townscape. With his paintings of London Bridge and of St. Paul's Cathedral, he did not fragment the subject matter, but gave it a heightened identity.

invention, the container, had killed them. For lack of trade, Wapping was closed in 1968, West India and Millwall in 1980, and the Royal Docks in 1981. These closures put an end to a cycle of adventures that had begun when the West India Dock was opened in the Isle of Dogs in 1800, the London Dock in 1802, the Greenland Docks in 1804, and the East India Dock in 1805. That cycle had lasted less than a hundred and fifty years, but Britain without it would have been a smaller and a feebler place.

The Royal Docks were larger in area than many a European city. In the 1930s, when a gigantic reinforced concrete structure called Millennium Mills was built in the Royal Victoria Dock, it really did seem destined to serve the century that was due to arrive seventy years later. So did that stately flagship of the Cooperative Wholesale Society, the CWS Granary, begun as late as 1938.

Everything about the prewar docklands seemed to be entered for a world championship of one kind or another. The gasworks at Beckton, near the Royal Docks, had been (and possibly was still) the biggest in Europe. Its neighbor, the sewage treatment plant, was no dwarf, either.

But during World War II the docklands lost a third of its warehousing by enemy action, and roughly half of its storage facilities. Enemy action had dealt savagely with private housing all over the area. The docks had outlived their original purpose. Where they had closed, warehouses were often left to rot. The death of a certain Britain was there for all to see.

Yet in recent years the docklands have entered upon a completely new phase. No one could have foreseen that the north bank of the Thames below Tower Bridge would one day become the equivalent of the Giudecca in Venice—a neighborhood in which one could live relatively cheaply and have glorious views across a broad stretch of water that even today is not at all dull.

On one level, this was related to the general transformation of central London

into a vast pleasure resort and lucrative hospitality center. London at the end of World War II had problems without precedent. But they were problems with possibilities. The former docklands could have sunk into dereliction, but in a time of relative optimism they could also be put to exemplary use.

Empty warehouses, in particular, often had huge interior spaces with a built-in potential for grandeur. They could be rehabilitated in ones and twos, as happened in 1972 when Oliver's Wharf on Wapping High Street was deftly turned into flats as magnificent in their scale and proportion as any in London.

There was also potential in buildings that had once enshrined institutions that had either gone elsewhere or faded away. An instance of this was Ivory House, that had looked down on the central basin in St. Katharine's Dock, hard by Tower Bridge, since 1854. Looking as if it had been magically forklifted from a major Italian port, it had served the European ivory trade very well. But after St. Katharine's Dock had been closed in 1966 there was no place for Ivory House, as such, in postwar London.

But, like Oliver's Wharf, it was just too good to lose. So, in 1973, it was the object of an elaborate conversion, with shops at quay level, offices in the mezzanine, and thirty-eight expensive apartments in the four floors above. It was all the more alluring for the fact that, wherever possible, the look and the materials of the past were integrated into the present.

Oliver's Wharf and Ivory House were role models. Nineteenth-century industrial architecture became, in effect, designer architecture, with already-existing features treated as heirlooms. Where those features did not exist—in new buildings, above all—property developers saw to it that marine echoes of one sort or another were simulated. If this was architecture in fancy dress, so much the better for the shareholders.

Initially, those conversions were aimed at the top end of the market, and to clients who saw themselves as immune to the possibility of pauperdom. A metropolitan wonderland freshened by salted breezes was within reach of any discerning individual who could afford it.

But before long the idea got around that the largely abandoned docklands could be rethought and made over in terms of an entirely new and very large section of London. Here were five thousand acres of potentially prime land, almost next door to the City of London. On those acres, people could live well and money could be made on the almost unimaginable scale that seemed well within reach in the 1980s.

Nothing was impossible. Whole towns would be built on virtually dead ground. There would be hotels, marinas, restaurants, schools, movie houses, sports grounds, arenas, health clubs on every corner, and campus-style parks in which every office would look out onto a landscaped view.

There would be thousands of new houses at every level of the market. People would fight for space in stylish offices equipped with every known mode of electronic communication. The largest shopping mall in Britain would fulfill their every need. Nineteenth-century industry would vanish, and in its place would be a whole new city, powered and prompted by the information industry.

All this, and architectural quality as well? It was not thought to be an impossible dream. The early postwar years in Britain were the age of the New Towns that were to be built in new places and make possible a new, happier, and more effective mode of life.

Where better than the docklands to bring the idea of the New Town to apotheosis? The local authorities concerned were anxious, each in their own way, to do right by their communities. Initially, there was a loyalty to the tradition of the East End as a primarily blue-collar or working-class area. The idea that it should be turned into a middle-class residential area, untainted by industry, did not win favor.

As against that, there was the fact that much of the East End was doomed or dead land, and that to rehabilitate it as a commercial area would cost an immense amount of money. The government of the day did not feel able to do it. Nor did private money come rolling in.

Investors preferred projects like the huge and hideous Tower Hotel, which is said to do very well with its eight hundred and more rooms within sight of Tower Bridge. Fancy apartments in places previously regarded as uninhabitable were also regarded as a good bet. So was new office space within walking distance of the City. The idea that the East End was about people, as much as about profits, was not popular in those days.

A key event was the formation in July 1981 of the London Docklands Development Corporation, which was intended to foster, regulate, and coordinate what would be by far the largest undertaking of its kind ever to be launched in Britain.

The next key event was the "listing" in 1983 of most of the dockyards' remaining nineteenth-century warehouses. Once on the list in question, those warehouses could not be pulled down. This had two results. One was that warehouse property was bound to rise in value. The other was that the warehouse, no matter how subtly adjusted, would remain the standard element on the docklands landscape. What the row house had been to Georgian London, the warehouse would be to the docklands. In this way, the cityscape might have a sense of continuity—and, with that, a certain generosity and simplicity of scale.

The conversion of warehouses attracted all kinds of people, some of them predictable, some of them not. One of the earliest and most distinguished conversions was commissioned by a young man of business called Andrew Wadsworth. In 1980, when he bought what was left of a late-Victorian group of warehouses in Bermondsey, he was only twenty-three years old. By 1984, at a cost of £3 million, and thanks to the participation of the architectural firm of Pollard, Thomas and Edwards, New Concordia Wharf in Mill Street, Bermondsey, emerged as a triumph of tact and discretion that was as pleasant to live and work in as it was to look at.

Elsewhere, timidity surfaced. What if not enough people had confidence in the new docklands? What if they were to peter out? What if the marshes were to take over again, and the docks reflood, and chaos be lord over all? Wouldn't it make sense to get the project moving at a bargain rate and with every possible inducement?

It was with this in mind that in 1982 the LDDC established an Enterprise Zone within which anyone who wanted to build an industrial or commercial building would be exempt from all planning restrictions. For the first ten years, they would pay no rates and enjoy one hundred percent relief on capital expenditure. The area in question covered primarily the former West India, East India, and Millwall docks.

These inducements took immediate effect—to an extent, in fact, that amazed many of those who had formulated them. ("We didn't believe our own publicity," one of them said later.) There was a sense that, on the terms offered, even quite small firms could do well in the docklands. Larger firms saw in the words "exempt from all planning restrictions" a license for lucrative, cheap big-scale building.

Concurrently, it became known that the American firm of Olympia & York was planning to develop the Canary Wharf area, just across the river from Greenwich. This news caused a vast euphoria, not only among those who were already

Nicholas Grimshaw & Partners, Ltd. Aerial view of new Waterloo Terminal, London. 1993

One of the most arresting of recent additions to London is the 400-yard-long terminal for trains that will run through the Channel Tunnel from London to Paris, and vice versa.

established in the docklands but among those who now could not get in fast enough. As Stephanie Williams said in 1990, "What began as a modest English confidence game, to encourage investment for a small new town, has turned into one riding on a whole new city center and the biggest development stakes in the world."

It would be a great gamble. But it was not the first great gamble that had been played out in the docklands area. Between the completion of London Dock House in 1805 and the building of St. Katharine's Dock in 1828, immense risks were taken. Acres of housing were razed. Thousands of people were turned out of their homes. Whole neighborhoods were robbed of their identities.

The wonderful plainness imposed upon London Dock House in Wapping by the unsung genius of Daniel Asher Alexander was restored in 1988. But not too much, otherwise, remains of the grand and sober manner in which Asher went about his work in the docklands. The fact that he also built Dartmoor Gaol has not made him loved. But in the docklands he did not mean to be charming, or amusing, or allusive, and he wasn't. He did not have in mind a society that might or might not come into being. Nor was he aiming to build housing, or shops, let alone leisure centers for the future inhabitants of docklands. He just wanted to make the damn place work for the next hundred or so years.

And he succeeded. It may be, though it is too early to say, that the thrust of the

Nicholas Grimshaw & Partners, Ltd. Interior of new Waterloo Terminal, London. 1993

new docklands will be most effective where it follows Alexander's pragmatic, dead-centered approach. The decisive move in that direction was made in 1986, when News International, the headquarters of the *Times, The Sunday Times, Sun, To-Day,* and *The News of the World,* was set up in central Wapping.

This signaled the end of Fleet Street as the center of the newspaper industry in London. Power, not beauty, was the aim of the building, and in this it won out. The *Daily Telegraph* moved into South Quay Plaza, on the Isle of Dogs, soon afterward, and the Mail Newspaper group moved to Rotherhithe.

A higher ambition lay behind the move of the *Financial Times* printing works to East India Dock Road in 1988. The printing of a newspaper is traditionally a secretive business, carried out in crowded quarters by a large and highly skilled work force. It was to be the particularity of the new Financial Times building that the entire printing process would take place in full view of the passerby and with a zero work force on the floor. Big rolls of paper would be fed in at one end. Complete newspapers, folded and neatly bundled, would come out at the other end, un-touched by human hand. As this building was designed by Nicholas Grimshaw and Partners, I can only say that it has been called "the finest building in the docklands, to date."

Among other distinguished arrivals in the information industry are two major buildings whose sole purpose is the international and, whenever possible, the instantaneous transfer of information, worldwide. One is the Reuters Dockland Centre, completed in June 1989, of which the shell and core are by the Richard Rogers Partnership. The other is the Telehouse, also finished in 1989, by Yorke Rosenberg and Mardall. Like the Financial Times building, these have a quality of immediacy and necessity that marks them out at once from the speculative buildings that have gone up all over the docklands and have yet to prove themselves.

When they look back on the last years of the twentieth century in the docklands, future historians may well reach for the oldest cliché in the book and say, "It was the best of times, it was the worst of times." Both cases can be argued. There may well be more new buildings of real distinction in the docklands than in all the rest of England put together. Here and there is the sense of community, of shared enjoyment, that comes about when people have struck out on their own and made a livable environment where none had existed before.

There was a moment in the 1980s at which a spirit of "Can do! Let it rip!" made itself felt here and there. A wild poetry ran free in buildings like John Outram's Storm Water Pumping Station (1988), the "Cascades" apartment building (1988) by Campbell, Zogolovitch, Wilkinson and Gough, and the brilliant blue Circle complex by the same firm on Queen Elizabeth Street on the south bank of the Thames near Tower Bridge. There was a feeling, rare in postwar Britain, that anything was possible.

Even in developments that are widely feared and disliked, poetry sometimes makes its way, uninvited. Cesar Pelli's tall tower in Canary Wharf is not universally loved, by any means, but its stainless steel exterior has turned out to be remarkably sensitive to London light. Sometimes it can blaze like a sunburst, and at other times it turns soft and fugitive, almost Whistlerian. (In gentle, mistlike rain, it can seem to vanish.)

As for the limitless ambition that went into the Royal Docks, it is not extinct, even if no one quite dares to tackle those docks today. To stand on the edge of those docks is to experience a sensation of loneliness that very few great cities can provide. One is there, on a patch of ratty grass. To right, to left, and as far as the eye can see, there is nothing except monuments of recent date that are as impressive, in their way, as their counterparts in Egypt or Mexico. They are not "great art," but in terms of valediction they are tremendous.

What has been built in the last few years is neither planned nor presented in comparable terms. At their best, the new constructions are brisk, efficient, and good to look at. If there is here and there an element of playacting, I can only say that after a day or two of roaming round the late-nineteenth-century City of London I had nothing against a well-thought-out and well-mounted charade.

Besides, there is at least one place in the docklands—Maconochie's Wharf, in the Isle of Dogs—where the human scale has triumphed and professional people have pooled their money and their skills to live as they wanted in the place that they wanted.

Elsewhere, Scandinavian affinities that date back to the eleventh century have been reaffirmed by the presence of a Danish developer, ISLEF, and churches for Finnish and Swedish sailors. In Beckton, a gigantic heap of rubbish from the former sewage plant has been turned into a dry ski slope. And what can be inferred from these miscellanea? Simply that, in the docklands, initiative (like wildflowers) may turn up where we least expect it.

As to the downside of the docklands, there is plenty of it. At the beginning of the 1990s, a time at which almost anything could be built gave way, almost overnight, to a time when nothing could be built. Imaginative large-scale schemes that had already been accepted were suddenly dropped altogether or put on indefinite hold. Greed, arrogance, and the craving for quick money have left many a mark.

Today, visitors can be within fifty yards of a heavily trafficked road and yet find themselves gazing up at a broken-down, boarded-up 1950s apartment block in which the centuries-old criminality of the East End of London has found a new nest. Everything about that apartment house reeks of ill-doing—theft, drug dealing, illegal entrances and exits. This is the heartland of the fraternity and the sorority of gangland, model 1994.

To make the docklands work, there had to be roads, trains (both overground and underground), buses, and an airport. Without a main line railway connection, the Victoria Dock would never have become what it once was—the natural center for Britain's imports of refrigerated meat, bananas, butter, and fresh fruit.

In its place, in the later 1980s, was the Docklands Light Railway, a contrivance that came straight out of the "Ealing comedy" movies of the 1950s. (It did not even stop at the City of London airport, by the way.) There was, therefore, an indispensable level on which the docklands simply didn't work.

There is also a social problem, too complex to be disentangled here but too unpleasant to ignore. Those who think of themselves as East Enders born and bred are often oppressed by a well-justified feeling of insecurity. Ancient ways of life and no less ancient occupations have disintegrated. Whole neighborhoods have gone blank on the map. For those who thought of them as their birthright they are blanker still.

These are people who feel dispossessed, disinherited, and robbed of their identity. That the docklands may become the financial capital of Europe does not encourage them. They will never be hired for work in an automated office. Nor is it the riverview apartment with its high-tech security system that will give them back their dignity.

People who feel thwarted and unloved often turn to hatred as their most reliable motivation in life. On the Isle of Dogs, which in the late 1950s pioneered the systematic beating-up of Pakistani immigrants, the population of Brick Lane had learned to live together with Asians. It was often taken as a symbol of a civilized turnaround in the docklands that over the last three hundred years one and the same building in Spitalfields had served successively as a Huguenot chapel, a synagogue, and most recently as a mosque. People took a pride in that.

But in the late summer of 1993 a member of the far-right British National Party came top of the polls in a local council by-election on the Isle of Dogs. There had previously been an upturn in the number of violent attacks by whites, both on individual Asians and on their property.

Thirty years ago, newly arrived immigrants tried primarily to keep out of the way of their tormentors. But their children have quite another attitude. They know their rights, and they are prepared to fight for them. They also know that racial hatred has lately reached a new level of systematic intensity, worldwide. There are areas in the docklands that come across as a backdrop for guerrilla warfare, and there are evil natures who would like nothing better than to see it break out.

This is the downside of what is good about the docklands—the sense of space, the freedom to reinvent the idea of big city life, and the "new frontier" that makes the City of London look stuffy and inert. That new frontier is one of the great metropolitan adventures of the late twentieth century. For the docklands to go down in failure would be the end of a certain idea of Britain.

Westminster Abbey

I N RESPECT OF WESTMINSTER ABBEY, I have for fifty years had a curious perspective. It dates from the year 1943, at which time it was thought desirable for Westminster Abbey to be patrolled during the hours of darkness by men who in one way or another were associated with art and architecture.

It was expected of us that we would show up at nightfall and stay until sunrise. We received a small dinner allowance, which most often we spent somewhere on Charlotte Street on anonymous chopped meats and a thimbleful of even more anonymous wine. On quiet nights, we had the use of iron bedsteads and rudimentary bedclothes in a dormitory that in normal times was part of Westminster School. When trouble was not expected, we roamed, we talked, we read, and we ruminated. As month followed month, we even dared to think about "after the war."

Specific duties were never laid down, but it was assumed that we could find our way around the Abbey. As a member of that bizarre but dedicated body of men, I blessed the turn of events by which, during our period of service, all nights were quiet and the air-raid alarm was never activated.

We might not have been so lucky. In September 1940 damage had been done by enemy action to the west window, the choir school, several houses in the cloisters, and the east window of the Henry VII chapel. None of these could be ranked as a feat of marksmanship, but the results were bad enough.

In May 1941, even more serious damage was done by incendiary bombs. In particular, there was a moment at which water supplies had temporarily given out and it seemed likely that flames might spread from the blazing roof of the Busby Library to the Abbey church itself. That possibility was not averted until the entire roof of the Library gave way and fell into the street, a hundred and thirty feet below.

If something of the sort had happened again, the chances of our being able to distinguish ourselves were not bright. Though awed by our putative role in the defense of the great building, we were untried, untrained, un-led, and unequipped. The idea that a gang of aesthetes could double as paraprofessional fire fighters did us too much honor.

Meanwhile, we were not merely privileged, but enjoined and expected to explore the Abbey in ways that are normally forbidden. On long summer evenings, we had the run of the enormous building, and we came to understand why Daniel Webster, the foremost American orator of his day, should have burst into tears when he first crossed the threshold of the Abbey.

I remember especially a first visit at twilight to the broad gallery from which one can look down, and up, and across. For the licensed intruder, this was a moment—hardly rivaled since—of pure, intense, and exalted astonishment.

Sometimes, admittedly, the objects of that astonishment had their comical aspect and were not to be found in the guidebooks. At one point in the gallery, and invisible from the nave below, was a series of enigmatic constructions—part wood, part canvas—as to whose function we were free to speculate. They were large, but portable—or, as could equally well be said, portable but large. They were a mode neither of transport nor of storage.

Louis Pierre Spindler. *London Interior*. 1834. Oil on canvas, 20¼ × 17″ (51.4 × 43.2 cm). Musée des Beaux Arts, Strasbourg

Only after many days did we discover that they were temporary lavatories that dated from the period in the eighteenth century in which one coronation followed another and it had become clear that there were bodily needs from which not even kings and queens, let alone dukes and duchesses, were exempt.

In this and other ways, we came to realize to what an extent Westminster Abbey is England in microcosm. To a quite exceptional degree, it engenders affection. This applies to the visitor, and it applies even more to those who serve the Abbey in one way or another. To spend time in Westminster Abbey is to be aware, within the first hour, of the pride and the unemphatic high style that go with a life spent in its service. There is in this great building a charge of emotion that has been banked up for close on a thousand years, and it would be a dull nature that did not respond to it.

It was during these tours of duty that I came to terms with a History of England that I cannot recommend too highly. For much of its great length it is wonderful and irreplaceable reading. (It cannot, however, be hurried.) It has hundreds, if not thousands of illustrations. It is history at first hand, history traced back to its sources, history that comes neither wrapped nor packaged but laid out on the counter for us to deal with as best we can.

In its form, this history is peculiar, though not unique. It cannot be bought. It will never turn up at auction. It does not come in fancy bindings. It is pointless to wait for it in paperback. We cannot borrow it, and it is not in the catalogue of the British Library. Ask for it in the Library of Congress, in the Bibliothèque Nationale in Paris, or in the great libraries in Moscow and St. Petersburg, and you will be looked at with a wild surmise.

With good reason, too. For the history in question is not in a book at all, but in the abbey church of Westminster that was founded in the very center of London almost a thousand years ago. It is a working church, a ministering church, a church with an everyday life that goes on almost round the clock. But it is also a three-dimensional walk-through history of England.

That history goes back a long way. The foundation stone of the present church was laid in July 1245. There was every reason for it to prosper. The Benedictine abbey of which it was a part could be traced back to around the year 970. London would not have been London without it.

In the eleventh century, when the royal court moved from Winchester to London, it became a private abbey that was directly under the royal protection and exempt, therefore, from episcopal control. How could the new church in the center of London not be the royal church, with the royal Palace of Westminster as its neighbor? It was a holy place, but it was also a worldly place, and in Henry III, who ruled England from 1216 to 1272, it had the ideal patron.

Henry III was nobody's idea of a good, or even of a competent, king. But he was an aesthete of cosmopolitan genius who lived for great architecture, and for beautiful and original objects, and didn't care how much they cost. He was not an absentee patron, either. In Matthew Paris's *Lives of the Offas* there is an illustration—self-evidently drawn from life—of Henry III right in there with his masons. In the words of an eminent historian, George Zarnecki, "the present Abbey owes everything to King Henry III."

He is thought to have spent about one-tenth of the entire wealth of his kingdom on Westminster Abbey. At his behest, and in short order, Westminster Abbey became not only a place of the first importance in English life but a building of splendor, intricacy, and far-ferreting invention.

Henry III loved sculpture, and he made sure that it was everywhere in the

William Torel. *Henry III (1207–1272).* c. 1291. Electrotype of effigy in Westminster Abbey. Height 44″ (111.8 cm). The National Portrait Gallery, London

Matthew Paris. Illustration from *Historia Anglorum,* c. mid-13th century, showing Henry III enthroned, holding in one hand his scepter and in the other a model of his new Abbey Church at Westminster. The British Library, London. Royal MS 14 C VII f9

Abbey—painted and gilded, more often than not, and virtually omnipresent as an extravagant and highly colored background in which angels, centaurs, and carefully recorded botanical posies found place alongside pioneer armorial shields.

Wherever instinct and expert opinion were in agreement, Henry III would try anything. In domestic politics he was one of the more outrageous failures in British history. His foreign policy was ridiculous. (Who was he to dream of rampaging all over Italy and Sicily and setting his sights on the Holy Roman Empire?) His attempted invasion of France in 1242 is best remembered for the great painting by Eugène Delacroix that depicts his defeat at the battle of Taillebourg.

In his last years, Henry III was a walking nobody, despised by opponents and supporters alike. Matthew Paris, the great historian of the first half of the thirteenth century, said of him that he had a heart of wax, and Dante—in the words of the English historian H. W. C. Davis—"relegated him to the limbo of ineffectual souls."

Ineffectual as he was in all matters of state, Henry III was the foremost English connoisseur of his day. Matthew Paris got it right when he showed him on the throne with a scepter in one hand and a model of Westminster Abbey in the other.

He also got it right when he showed Henry III in full session on the site of the new Abbey, with masons winding winches, building high walls, and in general doing their very best beneath the raised forefinger of the king. Senior masons, T-squares in hand, look terrified, as well they might, for this was the one department of life in which Henry III did not make a fool of himself.

If porphyry, jasper, and marble from Rome were in high favor, Henry III sent for them. He also sent for the craftsmen who excelled in what was called Cosmati work, the better to make of the shrine of Edward the Confessor one of the marvels of medieval England.

His was a universal curiosity. When it turned out that Pietro di Osiderio, who

Pietro Torrigiano. *Monument of Henry VII and Elizabeth of York*, Westminster Abbey. 1518. Gilded bronze

had come from Rome in 1268 to work on the shrine of St. Edward the Confessor, was capable of making a mosaic floor that would reveal the eternal pattern of the universe, Henry III told him to go ahead.

Such a floor would consummate the grand design that he had in mind for Westminster Abbey. As Richard Foster remarked in his *Patterns of Thought: The Hidden Meaning of the Great Pavement of Westminster Abbey*, the Abbey was to combine under one roof the royal functions that were performed in France by three separate national churches. Like the Sainte-Chapelle in Paris, it was to be a repository of holy relics within walking distance of the royal palace. Like the cathedral in Rheims, it was to be the coronation church. Like the basilica of Saint-Denis, it was to be the resting place of the royal dynasty.

In this grand design, the pavement before the high altar in Westminster Abbey would play a fundamental role. On Coronation Day, the new monarch who sat on the throne would literally have at his feet the secrets of the universe in coded but perfectly legible form.

It was a square pavement, exactly 11.73 meters on each side. In its design, it had an immense and almost impregnable complexity. Though stabilized on each of its four sides by a long narrow rectangular border, it expressed itself elsewhere as the apotheosis of the circle, the square, the hexagon, the lozenge, and the subdivisional triangle. In its whirling and whorling, geometry reached its highest point of contained energy. Even to the unbeliever, it is clear that these complications did not serve a merely decorative purpose.

In color, the pavement was rich and various almost beyond imagining. Once again, it is immediately clear that these colors did not correspond merely to a sophisticated and cosmopolitan fancy. Here and there, successive restorations have given a look almost of improvisation. (Concrete, green bottle glass, and a black tarlike substance were all pressed into service when the dilapidation of the pavement reached danger-point.) Problems also arose from the use of gray-green Purbeck stone instead of the white Carrara marble that was used in Cosmati work in Italy.

William Johnstone White. Hand-colored aquatint of the Cosmati-work pavement, executed by Pietro di Osiderio c. 1628 in front of the High Altar, Westminster Abbey. From William Combe's *The History of the Abbey Church of St. Peter's, Westminster, and its Antiquities and Monuments*. Published by Rudolph Ackermann (London: 1812). Plate, 9½ × 11¾″ (23.5 × 29.9 cm). Yale Center for British Art, New Haven. Paul Mellon Collection

The shrine of the Confessor no longer exists in the form that Henry III devised for it. Nor could it today be seen, in any case, by someone who stood on the pavement, since the altar screen blocks the way. Shrine and pavement long ago ceased to have the symbiotic relationship that Henry III had had in mind.

All this notwithstanding, there is something awesome about the choice of ingredients for the Great Pavement. Foremost among them is the purple porphyry that was quarried in the Porphyry Mountains in the eastern desert of Egypt. As the quarries in question were closed down in the fifth century B.C., purple porphyry, where found at all, had to be recycled from Roman buildings of classical date.

As Richard Foster points out, the phrase "born to the purple" dates from the tenth century A.D., when a future emperor was born in Constantinople in a room whose walls were of purple porphyry. It is not an accident that the tomb of Henry III of England stands high upon a monolith of purple porphyry.

Next came the seductive combination of green porphyry from quarries in Sparta, in Greece, and a golden yellow limestone called "antique yellow." To them were added a fine-grained carboniferous limestone, datable to around three hundred and fifty million years ago, and a greenish mineral called Genoise serpentine. It is from matings such as these that the pavement derives its fluid, ever-changing, almost fugitive character. In terms of color, nothing is set, fixed, or firm. Interplay between color and geometry is continuous.

To this, a fragmented compound known as *breccia giallo* or "yellow gravel" contributed. Its origins can be traced either to Asia Minor or to the Iberian

peninsula. A red limestone quarried in Britain also played a part, as did alabaster most probably found near Tutbury Priory in Shropshire. As for the glass—cobalt blue, turquoise blue, red, and white—that was used in the pavement, scientific analysis would seem to get nowhere with it. Did it come from ancient Rome itself, or from some remote Islamic outpost of the Roman Empire, or from Italy or England in the thirteenth century? "Any or all of the above" is the message from the labs.

Of the alternation, the binding, and the patterning of these multifarious materials, much could be said. But what mattered above all was not the composition of the Great Pavement, but its ultimate purpose.

Whether the universe is of finite or infinite duration is not a subject often encountered in conversation today, though it may be put to the test sooner than we would like. But in the thirteenth century it was a question of enormous urgency. What was it that had set the universe in motion? Would it be on the move in perpetuity? Did it make sense to think of it in terms of time, as we know it? Or did Robert Grosseteste—bishop, mathematician, and master of the natural sciences— have the right idea when he spoke of time as having set out from eternity and eventually returning thither, wearied by its long journey?

It is possible to see the Great Pavement as a map of the universe, with its central onyx roundel as symbolizing the chaos of undifferentiated matter from which the four Elements emerged. Around that central roundel, the Divine Order went whirling and whorling through sacred mysteries that take us to the threshold of Eternity and the threshold of Time.

From the four Elements, and from the concepts of mundane time, astronomical time, and eternity, the universe in all its diversity has proceeded. In the Great Pavement and the complicated and problematic texts that came with it, we grapple with questions that once had a fierce topicality and may one day have it again.

Anyone who doubts this should consider the implications of that great invention of the second half of our century: the radio telescope. It might be that mundane time, astronomical time, and the time of eternity are mere verbal figments, rigged up in the Middle Ages and long ago discarded.

But what if this is not the case? "Mundane" is mundane, more or less, even if its connotations now have a pejorative sense. "Astronomical" is astronomical, even if the word no longer has the all-knowing connotation that it used to have. But "eternity"? Are we to think of it as an unanchored superlative? A promissory note that will never be cashed?

It might have seemed so. But Sir Bernard Lovell's work on the radio telescope has proved that the universe as it exists beyond our unaided vision far exceeds the scope of astronomy as it was previously conceived. Unlike the optical telescope, the radio telescope can reach back into the very beginnings of time. What are those immemorial vibrations, if not the heartbeat of eternity?

And if that is so, is it not curious that the polychromatic enigma of the Great Pavement should have been laid at the feet of the kings and queens of England, more than seven hundred years ago, as if its secrets were to be communicated to them at the time of their coronation?

These are mysteries still unriddled. The pavement is almost never on public view, but on the rare occasions when it is uncovered thousands of people come to see it, as if magnetized. Speculation remains free, meanwhile.

It was Henry III's belief that nothing was ever to be beyond the reach of Westminster Abbey. If purportedly authentic drops of the blood of the Savior were on the market, Henry III paid the price and secured them for the Abbey. Two years later, he spared neither trouble nor expense to secure what was believed to be a footprint of the Ascension.

The tone that he set was part English, part French, part Italian. Raised in France, and the brother-in-law of Louis IX (later to be canonized as St. Louis), he was familiar—even if only by hearsay—with the latest developments in Amiens Cathedral, and in the Sainte-Chapelle in Paris. He also kept a shrewd eye on Canterbury Cathedral and did not much care to have competition from that quarter. His work in Westminster, and his hugely gifted work force, were what he prized most in life.

Westminster Abbey in general is remarkable for its straightforward, upfront, and on the whole egalitarian treatment of all those who are enshrined in it. So it may seem ironical that in his own monument King Henry III is literally upstaged by the lofty plinth that was designed for it by Pietro di Osiderio. Noble and unshowy as it is, it hoists the gilt bronze effigy of Henry III himself above the sight line of most visitors.

That is a great pity. As the effigy in question was made by William Torel in 1291, nineteen years after the death of Henry III, it cannot have an unquestioned actuality. But as a portrait of a vulnerable aesthete who in matters of state was a born loser it could not be improved upon.

It has to this day a quite exceptional finesse, even if vandals long ago made off with the orb and scepter that the king had originally had in his hands, and with the jewels that once studded his crown. Worse still has been the fate at one time or another of the shrine of St. Edward the Confessor, on which Henry III lavished so much thought and affection.

But it is not, of course, on one man's legacy that the huge, many-purposed complex of Westminster Abbey and its dependencies has relied for its continuance. It is central to the very idea of Britain, and on more than one count. For the pure-bred antiquarian, the burial of Harold Harefoot in the Abbey precincts in 1040 may be the earliest decisive step in that direction. But the unique status of the Abbey dates from the coronation of William the Conqueror in 1066. Since that time, every sovereign has been crowned on that same spot.

One of them, King Henry IV, died there, in the Jerusalem Chamber. Another, King Richard II, lost his temper in Westminster Abbey during the funeral of his wife, Anne of Bohemia. Thoroughly and inopportunely fired up, he set about one of his barons with a big stick and drew blood. (The funeral service was forthwith suspended.) A third, King Henry V, spent the night before his coronation in a hermitage within the precincts of the Abbey.

But the Abbey is central to the history of England in other ways also. It was in Westminster Abbey, in the octagonal Chapter House, that under Henry III, and from the reign of Edward III onward, the notion of parliamentary government began to burgeon. In that same Chapter House, where the vaulting is like tropical vegetation that springs from a single slender central tree, the subordination of the English Church to the English state was completed during the reign of Henry VIII.

It was in the Chapel of the Pyx that the nucleus of a national Treasury came into being. Money was kept there in great quantities, and seven successive keys were needed before the double-doored chamber could be opened. In that same chamber were kept the standard coins of the realm by which the purity and authenticity of all others were judged.

There was therefore a time at which Westminster Abbey was at once a great religious center, the seedbed of democratic government, the driving force of English music (thanks to the Chapel Royal and the example of Orlando Gibbons), and a safe

The Coronation Service of George IV, July 19, 1821. 1837. Colored etching, 19 × 14⅜″ (48.4 × 36.4 cm). By permission of the Trustees of the British Museum, London

deposit under august management. Within a few yards of the Abbey, the Houses of Parliament stand today. The Treasury—now a great office of state—is also still close to its place of origin.

Yet the Abbey is not only about power, though power has had a lot to do with it. Nor is it a museum, though it contains what may well be the single greatest work of medieval art in the country. But as a repository of monumental sculpture from the sixteenth century onward, it has no rival in Britain. And its memorial tablets form a dictionary of national biography that is wonderfully and memorably haphazard.

Among its other distinctions, it has waxworks far superior to those in Madame Tussaud's, or in the Musée Grevin in Paris. We cannot know Admiral Lord Nelson, the victor of the battle of Trafalgar, or William Pitt, the great statesman, till we have seen them in effigy, and dressed in their very own clothes, in Westminster Abbey.

In the tomb of Henry VII and his queen by Pietro Torrigiano, the Abbey has what John Pope-Hennessy called "the finest Renaissance tomb north of the Alps." It also has the most important thirteenth-century wall paintings in England, and a run of stained glass from the thirteenth century to that by Sir Ninian Comper in the 1960s.

Furthermore, it is still changing, growing, and renewing itself. Who would have believed in the 1930s that the sculptor Jacob Epstein—routinely ridiculed at that time by redneck officialdom—would in 1957 be entrusted with the bust of William Blake that is now in the Abbey? As for Poets' Corner, it should have had the "House Full" notice up for years, but ways are still being found of welcoming a new arrival.

Once inside, busted or profiled or seen at full length, people have to put up with the way they look. Editing is not allowed. The only exception known to me is the case of William Makepeace Thackeray, the author of *Vanity Fair* and much else besides.

Thackeray died in 1863. In that same year a bust of him by Marochetti (best known for his lions in Trafalgar Square) was put up in the Abbey. No time had been lost, therefore. His family and friends should have been delighted.

But his redoubtable daughter, Lady Ritchie, was not delighted. The bust was a travesty, she said. Her father's whiskers were never that long. Any other daughter would simply have made it a source of lifelong complaint, thereby boring everyone who came within earshot.

But Lady Ritchie was a doughty persuader. Quite some years later, she went to see the Dean of Westminster. She exerted her well-known and somewhat intimidating charms. The Dean agreed forthwith that the sculptor Onslow Ford, to whom the Abbey owes busts of General Gordon and John Ruskin, should be asked to shorten Thackeray's whiskers.

Ford didn't really want to do it, and in the end he left it to his assistant to go ahead under his supervision. Mary McCarthy, the wife of the literary critic Desmond McCarthy, was a witness to the occasion. Later, she told how "chip, chip, chip flew the bits under the white-bloused assistant's chisel . . . Finally, the bust was

British School. *The Coronation Banquet of George IV in Westminster Hall, 1821.* c. 1821. Oil on canvas, 39½ × 49⅞″ (99.8 × 124.5 cm). The Museum of London

flicked over with a cloth, as if after a shave, and it was carried back up the nave and back into its own niche."

The kings and queens of England had no such luck, and in any case the honors paid to them do not necessarily accord with their rank. William III and his Queen Mary deserved well of England. And it is Queen Anne whom we have to have thank for a gift of land on Manhattan Island, but we have to search for all three of them, as best we can, on the floor of the Mary Queen of Scots Chapel.

The Abbey is in a sense the private chapel of England's kings and queens, but in its human concerns it cuts a Tolstoyan swath. All England is there, if we know where to look for it. Not even in *War and Peace* shall we find a more comprehensive account of the ups and downs and the ins and outs of life.

At first glance the Abbey might seem to concern itself only with the great ones of the earth. Due honor is paid there to grandeur of spirit and station, to a warrior strain not yet extinct, and to the notion of public service both at home and in far places. The spiritual life well led, preeminence in literature and the sciences, and, not least, an occasional robust eccentricity—all have their place.

But if the Abbey at times has the air of a white marble charnel house, that impression will vanish as soon as we look closely at tomb and tablet. For the Abbey is not simply a place of privileged rest for the heavy hitter in this or that department of human activity.

Inventors and philosophers and men of science have a place in the Abbey. So do explorers, stonemasons, playwrights, sailors and soldiers, poets and lawyers, schoolteachers and country clergymen. Alongside of them are composers and colonists, actors and actresses, painters and sculptors and architects, novelists and martyrs.

There is an Italian composer, Muzio Clementi, and Sir Rowland Hill, inventor of the penny post, and Richard Busby of Lincoln, a great seventeenth-century bookman, and Dudley Carleton of Brightwell, near Oxford, who bought Dutch paintings in The Hague for King Charles I and swapped Christian antiquities with Rubens.

There is Isaac Newton, needless to say, but there is also the tomb of Jeremiah Horrocks, a curate of Hoole, in Lancashire, who died in 1641 at the age of twenty-two after having predicted and witnessed the Transit of Venus. And then there is the tomb of Dr. Livingstone, the African explorer, who spoke out from his gravestone against the traffic in slaves from Central Africa. "May Heaven's rich blessing," he said, "come down on everyone—English, American or Turk—who will help to heal this open sore of the world."

As we study this great message in its forthright High Victorian lettering on the floor of the nave of the Abbey, we expect to see Livingstone surrounded by like-minded people. (Candidates could easily have been found.) But not at all. Such is the chancy, unregimented character of the Abbey that Dr. Livingstone lies beside Thomas Tompion, the great seventeenth-century clockmaker. Tompion has no inscription, and was doubtless believed not to need one, such was his contribution to the ordering of time in England.

The size and character of tomb and tablet can never be predicted. Queen Elizabeth I is by every imaginable criterion one of the most important figures in English history, and in her white marble effigy in the Henry VII Chapel she is "every inch a queen." But her monument is sober, plain, unostentatious. It is her courtiers, and above all Lord Hunsdon, her first cousin, who make the running. "Festive in a provincial sort of way" was how Kenneth Clark summed up the Hunsdon tomb.

Henry Webber. *Monument to the Actor: David Garrick Taking a Curtain Call.* 1797. By permission of the Dean and Chapter of Westminster Abbey

Opposite:
Poets' Corner, Westminster
Abbey

Though continually brought up
to date, Poets' Corner still has
its original background, with
William Shakespeare, Samuel
Johnson, and Robert Burns
conspicuous.

William Kent (carved by Michael Rysbrack). *Monument to
the Scientist Sir Isaac Newton.*
1731. By permission of the
Dean and Chapter of
Westminster Abbey

Like most old-fashioned histories, this one deals primarily with a man's world.
But due honor is paid to Dame Mary Jones, an amateur pharmacist who died in
1677. There is also a tribute to Lady Elizabeth Ferrers, who died in premature
childbirth in 1731 after being frightened by a flash of lightning. Room is found for
Mary Kendall (1677–1710) who was "of a severe life, but an easy conversation"
and lived—so her tablet reminds us—precisely as long as the Savior.

Death in childhood was no bar to admission. The Honourable Rebecca Folliott
is there, though she was only ten years old when she died in 1697. Westminster
Abbey also reminds us that throughout the centuries many a clever Englishwoman
could have played her part in the great world but preferred a quiet life in the country.

There is Miss Anne Whytell, who died in 1788 and has exactly three words—
"Innocence and Peace"—as her memorial. And in the tablet that comes with James
Gibbs's memorial to Katharina Bovey of Flaxley, in Gloucestershire, who died in
1726, a vanished world is set out before us. Here is someone who "did not care to
run into any freedom of Thought in regard to revealed truths." Her domestic
expenses were "managed with a decency and dignity suitable to her fortune, but
with a frugality that made her Income abound to all proper objects of Charity." Her
distributions were made, moreover, "not only with cheerfulness but with joy."

For many generations, room was found for those who had lived simply and left
upon their times no more than a local and a limited mark. It is worthwhile to seek

them out, and to see for oneself that the elegant Latin inscriptions that were once almost mandatory in the Abbey do not always refer to people whose names turn up in the schoolroom.

Among the names now little remembered there are many that no nineteenth-century novelist could have left alone—the Belasyses of Dancepath Castle, Durham, for instance, with their motto *Bonne et Belle Assez*. There are dukes by the dozen, but in the cloister there is also "Philip Clark, plumber" who died in 1707, aged forty-two. The monuments of Westminster Abbey make up an honor roll, but they are also an indispensable part of the collective memory of Britain.

Westminster Abbey is grand—very grand, in fact—and it serves us to perfection when grandeur is called for. To be commemorated in Westminster Abbey is today the prerogative of the great and the (presumed to be) good. The rest of us cannot hope to sneak in.

But there was a time when that was not the case. In 1628, George Villiers, Duke of Buckingham, was buried in the Abbey in circumstances so outrageous to popular opinion that the ceremony had to be held privately in the middle of the night. For many years, there were those who did not care to be buried there, on the grounds that (as Field Marshal Henry Conway wrote to Horace Walpole) "vice and insignificance have entitled people to an interment in Westminster Abbey."

The advantage of this, from the point of view of the present-day visitor, is that the monuments and memorials in Westminster Abbey are a wonderfully evocative and often quite irrational jumble. There are those who are there—as was said of William Pitt the Elder—because they deserved to be "brought near to the dust of kings." But there are also those who are there for one reason only—that they could afford to pay for it.

Like many of the finest English achievements, Westminster Abbey is a patchwork, put together over many centuries and many times revised, "restored," amended, embellished, and (if there is no such word, it should be invented) disembellished. It was W. R. Lethaby, disciple of William Morris and Surveyor to the Fabric of Westminster Abbey from 1906 to 1928, who said that by his time the Abbey "had been so completely re-cased that to describe it will be to describe a series of modern works." But, re-cased or not, the Abbey engenders awe, as much for itself as for the scenes that it has witnessed.

In that context, I prize the example of Joseph Wilcocks, who was installed in 1731 as Dean of Westminster Abbey. Between 1735 and 1740, he watched the construction of the two towers on the west facade that had been designed by Nicholas Hawksmoor. He loved the Abbey, and though he could have become Archbishop of York he preferred to stay where he was. He also loved Hawksmoor's towers, to the extent that he asked to be buried beneath one of them and to have a bas-relief of them on his monument.

Not merely the construction, but the very notion of those two towers was one of the most tricky assignments of the day. The blunt, unadorned, untopped west front of the Abbey had weight, and substance, but it did not command the eye. At the beginning of the eighteenth century it was much as it had been two hundred years earlier. Fundamentally, it conformed to the ideas of Henry Yevele, who had taken the unfinished Abbey a stage further forward in 1375.

Yevele was no innovator. Basically he carried on with the style of building that had been employed between 1245 and 1269. The effect of this was that, as Nikolaus Pevsner put it, "the whole abbey from the chancel to the west towers looks to this day very much as if it had been built to one plan during a short period."

It was Hawksmoor's task to bring the Abbey into line with the second quarter of the eighteenth century without imposing upon the huge building a too-evident caesura. The task was the more difficult in that the focus of wealth and power in Westminster Abbey had always been at the south and the east end of the church, and not at the west end. A late-seventeenth-century engraving makes it clear that at that time the Abbey simply petered out at the west end.

The Abbey backed onto Whitehall at a time when Whitehall was the single most important street in London and Whitehall Palace its most impressive set of buildings. To this day, the approach to Westminster Abbey along Whitehall, past the Banqueting House, past Westminster Hall and the Houses of Parliament, is the one that sets a noble tone. Walking up the now almost incomparably hideous Victoria Street toward the west front of the Abbey gives us no more than a partial and a slanted impression.

When the occasion called for it, Hawksmoor was a master of the metropolitan gesture. (Nikolaus Pevsner called his church of St. Mary Woolnoth "the most original church exterior in the City of London.") As the amanuensis of Sir Christopher Wren, who had himself been in charge of Westminster Abbey from 1698

Canaletto. *Westminster Abbey with the Procession of the Knights of the Order of Bath.* 1749. Oil on canvas, 39 × 40″ (99.1 × 101.6 cm). By permission of the Dean and Chapter of Westminster Abbey

onward, Hawksmoor was well aware of Wren's views as to its eventual completion. The west towers should be "in the Gothic form," Wren had once said. "To deviate from the old form would be to run into a disagreeable mixture which no person of good taste could relish."

But it was not in Hawksmoor's nature simply to devise a painstaking coda for the stumpy little non-towers that gave the Abbey such a strikingly unfinished appearance. His job was to make the Abbey "tell" from a great distance. It could not be rich and grand and elaborate, like the fan-vaulting in the Henry VII Chapel, but it could be grand in quite another way—light, airy, fanciful, and drawn rather than sculpted. It could ride the upper air, rather than hold on to it. An elegant pallor and a freedom from chiaroscuro would add to the ease with which the two towers would rise above the rest of the huge fabric.

Hawksmoor went ahead and put all those ideas into practice, though he died before the work was completed. Today, the two towers have to compete both with Big Ben and with the Victoria Tower. But when Canaletto came to London in 1746 and began to paint the Westminster area it soon turned out that, from no matter what angle, it was around Hawksmoor's two pale towers that all else revolved.

Hawksmoor's contribution finds apotheosis in a painting by Canaletto that is called *Westminster Abbey with the Procession of the Knights of the Order of Bath*. Painted in 1749, at a time when the two towers were still squeaky clean, it brings out their finesse of line, their refusal to complicate, and their general air of heading toward heaven without an ounce of unnecessary baggage. They are not a pastiche, either. Hawksmoor was true to his own day and his nature.

Canaletto also took care to show that, whereas Hawksmoor's towers are seen in a flat clear light with only minimal shadow, strong shadows pass across the remainder of the west front, molding and modeling in terms of volume and relief. At street level, something close to darkness prevails here and there, but from the point at which Hawksmoor takes over the tall slender twinned towers, they look as if they had been mapped in the upper air with a very fine pen.

Canaletto also got the point that for all their traditional reticence the English are unexcelled at pageantry. As the Knights of the Bath march out of the Abbey, make a sharp turn to their right on the red carpet, and swing round past the neighboring church of St. Margaret's, Westminster, and on toward the House of Lords, we sense that for just a few minutes Canaletto might not have minded if he never saw a Doge again. In pageantry, England called the shots.

For that matter, it still does. And Westminster Abbey has had its full share of pageantry. But it is not for pageantry that it is remembered. The Unknown Soldier, just inside the west door, is as well treated as any of the Field Marshals whom he served. Musical visitors recall how, in 1791, Joseph Haydn was present at a mammoth performance of Handel's *Messiah*. (When the performers—more than six hundred in all—broke into the Hallelujah Chorus, Haydn burst into tears and said, "He is the Master of us all!") Readers of Samuel Pepys's diary do not forget the Sunday in December 1661 when he was allowed to sit in the choir and sing along with the choristers.

Historians and genealogists can unriddle even the most elusive of the references in tomb after tomb. As they grow older, Londoners find themselves going more and more often to Westminster Abbey as their contemporaries drop, one by one, like birds from the branch. To that extent, Londoners become part of the Abbey, and the Abbey becomes a part of them. The Abbey is, and has always been, "like family."

Reason and the record prompt much of what goes on there. People do not faint dead away in the Abbey, as they did when John Donne preached in St. Paul's Cathedral. It was with Donne, rather than with the learned but on the whole low-keyed Deans of Westminster, that the sermon became one of the great instruments of the English language. If grief finds flamboyant outlet in the Abbey, it is in stone and marble, rather than in spontaneous demonstrations by the living.

The Abbey has lived through some terrible times—notably in 1644, when a parliamentary committee authorized the destruction of the High Altar in the Henry VII Chapel and paid someone £7/16 to remove its stained glass windows. Even rougher goings-on occurred in 1660, when Oliver Cromwell and two of his closest colleagues were disinterred from their tombs in the Abbey. (Their heads were hoisted on poles set above Westminster Hall.)

There was also a time when—as happened with Dean Richard Cox in 1553—even the Dean of Westminster was sent to prison for political reasons and found it desirable to leave England and live in Frankfurt. In 1722, Dean Atterbury was arrested in the Deanery and exiled by a bill passed for that purpose in Parliament. (No friend of the Hanoverian monarchy, he had hoped to be able to proclaim James III as King of England at Charing Cross.)

It was with the Deanship (1864–81) of Alfred Penrhyn Stanley that the status of the Abbey became stabilized once and for all. In what were to be almost his dying words, Dean Stanley said that he trusted he had "sustained before the mind of the nation the extraordinary value of the Abbey as a religious, national and liberal institution." (All three adjectives, be it noted, had equal weight.)

A certain golden eccentricity has often been the mark of the Church of England, and it appeared at full force in the character and behavior of Armitage Robinson, who was Dean of Westminster from 1902 to 1911. Dean Robinson had freakish ways that endeared him to many. Though initially a New Testament scholar of high standing in Cambridge, he made over his life in ways peculiar to himself when he was appointed as Dean. Described by one of his colleagues as "a lot of fine china among rather coarse pots," he did not overdo his appearances in the Abbey itself.

Once a week he celebrated Holy Communion. Most evenings he attended Evensong. But it was his life as an independent scholar that took much of his time. According to his manservant at the Deanery, he asked to be given at ten P.M. precisely every evening a large supply of cigarettes and the means of making tea several times over.

Thereafter, his manservant said, "he would place what books he wanted on the floor in front of the fire, for he had the habit of crawling about the study from one book to another. He rarely retired until well after midnight. Often I heard him going to his room at 5 A.M., and sometimes later. He smoked at least fifty cigarettes during the night. He would remain in bed until 11 A.M. most mornings. I had to place his clothes in proper order for putting on. I am sure that if I had made a mistake by putting his gaiters on top of the pile he would have put them on first. I had to take care that he had money in his pockets."

A noctambular Dean! On all fours among his books until daybreak! And in the twentieth century! The tale inspires wonder, and awe. When Big Ben keeps the hours with its strong, slow, measured strokes, I often think of Dean Robinson stretched out on the floor, with the ash of fifty and more cigarettes around the room and a last cup of very strong tea close at hand. He, too, speaks for Westminster Abbey as the epitome of a certain England.

The Continuing City

Sir Christopher Wren. *West Facade, St. Paul's Cathedral, London.* 1675–1710

André Derain. *St. Paul's from the Thames.* 1906. Oil on canvas, 39½ × 32¼" (99.7 × 81.9 cm). The Minneapolis Institute of the Arts. Bequest of Putnam Dana McMillan

TO WALK ROUND A NARROW CORNER and see St. Paul's Cathedral almost within touching distance is one of the great metropolitan experiences. It is a part of the Londoner's birthright, and for many generations there seemed no limit to the number of twisty lanes that offered the stupendous sight.

It could not have been otherwise. For five hundred years and more, the City of London had been overcrowded and overbuilt. As a city of dead ends, it was second to none. When it come to processional ways like those favored in Greece and Rome, and to vistas judged (as in St. Petersburg) to the nearest centimeter, the City of London did not compete.

It didn't want to compete, either. It excelled with intimate, neighborly, almost conspiratorial spaces, and it saw no reason to change its ways. Vistas didn't make money. Nor did processional ways. The business of the City of London was business, and only in the case of St. Paul's Cathedral did it stand back a little and let great architecture have its say.

It was always so. Long before Sir Christopher Wren was born, an earlier St. Paul's was the biggest and the most conspicuous cathedral in Europe. When an artist from Antwerp called Anthony van der Wyngaerde was in London in the 1540s, he made the earliest drawings of the city that give us a more than cartographical idea of what it looked like. He stood on the south bank of the Thames, in Southwark, and he told us what he saw. At least fourteen large sketches resulted.

Where architecture is in question, there have been greater physiognomists than Anthony van der Wyngaerde. In his drawings, the fingers often did more work than the eye. But what the drawings do show, beyond question, is the primacy in sixteenth-century London of the old cathedral of St. Paul's. In a city still more or less shapeless, Old St. Paul's was the prime landmark. How could it not be so, when its spire—completed in 1315—was 489 feet high?

As time went on, Old St. Paul's was not at all the place of rest and meditation that we now suppose a cathedral to be. When Popish ways were forbidden, Old St. Paul's as a working church was summarily degraded. The High Altar was demolished in 1549 and a plain wooden table set up in its place. There was no money to repair the rest of the fabric, and its physical dilapidation was matched by a brisk downturn in its moral status. And then, in 1561, that heaven-storming spire was destroyed by fire.

Throughout the huge building, which was 585 feet in length, the sacred gave way to the profane. Services were still held in the choir, but prayer became the least of the cathedral's outward concerns. It functioned as a metropolitan thoroughfare through which load-bearing horses and mules made their way, heaped with meat, fish, and fruit and with baskets of bread and gallon upon gallon of beer.

It also functioned as a shopping mall, in which trade of every kind went forward. Rood-loft and tombs were strewn with merchandise, and shoppers knew exactly where to go for what they wanted. (Even the font was put to use as an improvised counter.)

You could do just about anything in Old St. Paul's. You could buy a horse and

118

ride away on it. You could consult a lawyer, hire a servant, spread false gossip, or get into a fight and settle it on the spot. Sinners outnumbered saints. Criminality was everywhere. (If you wanted to have someone killed, Old St. Paul's was the place to strike a bargain.)

This was the building which, in the 1620s, fired the imagination of Inigo Jones. Jones was one of the exceptional human beings who in the seventeenth century sometimes urged a certain modesty of statement upon a City of London that was by nature effusive, not to say boastful, about its achievements.

Inigo Jones in the 1630s was the top man in England in whatever he was asked to undertake. There never was anyone quite like him, whether as architect to the Court, as connoisseur, as antiquarian, as collector, or as draftsman. He also excelled as the inventor, decorator, and machinist of more than thirty of the airy and yet monumental entertainments in which both James I and Charles I delighted.

In the quality of his imagination, Inigo Jones was all fire and air. (We can think of him not only as he was drawn by van Dyck, in one of the great portrait drawings of all time, but as the "fiery spirit" whom he himself drew for one of his masques.) On the stage, with his sliding and revolving sets, he could complicate to unforgettable effect.

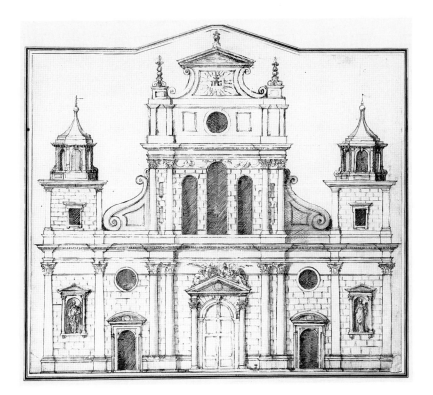

Above:
Inigo Jones. *Design for the Re-Fronting of St. Paul's Cathedral, West Elevation.* c. 1631. Pen, wash, and pencil, 18⅛ × 19¾″ (46 × 50 cm). The British Architectural Library, RIBA, London

Above right:
Inigo Jones. *Elevation for a New Termination of the Central Tower of St. Paul's Cathedral.* c. 1608. Pen, pencil, and watercolor, 29½ × 20¼″ (75 × 51.5 cm). The Provost and Fellows of Worcester College, Oxford

When learning had to mate with splendor, Inigo Jones worked his imagination at full stretch. The portico that he designed for the west end of Old St. Paul's has been described by the architectural historian John Harris as being "as grand as the Pantheon's, grander than any other portico north of the Alps, and perhaps even the noblest of any Renaissance porticoes."

But in 1638, when Inigo Jones was asked by Lord Maltravers to design a house for himself in Lothbury and a row of warehouses, about fifty yards long, for that same street in the City, he took quite another tack. Extravagance might have been in the air. Maltravers was the son of Jones's close friend and traveling companion, the Earl of Arundel. He had lately been granted a license to coin money—the royal farthing token—and to deal in it from his family property in Lothbury.

Here, if ever, was a moneyed patron. But did Inigo Jones let his fancy run free? Not at all. Such was the Tuscan plainness, the absolute simplicity, of the two projects that, if they had been built in Lothbury, they would have stood as a rebuke to later extravagances. But nothing came of them.

It was also in Old St. Paul's that the English language arrived at one of its highest achievements in the sermons preached by John Donne, then Dean of St. Paul's. Donne was in many ways the complete City-of-Londoner. He was born there in 1573 in the parish of St. Nicholas Olave. His father was a more than prosperous merchant who in 1574 became Warden of the Ironmongers' Company. (Donne himself came into a large fortune when he turned twenty-one.) When he went to Oxford as a child prodigy at the age of eleven, he was spoken of as the future equal of Pico della Mirandola, the Florentine philosopher and humanist.

Donne studied law in Lincoln's Inn. As a poet, he is known as the author of the *Holy Sonnets.* But he was also the author of some of the most lascivious poems in the English language. He was well known as a controversialist and pamphleteer, a master in the practice of civil and common law, and as someone who was much in brilliant (and sometimes in disreputable) company.

One of the most remarkable Englishmen of his age, he was as much a part of the London of his era as were, at other times, Samuel Pepys the diarist and public

Inigo Jones. *Torchbearer: A Fiery Spirit.* 1613. Pen and ink with watercolor, 11⅝ × 6⁵⁄₁₆″ (29.5 × 16 cm). Devonshire Collection, Chatsworth. Reproduced by permission of the Chatsworth Settlement Trustees

servant, Charles James Fox the statesman, Lord Byron the poet, and the first Duke of Wellington, the victor of the battle of Waterloo and later the Prime Minister of England.

Though often asked to take holy orders, John Donne hesitated to do so until in 1614 King James I sent for him and asked him to hesitate no longer. Once he was ordained, preferment was his almost by return mail, and in no time at all he became Chaplain to the King. In 1621 he was made Dean of St. Paul's.

In Old St. Paul's, as in the open air, Donne never lacked for an enormous audience. His sermons were events to which thousands of people craved admission. Among them were the Archbishop of Canterbury, Francis Bacon the essayist, and Lord Arundel the great collector. In the words of a later Dean of St. Paul's, "this congregation consisted, both of the people down to the lowest, and of the most noble, wise and accomplished of that highly intellectual age. They sat, or even stood, undisturbed, except by their own murmurs of admiration, sometimes by hardly suppressed tears."

Yet even in the days when people habitually read sermons for pleasure, Donne's were often rated as both tough and disconcerting. Today they pose even more problems. Everything about them seems to come from a vanished world—the idiom, the vocabulary, the hour-long span, the labyrinthine but perfectly balanced phrasing, the gigantic long-echoing metaphors, and the demanding and Latinate thought-sequences. We shall never hear anything like them.

Nor are we likely to hear or see anyone like John Donne—"a preacher in earnest," as his close friend Izaak Walton described him, "weeping sometimes for his auditory, sometimes with them; always preaching to himself, like an angel from a cloud, but in none; carrying some to Heaven in holy raptures, and enticing others by a sacred art and courtship to amend their lives; here picturing a vice so as to make it ugly to those that practised it, and a virtue so as to make it beloved even by those that loved it not; and all this with a most particular grace and an unexpressable addition of comeliness."

It was the fantastication of Donne's sermons that turned later generations against them. Plain words and plain talk were preferred. But when the occasion called for it, Donne could be as plain as any man. He could also be the author of phrases that are still current even among people who have never heard his name.

One and the same man was in question. The Donne of "No man is an island," and of "Ask not for whom the bell tolls" was also present in what an American expatriate, Logan Pearsall Smith, once called "the courtly, spectral figure standing with his hourglass in the pulpit of Old St. Paul's."

The plain-spoken Donne had one of his finest hours when in 1616 he preached before his patron King James I. James I at that time was in deep trouble. The wife of his closest and most prized friend, the Earl of Somerset, had engineered the murder by slow poisoning of a poet called Sir Thomas Overbury. Her four accomplices were hanged, and she herself was found guilty. But it did not escape notice that, as a late-Victorian commentator put it, the king "showed a hateful disinclination to bring the offenders to justice."

In the circumstances, many an ambitious preacher would have kept clear of controversy. But not John Donne. His hearers were riven to their seats as he spoke of God's implacable way with the wicked. "God is the Lord of Hosts," he said, "and he can proceed by Martial Law. He can sink down the Stage and the Player, the bed of wantonness, and the wanton actor into the jaws of the earth, into the mouth of Hell. Thou canst not lack examples," he went on, "that He hath done so upon others. And will no proof serve thee, but a speedy judgment upon thyself?"

Inigo Jones. *A Turkey and an Unidentified Animal*. Date unknown. Pen and brown ink, 9⅞ × 4¹⁵⁄₁₆″ (25 × 12.5 cm). Devonshire Collection, Chatsworth. Reproduced by permission of the Chatsworth Settlement Trustees

The genius of Inigo Jones did not exclude a sense of comedy that is still irresistible.

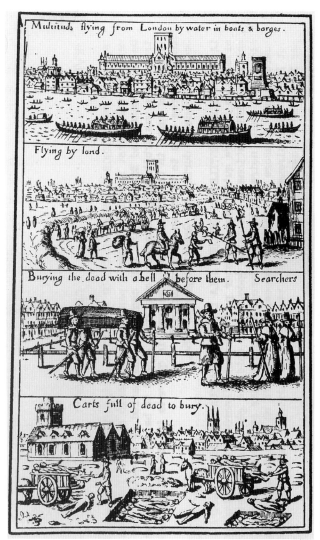

It was doubtless in part because he was himself no stranger to "the bed of wantonness" that Donne in his forties was able to strike such terror into a worldly and sophisticated audience. But it was also because terror, wild fancy, and an awestruck anguish were expected at that time of a great sermon.

Donne had to do for his hearers what Giuseppe Verdi was to do in his *Requiem* close on four hundred years later. But whereas Verdi had a huge orchestra, a full chorus, four soloists, and a printed score, Donne had nothing but his own sole voice, his beauty of feature, and a handful of notes. (He never spoke from a fully written-out text.)

His were prodigious performances. But there was only one John Donne. In 1631 he preached his last sermon, known to posterity as "Death's Duel." To this day we can be shaken to our very bowels by the passage that begins, "We have a winding sheet in our mother's womb, which grows with us from our conception, and we come into the world, wound up in that winding sheet, for we come to seek a grave . . . and when the womb hath discharged us, yet we are bound to it by cords of flesh, by such a string as that we cannot go thence, nor stay there."

This was the Donne who chose his own monument, ahead of time. Nicholas Stone was the sculptor who carved it in 1631. Still to be seen in St. Paul's, it shows him standing bolt upright in his shroud, like a specter come amongst us. This was

Above left:
Scenes in London During the Great Plague of 1664, from a late-seventeenth-century broadside. Pepysian Collection, Courtesy of the Clarendon Press, Oxford

Above:
Francis Barlow. *Mrs. Cellier in the Pillory*. n.d. Pen and brown ink, $3\frac{1}{8} \times 2''$ (7.9 × 5.1 cm). By permission of the Trustees of the British Museum, London

Rough justice in the open air, rather than in prison, was once an accepted feature of London life.

the Donne for whom people would stand by the thousand to hear him preach. If they passed out cold in a transport of emotion, as many of them did, they would be carried out at the end like dead men who might never wake up again.

But a certain moderation is the mark of the Church of England. What people would take from Donne, they did not care to take from anyone else. As Bishop Burnet was to say in his posthumous *History of His Own Time* (1724–34), congregations eventually grew weary of sermons in which "all was over-run with pedantry, piebald, and full of many sayings of different languages."

Besides, Charles II had come back to England as king in 1660. He had been in France, Burnet said, when the reform of the French language was much under discussion and "it soon appeared that he had a true taste for sermons that were clear, and plain, and short."

The preachers who came into favor were Tillotson ("a very prudent man," said his friend Burnet), and Patrick ("a great preacher, but a little too severe against those who disagreed with him"), and Lloyd ("ever grave and moderate," though he had in his care the richest living in England).

These were reasonable men who wanted to worship, undisturbed, in a limpid, uncluttered, un-mysterious interior. But in no time at all, as it must have seemed, their devotions were thrown into disorder by two metropolitan calamities that followed upon one another in rapid succession.

First, the plague bit deep into the City of London in 1665. Exactly how many died of the plague in 1665 will never be known, and it is likely that official returns, where they existed at all, were way below the true figure. In every generation, there are causes of death that people don't want to talk about, and nothing much came of an attempt in the late seventeenth century to enlist "discreet matrons" to keep a correct tally of plague victims.

From the 9 deaths from the plague that were reported for the week ending May 9, 1665, to the 7,165 that were reported for the week ending 19 September, the official rise was steep, and the real one probably steeper still. Thereafter deaths diminished, but it has long been a fact of London life that in a hot summer the fear of plague can never be discounted.

"Essentially," said E. S. de Beer in his majestic edition of the diaries of John Evelyn, "the plague was a disease of the badly housed poor. It is no diminution of the courage of the men of the upper classes who remained at their posts in London to say that they were not in such danger as they believed."

Evelyn himself did not leave London, and went about in infected places—"a dismal passage and dangerous," he wrote later, "to see so many coffins exposed in the streets and the streets thin of people, the shops shut up and all in mournful silence, as not knowing whose turn would come next."

The plague had haunted the central Londoner for centuries. There had been substantial outbreaks in 1258, in 1348–49 (the Black Death), 1407 (an estimated 30,000 deaths), 1499–1500, 1517, 1531, and 1532. In 1535, two-thirds of recorded deaths in London were due to the plague. In 1563, in 1593, and in 1603 there were further outbreaks. In the summer of 1625, 35,000 people died of the plague.

One of the more sinister of recorded illnesses, it was concentrated in a tumbledown, overpopulated, and insanitary quarter of London. So far from being isolated, victims were packed into hospitals so overcrowded that visitors had to clamber across bed after bed until they found the patient of their choice.

On house after house in what we would now call the East End of London, a red or a blue cross signaled bad news. Meanwhile, those who put their trust in the medical or pseudomedical profession laid fires with frankincense and rosemary and walked around with cakes of arsenic under their armpits.

Much good it did them. Once they had a bubo on their groin—or, as some called it, a black swelling the size of a nutmeg—their hours were numbered. The only remedy for the plague in London was to raze the entire area in which it had always thriven.

Just a year later, and as if in response to this evident need, there was the Great Fire of London in September 1666. The City has had more than its full share of fires, before and since, but there was London before the Great Fire, and London after it, and no one could mistake the one for the other.

The Fire itself was a remarkable phenomenon, and one that was preserved for posterity in two classic accounts. One of them is by Samuel Pepys, the other by John Evelyn. The two diarists have a double claim upon us. In their different ways, both Pepys and Evelyn were brilliant and reliable reporters. They also happened to be people of consequence on whom King Charles II had learned to rely. For that reason they can tell us, first, exactly what happened and second, what—if anything—the great ones of the English earth could do about it.

John Hayls. *Portrait of Samuel Pepys (1633–1703).* 1666. Oil on canvas, 29¾ × 24¾″ (75.6 × 62.9 cm). The National Portrait Gallery, London

Between them, Pepys and Evelyn constitute an incomparable resource as to what life in London in the 1660s was like. The merits of Pepys's diary have never been better summed up than in that paragon of its kind, the fourteenth edition (1910–14) of the *Encyclopaedia Britannica.* "The diary of Samuel Pepys," it says, "is a thing apart by virtue of three qualities which are rarely found in perfection when separate and nowhere else in combination. It was secret; it was full; and it was honest."

Pepys was, in effect, secretary to the British Navy almost uninterruptedly at a time—from 1660 to 1688—when the Navy was of sovereign importance to the security of the nation. His duties brought him into close contact with power and authority in all their forms. When accusations were laid against the Navy office in Parliament in 1668, it was Pepys who went down to the bar of the House of Commons and routed the opposition.

In 1684 he was elected to the Presidency of the Royal Society. He also compiled what can be called a diary within his diary of the plays that he saw, year by year. (He once saw *Macbeth* and *Henry V* on the same day, but did not disdain to see *Love in a Tub,* not to mention other even less reputable entertainments.)

In his diary—for which he used what he thought to be an unbreakable code— he presents himself involuntarily as one of the great all-time English comic characters. He was both a dedicated and effective public servant and, in domestic matters, a paradigm of human frailty. It is with delight and fascination that we keep step with him as he races round the London of his day. To that London—as much as to his own self—he is an irreplaceable guide.

As it happened, Pepys and John Evelyn were friends for nearly forty years. (Their friendship burgeoned when Evelyn's brother was about to be operated on for the removal of a stone. Pepys forthwith went over with the stone, "as big as a tennis ball," that had been cut out of him in 1658 and preserved in a specially made case.) In his will, Pepys asked Evelyn to be one of his pallbearers.

Yet no two men could have been more different. Evelyn was born in 1620, the second son of a country gentleman whose comfortable fortune was derived from the manufacture of gunpowder in Elizabethan times. (The family estate, which Evelyn inherited in his late forties, included a handsome house and around 7,500 acres of land.) Throughout his long life—he died at eighty-five—John Evelyn did a little bit of everything and did all of it rather well.

Dutch School. *The Great Fire of London.* c. 1666. Oil on panel, 35⅞ × 60⅝″ (89.7 × 151.6 cm). The Museum of London

Sometimes he went to work under grand auspices and by way of obliging King Charles II, of whom he saw a great deal. In 1662, he was appointed one of the twenty-one commissioners who were to supervise the paving, repair, or widening of certain streets in London. They were also to regulate the licensing of hackney coaches, but it would not appear that either of these duties was very taxing.

In 1663 he was appointed to the committee that regulated the affairs of the Royal Mint. He was more active, and more emotionally committed, as a commissioner for sick and wounded seamen, and he enjoyed the work (and, no less, the salary) of the Council of Foreign Plantations, on which he served from 1671 to 1674.

He also had a fine line in high-minded indignation, some of it well directed and some of it not. On metropolitan pollution, for instance, his every word is still valid. But he also thought it disgusting that an English gentleman should ever be overdressed, and he was convinced that the Swiss would never have attained nationhood if they had not kept to their "prodigious breeches." On that matter, his views did not carry the day.

But for much of his life, Evelyn operated as the most private of individuals and at the prompting of a vagabond curiosity as to a wide range of phenomena. He wrote very well on all manner of subjects, from numismatics and mezzotinting to the natural history of the salad and the beneficent properties of the artichoke, the broom bud, the melon, the nasturtium leaf, and the famed Egyptian onion.

When Evelyn was in London, which was by no means all the time, he made the very most of it. Curious happenings would fall into his lap. One day, for instance, he was summoned to an audience with Charles II and found that Samuel Cooper, the foremost miniaturist of the day, was drawing the king's portrait for use on the new milled money that was about to be issued. It fell to Evelyn to hold the candle that strengthened the shadows, "during which his Majesty was pleased to discourse with me about painting and graving, etc."

He would also go hunting for experience in ways that are still very much open to us in London. He knew, as so many Londoners have known since Adolf Hitler came to power in Germany in 1933, that much can be learned from those who come to England as refugees from tyranny. In his case, it was in the company of a Polish refugee, "the learned Mr. Hartlib," that he tapped many a new vein of miscellaneous learning.

It should be said that Evelyn had neither an original nor a vivacious mind. Excess in all its forms was abhorrent to him. He was aghast that the king should throw the dice at a gaming table and set an example of high play. And it enraged him, understandably enough, that when he dined out in the country his coachmen were given so much to drink in the servants' hall that they fell off the coach box in open country and were unable to continue.

And whereas his friend Samuel Pepys was notable for his almost robotic lechery, Evelyn in that context was circumspection itself. When his eldest son got married in 1680, he urged the bridegroom to "avoid carnal caresses on a full stomach, or in the day time." Nor was he to be one of those "who brag about how frequently they can be brutes in one night." Just to sum it up, he said that "Too frequent embraces dull the sight, decay the memory, induce the gout and shorten life."

As may by now be guessed, Evelyn was not a lot of fun, and we may doubt that he prized fun in others. Even when he heard a sermon preached by the Reverend Mr. Flea, the name seems not to have made him smile. But he had a steady, fair-minded way with him, and when he compared London to Paris—a city he loved—he said that "what our city of London has not in houses and palaces, she has in shops and taverns which render it so open by day and so cheerful in the night that it appears to be a perpetual wake, or wedding, to the beholder. So mad and loud a town is nowhere to be found in the whole world."

Evelyn published that in 1652. By the time the Great Fire broke out in September 1666 he had seen as much of the great world, and of the thinking world, as any man in England. Less than a week before the fire broke out, he had been to St. Paul's with Christopher Wren, among others, and they had debated what should be done about the great church, which was by then in a ruinous state.

Wren had been in Paris from July 1665 till the spring of 1666. On his return he had no doubt as to what should be done about St. Paul's. "Pull it down and start again," was essentially his advice. Some of his colleagues on the commission were for patching, and straightening, and keeping the old steeple, and in general for leaving things much as they were. But at their meeting on August 27, 1666, Wren's ideas won the day.

Writing in his diary that evening of the proposal to delay and defer, Evelyn said that "we totally rejected it and persisted that it required a new foundation. The shape of what stood was very mean, and we had a mind to build it with a noble cupola, a form of church building not as yet known in England, but of wonderful grace."

That was Monday, August 27. On Wednesday, August 29, 1666, the Royal Society's meeting was as rewarding as ever—more so, if anything, in that on that afternoon Mercator himself demonstrated a clock that showed the difference between solar time and mean time. During the next few days, Evelyn may well have wondered if Wren's "noble cupola" would ever get built, so contrary was it both to English practice and the form of St. Paul's as it then existed. Nor had the opposition said its last word.

But then, around two A.M. on the morning of Sunday, September 2, a fire broke out in a baking house on Pudding Lane. The season was dry, the air already hot from a long summer, and the east wind very fierce. The area was overbuilt and overpopulated. When the fire spread, it burned, so Evelyn wrote, "both in breadth and in length, with the churches, public halls, exchange, hospitals, monuments and ornaments, leaping in a prodigious manner from house to house and street to street, devouring after an incredible manner houses, furniture and everything."

Though steady and exact by nature, Evelyn was carried away by the dimensions of the catastrophe, the universal terror of the inhabitants, and the biblical overtones of the scene. The City of London was a place of business, but it had also the character of a gigantic warehouse, in which huge stocks of coal and wood and oil and brimstone and other inflammatory materials went up in flames, one after another.

The night skies were "of a fiery aspect, like the top of a burning oven, and the light seen above 40 miles around." In the afternoon, the flames reminded him of "Sodom, or the Last Day." When he got back home unharmed, he thought of the nineteenth chapter of Genesis and likened himself to "Lot, in my little Zoar, safe and sound." Virgil haunted him, too, with his laconic "Ilium fuit" ("Troy once was") in the second book of the *Aeneid*.

It really did seem to him, for a moment, the end of London, and he remembered the words of St. Paul in his Letter to the Hebrews: "For here have we no continuing city." But when Samuel Pepys went about the blazing city, day after day, he stuck to the then and there. He could have presented himself in his diary (though he did not) as a key figure, inasmuch as he was the first person to go to Whitehall Palace and give King Charles II a reliable account of what was happening.

The King at once asked Pepys to find the Lord Mayor of London and tell him to pull down, without hesitation, every house that was in the path of the fire. Only in that way, he believed, could the fire be contained. Pepys was also asked to tell the Lord Mayor that if he needed the army to come and bring gunpowder to bear, he had only to ask.

There followed a scene of classic poignancy. Pepys finally caught up with the Lord Mayor, who had been up all night, on Canning Street. He looked "like a man spent, with a handkerchief about his neck. To the King's message, he cried, like a fainting woman, "Lord, what can I do? I am spent! People will not obey me. I have been pulling down houses. But the fire overtakes us faster than we can do it."

The Lord Mayor was further inhibited by the fact that there were prominent people who did not see why their houses should be destroyed when they were still quite some way from the flames. They were men in a big way of business, and would certainly expect to be compensated. Who would pay for it? Meanwhile, an estimated 200,000 refugees were flooding into Islington, and up the hill to Highgate, sleeping on the bare ground or in improvised tents.

Pepys in the days of the Great Fire was both prompt and effective. He thought of everything. If he had stocks of wine, and of Parmesan cheese, that were too good to lose, he dug a pit in his garden and buried them. If it was necessary to load his silver and other precious possessions onto a cart at four in the morning and take them to safekeeping in Bethnall Green, he got into the cart in his nightshirt and rode along with them. As for his private holdings of gold—and they were massive, by the way—he put them on board a boat, took them down to Woolwich by

128

moonlight, locked them up and had someone stand guard by it, night and day, until normal life was restored.

Nor was he the type to brood on Sodom, Troy, or the Last Day. On the 4th of September, he had an impromptu dinner for four in his office, "a shoulder of mutton from the cook's, without any napkin or anything, in a sad manner, but we were merry." On the 6th, things went even better. At the house of his neighbor, the East India merchant Sir Richard Ford, and in the company of Sir William Batten, surveyor of the Navy, and of one or two of the men of fashion who had not fled the city, there was a large and convivial dinner at which a fried breast of mutton was served on an earthen platter. "Very merry," he wrote, "and as good a meal, though as ugly a one, as I ever had in my life."

Going about the burning city, he missed nothing, great or small. Sitting at nightfall in a little ale house on Bankside, he watched the fire sneaking round corners, and up steeples, and in the narrow places between churches and houses, and up toward St. Paul's Cathedral with "a most horrid malicious bloody flame, not like the fine flame of an ordinary fire."

He crossed the river to Southwark in hopes of buying a clean shirt and a pair of gloves, but found nothing. He bought two eels, on the river, and noted their price (six shillings). Holed up with a friend for the night, he for the first time in his life lay down in "an empty bed, with only my drawers on." But he made the best of it.

Ever curious, he remembered "a poor cat taken out of a hole in the chimney joining to the wall of the Exchange, with the hair all burned off its body and yet alive." To borrow a clean shirt, to wash with soap and fresh water, and to be able to shave more often than once a week, were momentous events.

So were other things that did not rank high in the scale of human misfortune but at that moment seemed extraordinary. After making short work of a barrel of oysters, he noted the next morning that it was "strange, with what freedom and quantity I pissed this night."

In a remarkably short time the City of London began to put itself into something like order again. Pepys was once again able to prepare to answer to Parliament about the conduct of naval business. The Royal Society met. Pepys dug up his wine, had his every window reglazed, got his curtains hung the way he liked best, and even found a gilder to put his bookbindings in order.

Meanwhile, a most remarkable thing occurred. On Tuesday, September 11, no more than nine days after the outbreak of the Great Fire, King Charles II received two separate sets of plans for the rebuilding of the City of London. One was by Christopher Wren, the other by John Evelyn. Each of them, independently of the other, had in mind a new-model London. Either way, order and reason would prevail, in company with regularity of design and limpidity of spatial planning.

In Wren's case there was something of Roman town planning, as it had been initiated by Pope Sixtus V, and something of the formal gardens of France that Wren had marveled at only a few months before. It was Evelyn's hope that his new-model London, if adopted, would be mapped and engraved by Wenceslaus Hollar, the foremost European engraver of the day, by virtue of his new office as Scenographer to the King.

As intellectual constructs, both were clearheaded, serene, and civilized. To this day, there is something Mozartian about the speed, the wit, the elegance, and the understated power of Wren's formulations. As for Evelyn, he is the epitome of the gifted nonspecialist.

Had Wren's design, in particular, been adopted, we could think of the Great Fire as a cleansing agent, rather than as a catastrophe. It might not have replicated

Georg Braun. "Bird's-Eye View of London" from the atlas
Civitatis Orbis Terrarum. c. 1574. Courtesy of the Folger
Shakespeare Library, Washington, D.C.

Sir Christopher Wren's town plan for the rebuilding
of London after the Great Fire. 1666

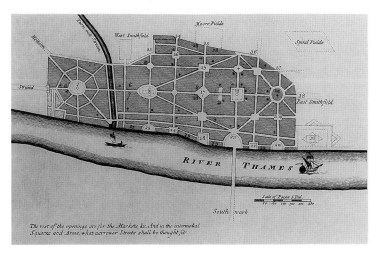

John Evelyn's alternative town plan for the rebuilding
of London after the Great Fire. 1666

Dryden's vision of a city "with silver paved and all divine with gold," but it would have been the next best thing.

As will be seen, there was never a chance that Wren's plans would prevail. Had he been a specialist—a professional architect battling for the job with other professionals—he might have felt the rejection as keenly as we do.

But he never spoke of it. We are entitled to imagine that he drew up those first plans from sheer delight in his intellectual capacities. Could it not have been with them, as it was with the meticulous colored drawings that he submitted for the rebuilding of St. Paul's? Whether or not they were accepted, he said, "I shall not repent the great satisfaction and pleasure I have taken in the contrivance, which equals that of poetry or compositions in music."

In Christopher Wren, London had someone who was, in all the ways that matter, a poet, a composer, an architect, and much else besides. Thanks to him, London in the last years of the seventeenth century does not remind us of Sodom, overwhelmed by artillery from on high, or of Troy, laid waste by one of the more conspicuous wars. It is, against all odds, the archetypal "continuing city," and one in which wild fancy and sublime contrivance both played a part.

This was not a matter of "taste." It was a moral matter. As the architectural historian Kerry Downes has said, "For Wren, architecture was not the highest form of scenery. Rather, it was a visible demonstration of the underlying and immutable truths of geometry—and therefore a statement about the Creator of the Universe—and it was made in the visual language of his own day and of his own invention."

It was in St. Paul's Cathedral that Wren the moralist took the high ground and held it for almost half a century—from 1666, when he first recommended a domed crossing for the projected cathedral, until 1711, when Parliament declared that the great building was finished.

In his fifty-two parish churches, Wren wrought marvels of wit and agility in contexts that basically were set for him by others. But in St. Paul's he had, by contrast, the single greatest and most conspicuous site in London and he could dictate precisely the angle at which the huge building would look down at the city.

While in France, from June 1665 until the spring of 1666, Wren had met—however briefly—Gianlorenzo Bernini, the great sculptor/architect. In the Louvre, he had for the first time watched a major building operation in progress. He noted the size of the work force, the complication of the machinery, and the regular attention of Colbert, who was to Louis XIV what Wren was to be to Charles II in London—the superintendent or Surveyor-General of "the King's works."

Wren's passion for the dome dates back to his sojourn in Paris. Wren had just seen the baroque churches of the Sorbonne and the Val de Grâce in Paris, and he knew that they worked. Standing under their domes, he knew that they, too, worked. Very few people in England at that time had stood beneath an executed dome.

These adventures gave him a new idea of what was involved in a major architectural undertaking. And he made up his mind, when in Paris, that architecture should have the attributes of the eternal and be impervious to changes in fashion.

That is the rationale behind St. Paul's. In 1657, when he was only twenty-three, Wren said that "the impregnable foundations of Geometry and Arithmetic are the only truths that can sink into the mind of man, void of all uncertainty." It was to geometry and arithmetic, rather than to fugitive notions of style, that he turned in St. Paul's for an assurance of finding "the eternal." And they served him well. Dr. Robert Hooke, F.R.S., did not exaggerate when he said that "since the time of

Archimedes there scarce ever has met in one man, in so great perfection, such a mechanical hand and so philosophical a mind." St. Paul's, inside and out, speaks for those hands, and for that mind.

St. Paul's is a stupendous achievement, but at first sight it may not seem a lovable achievement. Its exterior does not reach out to us. It lives a life of its own, in which we can function as admirers from a distance, but are not invited to participate. Wren covered his tracks, too. It is not at a first glance that we shall spot the well-judged impertinence of the make-believe walls that rise to nave height above the aisles. But, without them, the whole balance of the great building would be skewed.

When it came to choosing his collaborators, Wren had a magical instinct. The carvings by Grinling Gibbons and Caius Gabriel Cibber, way up on the exterior, do much to animate the grave music of Wren's designs. It takes time, too, to master the relief of the *Conversion of St. Paul* by Francis Bird on the pediment of the two-storied west front.

Once indoors, visitors often find that St. Paul's has not a hospitable interior, in the sense that Westminster Abbey has a hospitable, all-welcoming interior. In Westminster Abbey we feel as if we had been invited to an enormous block party, in which everyone that we have ever wished to see will turn up around the next corner, if we only keep looking. The Abbey never makes us uneasy.

In St. Paul's, on the other hand, our first impression is, as Nikolaus Pevsner said, "one of ordered spaciousness and somewhat cool perfection." We may even feel inadequate, if not actually rebuffed. "In St. Paul's," James Pope-Hennessy wrote in 1939 in his book *London Fabric*, "people tend to look silly and dwarfed. Beside the visible proofs of Wren's symmetrical vision, the slightest physical defect is magnified, and human beings look badly made."

The scale of the interior is admittedly daunting. The bishop's throne and the choir stalls by Grinling Gibbons, the screen by Jonathan Maine for the chapel of St. Michael and St. George, and the lofty wrought-iron gates by Jean Tijou—all these are majestic, but they are not at all companionable.

But then Wren did not mean them to be companionable. He meant them to stand out in great spaces. Awe, not admiration or affection, was his objective, and he did not wish it to be diminished or abated by additions not sanctioned by himself. When in Paris, he deplored the fact that, because of the influence of women in high society, "little knacks were much in vogue." He didn't want little knacks in St. Paul's, and he didn't want big knacks, either.

From 1790, however, and with Wren dead since 1723, monuments and sculptures began to infiltrate his noble spaces. They began very commendably in 1794, with sculptures of four "benefactors of the English people"—Sir Joshua Reynolds, painter, John Howard, prison reformer, Dr. Johnson, giant of letters, and Sir William Jones, orientalist and jurist. (A civilized and pacific list, by the way.) Among other monuments in St. Paul's, the effigy of Admiral Lord Nelson by John Flaxman may well be our finest reminder of a supreme sea warrior.

The crypt is well worth a visit, not least for the wonderfully laconic summations of some entrants of recent date. But St. Paul's as the visitor sees it is above all the glorious dome. It is, in reality, three structures in one. But what we see, and what we remember, is what Kerry Downes calls "the outer cupola of lead-covered timber that proclaims the majesty of God to London and the might of London in the world."

The might of London may be somewhat in decline, but the majesty of Wren's dome is not.

After the Great Fire

THAT LONDON IN THE LATE 1660s could be a wonderful place in which to live may seem ridiculous. Was this not a decade in which the center of London endured a particularly unpleasant epidemic? Yes it was. In the year 1665 a very large number of Londoners died of a plague that was passed not from one human being to another but by fleas from the feet of infected rats.

And was not the City of London burned virtually to the ground in September 1666? Yes it was. But, between them, the plague and the fire made it possible for London to be redesigned on esthetic and philosophical lines that would have done away forever with the old, rickety, ever-dangerous medieval inner city.

In its place would have been a London made up of long uncluttered vistas, and of circuses toward which six, seven, or even eight straight new streets would lead. The ground-plan would be a metaphor for order and lucidity. Brick and stone would stand tall and straight forever. As for crime and disease, they would summarily take their leave.

The poet John Dryden set out that point of view in his "Annus Mirabilis, 1667." In the end, he thought, the Fire could have done only good. "Methinks," he began,

> already from this chymic flame
> I see a city of more precious mould,
> Rich as the town which gave the Indies name,
> With silver paved and all divine with gold . . .
>
> More great than human now, and more august,
> Now deified she from her fires doth rise:
> Her widening streets on new foundations trust,
> And opening, into larger parts she flies.
>
> Before, she like some shepherdess did show
> Who sat to bathe her by a river's side,
> Not answering to her fame, but rude and low,
> Nor taught the beauteous arts of modern pride.

In all this, Dryden was nature's optimist, just as others were, close on three hundred years later, when they dreamed of a new London at the end of World War II. The aesthetics, the town planning, and the pragmatics of a new society—all were subject, in the 1660s as in the 1940s and 1950s, to the day-to-day necessities of a large commercial city that had been left in ruins. But to see the original plans from the year 1666, and to know how rapidly they were put together in the face of disaster, is to realize that London in those days was one of the heartlands of pure intelligence in human affairs.

This was a time, and a place, in which human affairs were thought to be perfectible. To every problem, there had to be an answer. That answer was within the reach of a group of intelligent and versatile men in whom King Charles II had

Canaletto. *London: Whitehall and the Privy Garden from Richmond House.* 1746. Oil on canvas, 42 × 46″ (106.7 × 116.8 cm). From Goodwood House by courtesy of the Trustees full confidence. They were the Fellows of the Royal Society, which had received its charter from Charles II in July 1662. Originally they numbered in all ninety-eight, plus King Charles II, who offered himself as a candidate for admission and, needless to say, was not turned down.

The members of the Royal Society were enjoined "to make faithful records of all the works of nature or art which can come within their reach." Thus informed and equipped, they were to establish "a philosophy of mankind" that would last as long as mankind itself.

The Society had begun small, and it had begun private. In 1645, with King Charles I still on the throne, a bishop, a mathematician, an astronomer, and one or two others had agreed to meet once a week in London. They would discuss, among other things, "the circulation of the blood, the Copernican hypothesis, the weight of air, Nature's abhorrence of vacuities, the Torricellian experiment and the descent of heavy bodies."

This was the germ of what later became the Royal Society. It might have been simply a historical curiosity, to be superseded in time by the multitude of learned and not-so-learned societies that every capital city spawns. But its charter was a key event in the history of London, and it has never been superseded. Membership of the Royal Society is to this day what it was meant to be—a brevet of high achievement in one or another of the sciences. To have the initials F. R. S. after one's name is owed to one thing, and to one only: true merit. And London has other, more specialized learned societies of which the same can be said.

If we know what the Royal Society stood for at its foundation, and what it has stood for ever since, it is in part because the first wave of its membership included two great diarists: Samuel Pepys, who was its President from 1684 to 1686, and John Evelyn. Thanks to them, we know the Royal Society as it existed week by week in its first years.

The original Fellows included a poet of the first order, John Dryden; Elias Ashmole, the founder of the Ashmolean Museum in Oxford; Christopher Wren (initially known as an astronomer); and John Aubrey, the antiquarian and future author of *Brief Lives*.

Assorted grandees were also included. There were the 2nd Duke of Buckingham and the 1st Marquess of Dorchester. There were bishops and soldiers and courtiers. This was the very heyday of the new idea as a generative force, and the Fellow was rare who had not something of substance to contribute to the Wednesday meetings of the Society.

There was Dr. Glisson, soon to be president of the Royal College of Physicians. There was Sir Edward Ford, who has his place in history as a lifelong royalist and a distinguished soldier. But he also invented a new way of coining small change, an engine that would "transport the waters of the Thames into the higher streets of London," and the prototype of a drogue ("an umbrella-like invention for retarding a ship when she drives in a storm").

These men were not specialists in our sense of the word. (That sense is not recorded in the *Oxford English Dictionary* until two hundred years after the Society was founded.) They were there because of the English belief—only lately discarded—that there is no limit to what can be asked of someone who knows ancient history and philosophy in the original and can write Greek and Latin verses in his head.

In the second half of the seventeenth century a prestige of the same order was also attached to mathematics. There was nothing that could not be expected of a

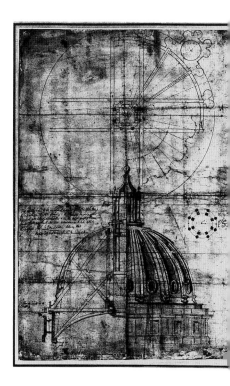

Sir Christopher Wren (drawn by Nicholas Hawksmoor). *Design for the Dome over the Painted Hall in the Royal Hospital, Greenwich.* 1702. Sepia pen and gray wash, 27 × 18½″ (68.6 × 47 cm). The British Architectural Library, RIBA, London

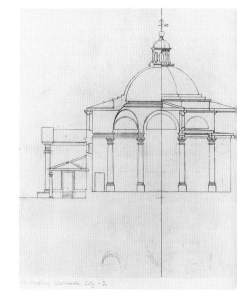

Sir Christopher Wren. *Design for the Church of Stephen Walbrook, City of London.* c. 1671. Half sections looking east to a scale of approximately 1¹⁄₁₆″ to 1′. Pen, 14¼ × 20⅛″ (36.2 × 51.1 cm). The British Architectural Library, RIBA, London

Sir Godfrey Kneller. *Sir Christopher Wren (1632–1723)*. 1711. Oil on canvas, 49 × 39½″ (124.5 × 100.3 cm). The National Portrait Gallery, London

major mathematician. If words like *algebraist* and *trigonometrician* awed all who heard them, it was because it was taken for granted that, singly or collectively, learned men would shortly crack the secrets of the universe, one by one.

A prime instance of this omnicapacity is Robert Boyle, a founder-member of the Royal Society who single-handedly and in his own laboratory made himself the father of modern chemistry. Boyle was in the highest possible degree a man who liked to get to the very bottom of every subject. To master the Gospels, he taught himself Greek and Hebrew, with Syriac and Chaldean grammar on the side.

In this, he personified the spirit of the Royal Society, which was urged by King Charles II to promote what was then called "physico-mathematical-experimental learning." There was no end to the applications of that threefold adjective.

Sir Christopher Wren, for example, has many claims upon the Londoner, but he hoped to rack up one more when he invented a machine that would manufacture at least seven pairs of silk stockings at a time. When he demonstrated it to the silk-stocking makers in the City of London they turned it down, on the ground that it would lower prices and ruin their trade. (When he heard that, Wren flew into one of his rare tantrums and destroyed the model under their very noses.)

Bizarre as some of the proceedings at those Wednesday meetings may now seem, they stood for a decisive change in human affairs. As of 1662, all knowledge was to be the Society's concern. Its purpose was to give London a new and specific distinction—that of a great city in which there was nothing that could not eventually be known.

It has, of course, had rivals for that title in the last three hundred years, and the role of the specialist has become paramount. But from Isaac Newton (elected a Fellow in 1671, and president from 1701 to 1727) to T. H. Huxley and Ernest Rutherford, it has had many a great man of science among its members—and at least one great woman scientist, too, in the person of Dr. Dorothy Hodgkin, who in 1964 was awarded the Nobel Prize for chemistry.

There was an inexhaustible variety about the weekly meetings of the Royal Society. One time, they would argue about the best way to make French bread. The next time, they would look into the problem of how to design a coach that would give them (and everyone else) a smoother ride.

One of their members, Dr. Robert Hooke, could lecture on anything from the making and marketing of felt to the operation of gravity (a subject on which he is said to have given Isaac Newton a pioneering tip or two).

Robert Hannah. *William Harvey Demonstrating his Researches on the Deer to Charles I and the Boy Prince*. 1848. Oil on canvas, 31¾ × 36″ (80.7 × 91.4 cm). By permission of the Royal College of Physicians of London

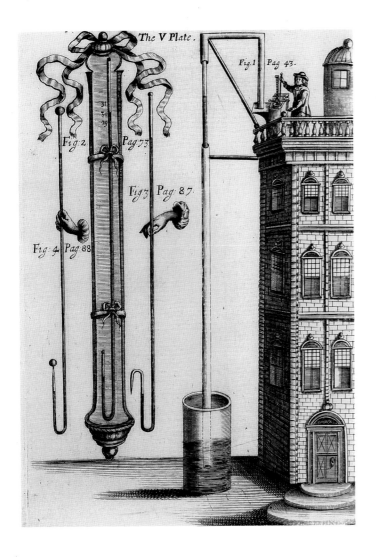

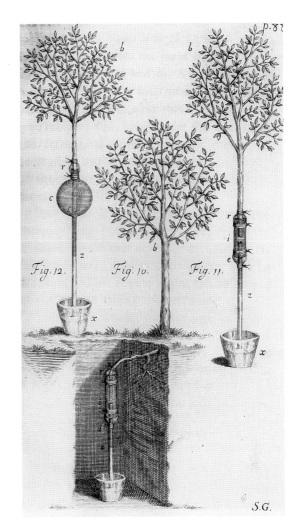

Above:
Robert Boyle. "The Spring of the Air." 1680. From Robert Boyle's *A Continuation of New Experiments, Physico-Mechanical, Touching the Spring and Weight of the Air, and Their Effects* (1669–82). Library of Congress, Washington, D.C., Rare Book Collection

Above right:
Stephen Hales. "Up the Trunks of Trees: Investigation of the Way Sap is Drawn." 1727. From Stephen Hales's *Vegetable Staticks* (London, 1727). Special Collections Branch, National Museum of American History, Smithsonian Institution Libraries, Washington, D.C.

One week, the uses of treacle in medicine were on the agenda. Another time, they tested a harpsichord in which the strings were not plucked, but brought into contact with a revolving wheel covered with parchment. (Evelyn thought that this sounded like "a consort of viols with an organ," but the instrument never went into production.) And sometimes they vied with one another as to who could produce on demand a smokeless fuel, a new mode of rigging for big ships, or "a wheel to run races in."

There was no small competition at such times. While still at school, Dr. Hooke had invented thirty different ways of flying. Sir William Petty, the inventor of "Political Arithmetic" (statistics, as we would call it), was also the inventor of the hinged keel and the double-bottomed ship. Though himself more at home with the advancement of the English fruit tree—a subject on which he knew a very great deal—John Evelyn took careful note of the day on which two concave globes filled with sand were manipulated to represent the respective motions of the earth and the moon.

Blood transfusion interested them, though an early effort involving the use of sheep's blood on a human invalid ended in disaster. If poisons were never far from the Fellows' thoughts in the 1660s, it was not because they were a gang of assassins. It was because they believed that certain poisons—notably one sent to London by "the King of Macassar in E. India"—had curative powers. (Sir Christopher Wren was particularly keen on that idea, and once whipped a dying dog round his garden in hopes of restoring him to health.)

It would be possible to regard many of those early experiments as both freakish and profitless. In our century, after all, Lytton Strachey thought that the

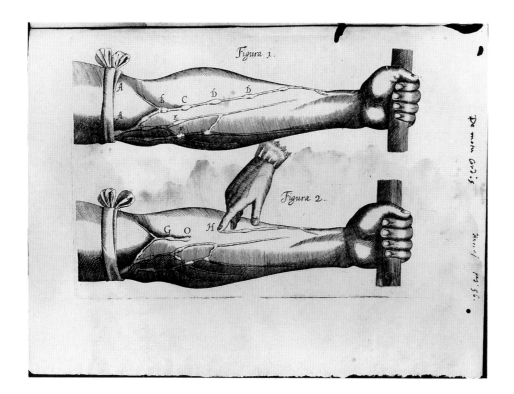

philosopher and essayist Francis Bacon had gone off his head when he jumped out of his coach at the bottom of Highgate Hill on a bitter cold day and insisted on standing in the open and stuffing a chicken with snow.

But he wasn't crazy at all. There had come to him, in a flash, the first principle of refrigeration. As John Aubrey said in his *Brief Lives,* Bacon had suddenly had the idea that flesh might as well be preserved in snow as in salt. In the same way, the apparently nonsensical fancies that were recorded at early meetings of the Royal Society have brought lasting advantages to every one of us.

Attitudes that began as the province of an exclusive club ended by being second nature to a great and thriving capital city. Why did London until 1914 have standards of intellectual energy, many-sided inventiveness, and mercantile near-genius that kept a huge empire in business? Because a handful of very clever men had sat round a table every week and bounced ideas off one another. In time, their ambition, their competitive spirit, and their universal curiosity became the blason of London.

Given that Christopher Wren had both a practical and an august and almost unearthly turn of mind, it was a magical moment in the history of the City of London when he was put in charge of rebuilding its churches after the Great Fire. It was owed primarily to him that not far short of three centuries ago the City of London was shaping up as a cosmopolitan paradise for those of its inhabitants who were at the top of the heap.

The Great Fire of 1666 was a thing of the past. The new St. Paul's Cathedral had been finished in 1711 and was the unchallenged flagship not only of the City of London, but of London itself. Sir Christopher Wren had designed more than fifty churches for the rebuilt City—a City that measured no more than two miles in any direction—and they set a standard of originality, abundance, amenity, and wit that will never be paralleled.

Wren's parish churches for the City of London were built for reasonable people. They were churches in which everyone would have a clear view of the

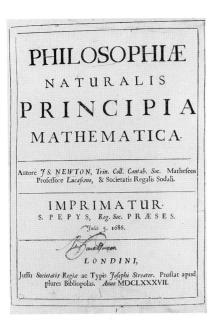

Sir Isaac Newton. *Philosophy.*
First issue of first edition.
July 5, 1686. Library of Con-
gress, Washington, D.C.

Sir Isaac Newton. "A Reflecting
Telescope." 1672. From Sir Is-
aac Newton's *Correspondence.*
Collection The Royal Society,
London

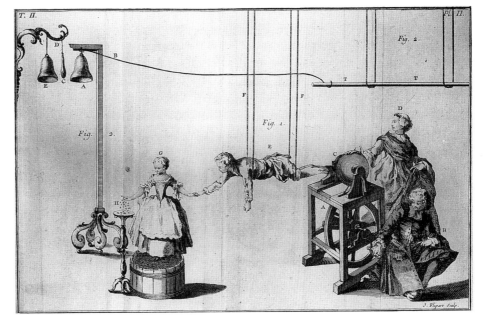

Sir William Watson. "Electro-
statics Demonstration." 1748.
From F. H. Winckler's *Essais
sur l'Electricité* (1748). The
Burndy Library, Norwalk,
Connecticut

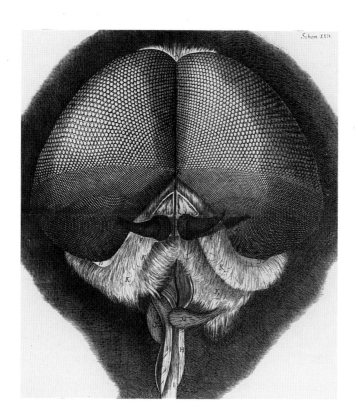

Robert Hooke. "Eye of a Fly." 1665. From *Micrographia* (The Royal Society: London, 1665). Collection The Royal Society, London

preacher and the sermon would not scare the wits out of them. Stained glass was discouraged. Walls were to be left as plain as possible. (Wren's intentions were to be falsified over and over again in the next three hundred years.)

The particular challenge of the City of London as a site for church architecture was that more often than not the sites were preordained, awkward, and ungrateful. Land was land, and no one who owned a piece of it was going to give it up.

It was for this reason that new churches in the City of London could not close great vistas. Nor could they signal to the saints in privileged communication, with light and air all around them. Most often, Wren was given a runty little site and had to make the best of it.

Almost from the very beginning of his career as an architect he was the master of that situation. Problem-solving had been his business ever since—still in his twenties—he had first made his mark as an astronomer. Nothing fazed him. His task was enormous, but he did not see it as in any way beyond his capacities.

Of the 108 churches that had existed in the City of London before the Great Fire, 87 had been destroyed or damaged in the fire. Thirty-two were abandoned. The others were redesigned by Wren, together with 3 more that lay to the west of the City (St. Anne's in Soho, St. Clement Danes at the west end of Fleet Street, and St. James's in Piccadilly).

No man could have had a more majestic brief. In a single year, 1670, Wren designed 16 new churches. Even after he had begun to design St. Paul's Cathedral, in 1672, and to supervise its building in 1675, he went ahead with the parish churches. He did not have to compete for the honor. Nor did he build the churches of his choice and leave the rest to others. His alone was the job, and he built them all, without exception.

He did not do it for money either. Anyone who is familiar with present-day architectural practice will be amazed to learn that although Wren was paid £200 a year for his work on St. Paul's, he was paid nothing at all for his work on the parish

Robert Hooke. *Microscopy.* 1667. Engraving. National Library of Medicine, Bethesda, Maryland

churches. It was as if the honor of being given the job was payment enough, though there were parishes that gave him presents of money or plate on the side by way of keeping his mind on their affairs.

He knew that every parish church had its rights, its dignity, and its difficulties. Faced with St. Mary-le-Bow, in Cheapside, he saw at once that this was, or had once been, one of the key buildings among the City churches. It went back to the eleventh century and had played a grand role in the life of London. But in relation to Cheapside—no mean street, by the way—it did not "tell" as it should have.

So Wren saw to it that anyone who walked along Cheapside would know at once where he was. He discovered that there was a Roman gravel roadway to the north of the church that would not sink beneath the monumental construction that he had in mind. He then designed a tower, 225 feet high and broad and strong at its base, that had two monumental doorways. Gerald Cobb, the historian of the City churches, described them as "perhaps the two finest Classical entrances in England," and it is true that they rank with the work of François Mansart, the great French architect whose work Wren had glimpsed in Paris.

This tower and those doorways gave Wren a stronghold on the street that the church had never had before. The task was one in which, as the saying goes, he had "nowhere to go but up." And go up he did, in a free-floating aerial manner that must have caused amazement when the tower first rose above the stumpy town houses of Cheapside. Column and colonnette, each in batches of twelve, step out above the coupled pilasters of the belltower itself. Fancy upon fancy rides high and lightly, with just enough contrast in the color to make us aware of the elegance with which the white stone has been carved.

Wren worked from finesse, but he also worked from strength. He and his masons, Thomas Cartwright and J. Thompson, wrought so well in St. Mary-le-Bow that the structure as a whole held firm even during World War II, when the steeple was wracked by fire and the bells came tumbling down the tower.

There is no such thing as a generic "Wren church" in the City of London. In every case, he played with the cards that fate and the laws of real estate had given him. If he thought that in the context of St. Mary-le-Bow the basilica of St. Maxentius in Rome had something to give, he went ahead and took it. If he thought that the design of the Jesuit church in Antwerp could be adapted to a London setting, he did not hesitate. If he had on his staff an incomparable bricklayer, in the person of Thomas Horn, he made sure that the church of St. Andrew-by-the-Wardrobe in Queen Victoria Street would show off his skills to perfection.

In the interior of St. Martin Ludgate, hard by St. Paul's Cathedral, there is a kinship with the Nieuwe Kerk in Haarlem. It was in St. Stephen Walbrook that he tried his hand at a great dome, thereby raising his confidence in the design for St. Paul's. He could come on like a visiting Dutchman, as in St. Benet's, Paul's Wharf, and in St. Michael's, Paternoster Royal, he could lift a special something from Borromini's S. Ivo della Sapienza in Rome and make it his own.

He did nothing twice. No matter how bothersome the site, he produced a design in which reasonable men and women could get both an eyeful and an earful of the reasonable tenets of the Church of England. Ground plans like the ones for the decagon of St. Benet Fink and the octagon of St. Antholin have a Mozartian fluency that makes them look easy. But we know that they were nothing of the kind, and that Wren would have preferred to build churches that would be seen at the end of a vista of houses, and be dispersed in such a way as to appear "neither too thick, nor too thin, in prospect."

The men of property put an end to that. But when it came to spire and steeple Wren never failed to fox them. In his eightieth year he was still making the case, in writing, for "handsome spires, or lanterns rising in good proportion above the neighboring houses." It was there, in the upper air, that his fancy roamed free and his wit met with no impediment.

At the time of his death, Wren was already out of fashion. Old and enfeebled and long out of office (but, as his son wrote, "cheerful in solitude"), he liked to go and sit beneath the dome of St. Paul's. If he was never pestered, it was not from good manners. It was because, by then, nobody knew who he was.

He died in 1723, in his ninety-second year. For a long time, and to an astonishing degree, his work dominated the skyline of the City. The City was still a dumpy, twisty, low-slung sort of place. Built like a basset hound, and with no thought of storming the heavens, it could have fallen as flat in emotional as in literal terms.

James Boswell felt something of that when, in July 1763, he climbed up to the dome of St. Paul's and "went out on the leads, and walked around it. I went up to the highest storey of roof. Here I had the immense prospect of London and its environs. London gave me no great idea. I just saw a prodigious group of tiled roofs and narrow lanes opening here and there."

That was the context within which Wren worked. But with his spires, his steeples, and the 200-foot-high Roman Doric column that was his monument to the Fire of London, he gave the City of London the look of a brick-and-stone regatta that might at any moment break out its sails and move off toward the sea. It looked trim, festive, and slightly impertinent—and never more so than in the view of the City from Somerset House by Canaletto that is in the royal collection.

Impossible as it may be today to see the City as Canaletto saw it, Wren can still raise our spirits as we stumble from one hideous new vista to another. He was a man of reason, a man of fancy, a man of wit, and a man of genius. Of how many of us will as much be said?

Anonymous. *St. Mary-le-Bow, Cheapside.* c. 1867. Albumen print, 8³/₁₆ × 5¼" (20.8 × 13.3 cm). Gernsheim Collection, Harry Ransom Humanities Research Center, The University of Texas at Austin

Putting It All Together

WITHIN A FEW YEARS of the Great Fire, the City companies were putting themselves together again, in architectural terms. By 1670 the Apothecaries, the Innholders, the Skinners, the Stationers, the Tallow Chandlers, and the Vintners were making a brave show. (It was a sign of the advance of specialization that the members of the Blacksmiths' Company were no longer expected to double as dentists, as had once been the custom.) Town houses of great splendor were being built—notably nos. 1 and 2, Laurence Pountney Hill, dated 1703 and still standing.

As Nikolaus Pevsner pointed out, it was not thought necessary in the sixteenth, or even in the seventeenth, century for big companies to have flamboyant corporate headquarters. ("The Muscovy Company, the Turkey Company, the Levant Company needed no office premises.") Even the East India Company—prepotent among English commercial enterprises—did not get its headquarters on Leadenhall Street until 126 years after it was founded in 1600.

In the first half of the eighteenth century, the City of London began to opt for monumentality. Though in operation from 1694 onward, the Bank of England did not have a house of its own until 1734, when it opened for business on Threadneedle Street—an address that was to twist many a foreign tongue for more than two hundred years. Majesty of a medical sort was the aim of the rebuilt St. Bartholomew's Hospital, by James Gibbs, which was begun in 1730. Against all the odds, in the eighteenth century, Gibbs wanted men and women to die in dignity.

A conspicuous lacuna was filled in 1739, when the Mansion House began to come into being and the Lord Mayor of London at last had a home of his own in the City of London during his year in office. No one could call the Mansion House a masterpiece of refinement, but it has a lot of bounce. (John Summerson described the two enormous arklike attics that originally rounded off the building as "an exciting touch of millionaire enormity.") But excitement was what the Mansion House was all about, and it was with amazement and high expectation that visitors in the 1760s climbed the deceptively narrow staircase up to the stupendous portico.

In a moment or two, they saw before them a succession of state rooms that went straight through the big building from front to back. The giant order of columns on all four sides of the Egyptian Hall had been meant to stun, and it succeeded.

The City of London had always been a place in which some people made an enormous amount of money, and as the eighteenth century proceeded the City took on a look of well-justified self-confidence. By the 1720s, Daniel Defoe was able to describe the City of London as "the most glorious sight without exception that the whole world at present can show." Since the sack of Rome and the burning in 586 B.C. of the great Temple of Jerusalem, there had in Defoe's view been nothing to compare with the City of London.

This estimate was perfectly acceptable to the great men of the City, who saw their two square miles as virtually a state within the state. To this day, the Lord Mayor of London brings his scepter to Westminster Abbey on Coronation Day and holds fast to it throughout the proceedings. His chain of office, with its enameled

Joseph van Aken. *The Old Stock Market*. c. 1730. Oil on canvas, 39½ × 49¼" (100.3 × 125.1 cm). Courtesy of the Governor and Company of the Bank of England, London

Tudor roses and knots, dates from the 1530s, and in 1799 it was further orna-mented by a pendant sardonyx carved with the arms of the City and set in diamonds. It is not every Lord Mayor who can carry off that chain. Even rarer may be the Lord Mayor who can convince us that he was born to wield that glorious and elaborate product of the 1550s, the Pearl Sword. The Sword of State and the Great Mace also speak for the days when the Lord Mayor of London was a great personage in his own right, and not to be trifled with.

There was a time when the City of London did, indeed, act as a counterweight to the arrogance of Parliament. Among the plate owned by the City Corporation there is, for instance, the Brass-Crosby Cup, made by John Romer in 1772. This commemorates the occasion on which the Lord Mayor of the day and his aldermen faced down the demand of Parliament that its debates should not be reported in the public prints.

Inconceivable as this may seem in an age in which parliamentary and other proceedings are routinely presented the world over on television, this fiat might well have gone unchallenged without the protests that were initiated by the printers of the City of London.

The Bank of England is by many criteria the most important building in the City, if not in Britain as a whole. The Bank of England is the government's bank, the bankers' bank, the source of all currency, the manager of the national debt, and the guardian of the nation's gold reserves. Its windowless walls give it the air of a metropolitan Fort Knox. In economic terms, it was long regarded as the nation's family physician.

In that context, its every bulletin struck awe and its every maneuver was discussed and rediscussed, nationwide. When Montagu Norman was governor of the Bank of England, he was regarded as a combination of magus and diagnostician. If he crossed the English Channel, his every move was monitored and analyzed. The future of the nation could be foretold—so it was thought—by the precise tilt of his unmistakable hat. To be "something in the City" was to be the liege lord, in no matter how small a way, of Montagu Norman.

As architecture, the Bank of England has now virtually no merit whatever. Anyone who is looking for a three-dimensional metaphor for national indignity and demoralization need look no farther than the Bank as it was virtually rebuilt between 1921 and 1937.

Nikolaus Pevsner was a great judge of architecture, and a man who measured his words. In his opinion, the rebuilding of the Bank of England was "in spite of the Second World War, the worst individual loss suffered by London architecture in the first half of the 20th century." And he went on to say that the Bank of England as it had been built by Sir John Soane between 1788 and 1833 was "the only work on the largest scale by the greatest English architect of around 1800, and one of the greatest in Europe."

It is unlikely that anyone now alive can remember the look of Soane's Bank of England as it existed at the end of World War I. Guarded at night by a detachment of the Brigade of Guards, and difficult to get into by day, it was about as secret as a public building can be.

A high-ceilinged, single-storied construction, it covered three acres of prime land in the center of the City. Soane did not build for the bankers' convenience. He built for poetry. A wild, sepulchral fancy went into the 5 pound note Office, the 3½ percent Consols Office, the Discount Office, and all the other places in which business was done. The scale was gigantic, the light infused with high drama, the vaulted spaces contained with a mysterious and a palpable passion.

Sir John Soane. *The Bank of England, the Lothbury Front as Completed in 1805.* 1807. Watercolor, 12³⁄₁₆ × 36⅛″ (31.9 × 91.7 cm). By courtesy of the Trustees of Sir John Soane's Museum, London

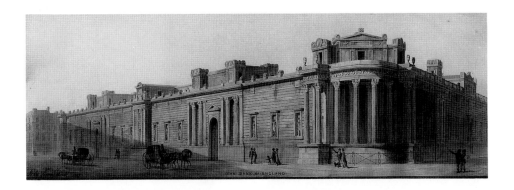

Sir John Soane. *The Bank of England, from Lothbury Court.* 1797. By courtesy of the Trustees of Sir John Soane's Museum, London

There were smaller offices, too, in which what Sir John Summerson called "the precious, mercurial marrow" of Soane's genius was precipitated. Though ideal for the hermit, the visionary, and the fastidious worldling, Soane's bank was not perfectly adapted to a money market that was in continual expansion.

After World War I, the down-to-earth won out over the poetical, and Sir Herbert Baker, an architect now universally derided, was allowed (in Pevsner's words) to use Soane's masterwork as a footstool.

Even so, it is the Bank of England, with St. Paul's Cathedral and the Mansion House, that puts the case for the City of London as a place in which people can get rich in a lawful and orderly way, live to enjoy the respect of their peers, and grow old in holiness. That particular grand slam is not common, but it gives exaltation to the idea of being "something in the City."

The City was always a place of opportunity. If you had enough money, it could be as wonderful to live in as it was, in Defoe's view, to look at. You could have a big house with a big garden. Just a mile or two to the north, there was open country. Churches were full on Sunday, and the congregation of one of them, St. Dionys Backchurch, had been prized by Samuel Pepys for its "very great store of fine women."

The City has, moreover, an essential character that is not ignoble. Though riven from time to time in the Middle Ages by an implacable xenophobia, it is by its nature hospitable. Though once walled, it is in essence an open house for universal

Hans Holbein the Younger. *Portrait of Georg Gisze, Merchant.* 1532. Oil on wood, 38 × 33¾" (96.3 × 85.7 cm). Staatliche Museen zu Berlin-Preussischer Kulturbesitz, Gemäldegalerie

The City of London has always had its share of foreign merchants, but only one of them was lucky enough to be painted by Holbein.

trade, in which all languages can be spoken and (at the right rate of interest) all demands can be satisfied. The very name of Lombard Street, hard by the Mansion House, speaks for the early medieval times when bankers from Lombardy cast a long shadow northward across the Alps.

Queen Elizabeth I may have expelled the Hanseatic merchants from England, but the City allowed the Hanseatic League to keep its steelyard on Cannon Street till 1853. When the Spanish and Portuguese Synagogue was built on Bevis Marks in 1700–1771, Queen Anne gave one of its main beams and the builder returned his fees to the congregation.

Foreign firms and foreign ideas were never outlawed. Until World War I, the German company called Metalgesellchaft, which dominated the market in zinc worldwide, was happy to have its trading headquarters in London. In 1914, a Dutch shipping company was made welcome at no. 32 Bury Street, and its premises were designed by Berlage, the most inventive Dutch architect of his generation. It did not look like anything else in the City of London, but in those open-minded days nobody complained. As recently as 1961–63, the Moscow Narodny Bank was set up on King William Street. ("A satisfactory design," Nikolaus Pevsner noted.)

This was also a city in which great adventures began. Until it was destroyed in an Irish terrorist bomb attack in 1993, the tiny church of St. Ethelburga, in Bishopsgate, looked like what it had been for six hundred years—a neighborhood church that amply predated the Great Fire. For three hundred years, until around

1931, the only entrance to it was beneath and between two equally tiny shops in which an optician sold spectacles. (To that, big signs attested.)

St. Ethelburga's could have been no more than an ancient curiosity, to which had been added in the seventeenth century some fine heraldic glass and in the nineteenth century a font that had a Greek inscription that could be read both backward and forward by those who could read it at all. But it was in this miniature church that in 1607 Henry Hudson and eleven of his crew went to Holy Communion before going off to search for the North-West Passage.

In time, the idea got around that in terms of international trade the City of London was the epicenter of the world. Not to have your headquarters in London was to lengthen the odds against your success.

It also got around that fair dealing was fundamental to the City of London. It was not simply that the merchants of London got rich. What mattered in the long run was that they got rich by behaving well.

That they still behave well today is a notion stoutly upheld, though much contested since that decade of misdeed and malfeasance, the 1980s. The notion has never been better or more succinctly put than by John Betjeman, who wrote in 1977, "What makes the City so different is its secrecy. It is really a village of about four hundred people who know each other and whose words are their bond. If they break their word, they are out."

By "secrecy" Betjeman meant the invisible and unwritten bonding that exists between people of good character who have known one another forever. Between such people, nothing needs to be spelled out. A fractional hesitation, a momentary intake of breath, an almost involuntary droop of an eyelid, and the wordless work is done.

Londoners occasionally get high on this state of affairs, but very few of them have got as high as Joseph Addison in 1711. In his essays, Addison in general took a comfortable view of human nature, but when he wrote about the Royal Exchange he went somewhat over the top. It gratified his vanity as an Englishman, he said, "to see so rich an assembly of countrymen and foreigners consulting together upon the private business of mankind, and making this metropolis a kind of emporium for the whole earth."

On formal occasions in the City of London, Addison by his own account could not restrain the tears that flowed down his cheeks. "I am wonderfully delighted," he said, "to see such a body of men thriving in their own private fortunes, and at the same time promoting the public stock; or, in other words, raising estates for their own families by bringing into their country whatever is wanting, and carrying out of it whatever is superfluous."

As for the amenities that resulted, Addison simply couldn't get over them. On the Englishman's table, he said, "the food often grows in one country, and the sauce in another. The fruits of Portugal are corrected by the products of Barbados, and the infusion of a China plant sweetened with the product of an Indian cane. The Philippine Islands give a flavor to our European bowls."

The image of London as Cosmopolis did not stop there. Addison said that "the single dress of a woman of quality is often the product of a hundred climates. The muff and the fan come together from the different ends of the earth. The scarf is sent from the torrid zone, and the tippet from beneath the pole. The brocade petticoat rises out of the mines of Peru, and the diamond necklace out of the bowels of Hindustan."

As a pioneering eulogy of London as the headquarters of multinational and intercontinental commerce, that would be hard to beat. Those who live by the import-export business should have it by heart. We may wonder to what extent the population of London in Addison's day had access to the gourmet foods that he talked about, let alone to the couture costumes that he saw on the back of every "woman of quality." But his was a wild euphoria, and it carries us along.

As Addison implied, importing at that time and for many generations to come was a highly specialized activity. The visitor had only to put his nose inside a warehouse within range of the Thames waterfront to know at once what kind of traffic was carried on there. To this day, in London's docklands, where no cargo will ever again be unloaded, we can often still feel our way by smell alone.

In these intimations there is a vestigial echo of what Charles Dickens remembered from his Sunday walks in the City of London in the 1850s. "In the churches about Mark-Lane, for example, there was a dry whiff of wheat; and I accidentally struck an airy sample of barley out of an aged hassock in one of them. One church near Mincing Lane smelt like a druggist's drawer. Behind the Monument, the service had a flavor of damaged oranges which, a little further down the river, tempered into herrings and gradually toned into a cosmopolitan blast of fish. In one church, the exact counterpart of the church in the Rake's Progress where the hero is being married to the horrible old lady, there was no speciality of atmosphere until the organ shook a perfume of hides all over us from some adjacent warehouse."

The City of London in Addison's time was not what it is today—primarily a financial center. It was a place where things were made, most often by hand. (More than two hundred occupations were listed in the City in the year of the Great Fire.) It was also a place where things were imported and warehoused. Bargains were not struck, as they are today, in respect of imports that would never cross the boundaries of London. The deal done and the things bought belonged in the same square metropolitan mile.

As to that, the great monument (now occupied by the Port of London Authority) is the six-storyed and five-acred construction on New Street, off Bishopsgate, that was built from 1769 onward as the warehouses of the East India Company. The East India Company was at that time—here I quote from Lucy S. Sutherland's definitive survey of the subject—"not only far and away the biggest and most complicated trading organization in Britain, but (together with the Bank of England and the South Sea Company) the center of the financial market then rising in

John Rocque (engraved by John Pine). *A Plan of the City of London and Westminster.* 1744–46. Facsimile published by London Topographical Society 1913–18

London, and of the Government's political and financial interest there."

Like the great multinational corporations of today, the East India Company functioned almost as a sovereign state. In India itself, the armed forces of the crown were at its service. It did not need to have a flamboyant building. Bare red brick, and plenty of it, was quite enough, and in the late eighteenth century it must have stunned many an imaginative observer.

To the casual visitor, the City of London today is almost indecipherable. When we stand in the City with our heads bowed above that invaluable compilation, the *London A to Z*, we wish ourselves back in the year 1746, when John Rocque's brand-new map of London offered the first-time visitor a peerless orientation.

Though not exactly portable—it was on a scale of twenth-six inches to a mile—it was a masterpiece of the engraver's art. It brought lightness and order into conglomerations that took forever to disentangle. Where a big city was concerned, Rocque knew what was garnish, and what was fundamental, and he never mistook the one for the other.

He knew that a capital city, however small, needs a city hall, a church, a bank, a court of law, a hospital, a counting house, a school, and a marketplace. It needs a point of arrival, a point of departure, and a place of assembly. It also needs a place to eat and a place to sleep.

Rocque thought the matter through, and eventually he flagged the addresses in question in one limpid typeface after another. If there were big private houses with gardens of their own, he had unmistakable symbols for them. His type came in many sizes, and even the smallest of them sang out, neat and clear. Wherever you wanted to go in the City of London, John Rocque would make sure that you got there. (In the matter of somewhere to sleep, he did rather fall down. But then the City of London was not then hotel country, and never has been.)

To a remarkable extent, the City is still the center of London. The Old Bailey is what it always was—the Central Criminal Court—and it stands on the site once occupied by Newgate Prison. Abbeys and cathedrals notwithstanding, St. Bartholomew-the-Great is still what it was in the twelfth century—the grandest and the plainest of London's churches. The dignity of dying still permeates St. Bartholomew's Hospital, built by James Gibbs between 1730 and 1759. It was Gibbs's intention that the sick, too, should have their palace, and it looks, as Nikolaus Pevsner said, "very much like the 18th century beau ideal of a Cambridge college court."

One by one, the great markets of the City of London have been phased out and moved elsewhere. This is not because they had ceased to be important. It is because they no longer made sense. Billingsgate Market survived until 1982 as the center of London's trade in fish. As recently as 1963 the City of London Corporation renewed the claim of Smithfield to be the center of the trade in meat. Until 1991, Spitalfields Market was the place to go for fruit and vegetables. (Since 1928, people had relied on the heated cellars in which bananas lay ripening.) As for Beaver Hall in Great Trinity Lane, it held fur sales even on Sundays, when everyone else in the City had shut their doors from Friday till Monday.

These were places of legend, fixed centers of a craving for baron of beef and Dover sole, year-round, for strawberries in midsummer, and for a fur tippet on brisk mornings in October. It was not from nostalgia, but from actuality, that John Betjeman could write in 1977 of Smithfield's "Chaucerian characters and medieval-looking hand-barrows." Visitors who tried the patience of the porters in Billingsgate will never forget how—well into the late twentieth century—this was a veritable theme park of British invective. Not for nothing in the 1670s did "billingsgating" become a synonym for bad language.

But then, one by one, those great markets disappeared. A new technology made it both more convenient and more profitable for meat, fish, fruit, and vegetables to be traded elsewhere and in other conditions. The age of the container and the articulated lorry was not one in which Chaucerian characters, let alone handbarrows, medieval or otherwise, could flourish.

To that extent, John Rocque today would have to redraw his map. One or two other defections should be mentioned. St. Paul's School, founded in 1509 in the shadow of the east side of St. Paul's Cathedral, was in its day the largest school in England and provided free education for 153 children, who were to be "of all nations and countries indifferently."

How it is today I cannot say, but when I was at St. Paul's School in the 1930s its original and exemplary mandate was still in force. Refugees from Nazi persecution were made welcome, a grandson of Sigmund Freud sat at the next desk to mine, and roll call was enlivened by names like Qadir, Aserappa, and ffennell—exotic novelties, one and all, for those who had grown up with Smith, Brown, and Robinson. But by then the school had long since moved out of the City to Hammersmith, and links with the Cathedral were no more than nominal.

The centrality of the City in medicine was established in 1509 with the encouragement of Henry VIII. Like most of the major institutions in London, it began slowly and quietly, with meetings of just a handful of people in a private house. (The householder in question was Thomas Linacre, a scholar and gram-

Pieter Angillis. *Covent Garden Market*. c. 1726. Oil on copper, 18¾ × 42¾" (47.8 × 63 cm). Yale Center for British Art, New Haven. Paul Mellon Collection

marian who was friendly with both Erasmus and St. Thomas More.)

A hundred years later, in 1616, William Harvey, a physician to St. Bartholomew's Hospital, in the very heart of the City, cracked the secret of the circulation of the blood. The College of Physicians had thereafter an international resonance, and when its headquarters were rebuilt in the 1670s after the Great Fire it was one of the more imposing collegiate constructions in the City of London.

It was designed by Robert Hooke, a man of almost universal genius who researched the nature of combustion, discovered the fifth star in Orion, asserted the true principle of the arch, hypothesized the possibility of telegraphy, planned to measure the force of gravity with the help of a pendulum, and invented, among much else, the marine barometer and the watch spring. In John Aubrey's opinion he was "certainly the greatest Mechanick this day in the world," and when Aubrey asked him how many inventions he had made he said, "Not less than a thousand," but could not be bothered to list them.

After the Great Fire, when Hooke was made one of the two Surveyors to the City of London, he was in demand as an architect. His Bethlehem Hospital, better known as Bedlam, had a truly palatial air (John Evelyn compared it to the Tuileries). He may have had at least a hand in the design of the Monument, and Sir John Summerson once suggested that he, and not Wren, might have been the architect of the city church of St. Edmund the King.

Thomas Rowlandson. *A Meeting of Creditors.* c. 1775–88. Pen and gray-black ink and watercolor over traces of pencil. 11½ × 17" (29.8 × 43.2 cm). Fitzwilliam Museum, Cambridge

His College of Physicians no longer exists, but an eighteenth-century engraving suggests that it was midway between a metropolitan palace and a college in Oxford or Cambridge. If it was incoherent in style, that was doubtless because Hooke was too restless to leave any idea alone.

What mattered was that it was clearly a place in which highly educated men came and went, secure in the possession of gowns, hoods, and validated degrees that set them high above the rabble of "midwives, folk-healers, seventh sons, strokers, bone-setters, lithotomists, astrologers and hawkers of pills and potions" who aspired to double as doctors. (I owe that impressive list to Dr. Harold E. Cook of the University of Wisconsin.)

The stately ensemble of the College of Physicians was in line with the ambition of the City's physicians to act as sole arbiters in medical matters. By the 1680s, they were empowered to examine and license all medical practitioners in London. Once licensed as learned professionals, the new entries made the most of their position as monopolists. This was, in fact, the high point of the City of London as a center of virtual dictatorship in the profession of medicine.

Under Charles II and James II, the College was allowed a free hand. But with the arrival in 1688 of King William III, quite other policies prevailed. William III had his own ideas about doctors. He was not impressed by the university status to which the London doctors aspired. He liked free and practical spirits—men who had worked with the army or the navy and had proved their worth in times of emergency.

Book learning was not his criterion, and he did not admire doctors who walled themselves up in their studies and pored over the classics of the past. Rather than give priority to doctors of philosophy, he liked doctors who went out into the world, and preferably to the battlefield, and got on with the day-to-day difficulties of healing. If they had new ideas, he fostered them. If they rose from the ranks, as often happened with naval surgeons, he applauded them. If they were ready to try new drugs, new instruments, and new hypotheses, so was he.

In short, he wanted a free medical marketplace in the City of London, and he got it. For this and other reasons, the center of medical gravity eventually moved westward in the 1840s, to the long straight streets named after Edward Harley, the 2nd Earl of Oxford, and Welbeck, the seat of the Cavendish family in Nottinghamshire. Behind those august but almost anonymous facades, moneyed patients could be received with all discretion and the phenomenon of the fashionable physician could burgeon at leisure.

An unregretted absentee from present-day maps of London is the irregular shape that stands in Rocque's map for the Fleet Prison, to which debtors were consigned. Somewhere within all true-born Londoners there lurks to this day an ancient and ineradicable horror of debt. They may live within their income. Their bills may be paid by return mail. They have been in the black at the bank since they first opened an account. But none of this makes any difference. For the true-bred Londoner, DEBT is the ultimate four-letter word.

Elsewhere, debt is a way of life. In how many developed societies could life be carried on today without the mortgage, the bank loan, the hire purchase agreement, the deferred payment, and the credit card? Not to be in debt to the bank in the United States is to be some kind of freak.

For that matter, how many countries are without a national debt that they must live with as best they can? There are even those who see the size of that debt as an index of national vitality. But the true-born Londoner sticks to his inherited ways. Buried deep within him is a dread of the debt collector. "Be regular, sir! Do be regular!" was what the debt collector said to a young man in one of Anthony Trollope's novels, and his whisper still echoes down the wind.

Folk-memory reinforces that terror. The true-bred Londoner bears within him a subliminal recollection of the days when debtors could be sent to prison. If they went into hiding to escape arrest, they could be hanged for it. Once arrested, they could be dragged to prison, feet first and flat on the ground, in a kind of cage. Once in jail, they could be kept there forever in disgusting and degrading conditions.

Of those conditions the best known and possibly the most blatant example was the Fleet Prison, which until it was pulled down in 1846 stood on land that is now part of Farringdon Street. Those who were shut up in the Fleet Prison for debt were not all common crooks. One of them, in 1777–79, was William Penn, the founder of Pennsylvania. Another was William Wycherley, the author in the 1670s of *The Country Wife*, one of the funniest plays in the English language. Yet another was Richard Hogarth, the schoolteacher father of William Hogarth, painter and printmaker.

So we still shiver when we study John Rocque's map of London and see, just north of Ludgate Hill, the outline of the Fleet Prison. For years, Daniel Defoe was in danger of what he rightly called "Perpetual Imprisonment for Debt." Dr. Samuel Johnson said in 1758 that "the confinement of any man in the sloth and darkness of a prison is a loss to the nation, and no gain to the creditor." Charles Dickens in his *Pickwick Papers* leaves us in no doubt of the horrors of the Fleet Prison.

Yet it was not until the Debtors' Act of 1869 that imprisonment for debt was abolished in England. Meanwhile, the City of London flattered itself that it lived in what Dr. Johnson called "an age of commerce and computation." But if any of its turtle-eating aldermen ever computed the cost, in human terms, of the Fleet Prison, nothing ever came of his calculations.

Yet it could be said that, without the Fleet Prison, William Hogarth would have lacked a hideous but vital ingredient in the portrait of London life that he passed down to us. Had his learned but perennially unsuccessful father not been sent to the Fleet Prison for debt, the adjective *Hogarthian* would not have had so swift and so sure a passage into the English language.

Hogarthian is one of the great English adjectives. It looks well. It sounds well. And it is the epitome of something very important about Londoners—and, above all, about City-of-Londoners.

William Thompson. *The Upper Condemned Cell at Newgate Prison in the Morning of the Execution of Henry Fauntleroy.* 1828. Oil on canvas, 40⅛ × 50¼″ (101.9 × 127.6 cm). The Museum of London

William Hogarth knew the life of inmost London as well as any man. He was born in 1697 on Bartholomew Close, West Smithfield. He was raised within two minutes' walk of the grandest of all London parish churches, St. Bartholomew-the-Great. Just around the corner, the annual Bartholomew Fair made him a co-conspirator in a spectacle unmatched, then or since, for its displays of civic devilry.

In the words of Hogarth's biographer, Ronald Paulson, the fascination of the fair lay in the fact that "people of whatever age and class could lose themselves in a world where their imaginary projections coincided with reality and their most anarchic and aimless desires could be explored. The fair was a last place, short of the gin shop, where man could escape civilization and return to his instincts and primal chaos."

Smithfield Market was as educational, in its way, as any formal classroom. Hogarth had in his birthplace a horse and cattle market that likewise had many a lesson in life to offer. St. Bartholomew's Hospital was so dear to him that when there was a question of an Italian painter, Jacopo Amiconi, being asked to decorate it Hogarth offered to paint the two large pictures himself, for free. (His offer was accepted.)

In his professional activities Hogarth eventually drifted westward, living in what is now Leicester Square and running an art school on St. Martin's Lane. But it was in the City of London that he formed himself as a moral observer. The City as he portrayed it was a ruthless, rascally, undependable place in which men and women alike could go up fast and come down even faster. Fair dealing, sweet good nature, and forgetfulness of self played no part in his narratives. In them, as in a proverbial Latin phrase, man was a wolf to man, and women didn't always behave too well, either.

He knew the City of London as an overcrowded place in which there were just too many people, too many belongings, and too many bad smells. All human encounters were potentially dangerous. The struggle for life was as ugly as it was unremitting. Indoors and out, privacy and London were mutually exclusive.

To make all that clear in his prints, Hogarth developed a mode of expression

Anonymous. *Bartholomew Fair.* c. 1730. Fan design providing a comprehensive survey of the fair from Lee's and Harper's platform stage and the famous conjuror Isaac Fawkes. The Museum of London

that was nothing short of graphomaniacal. In the storytelling prints that he produced in one series after another, there is so much to look at and so much to decipher that we are constantly on the edge of informational overload. Hogarth has just too much to tell us, and most of it is bad news.

Much of his work was, in effect, an encyclopedia of ill-doing. Nowhere in art is the dark underside of the City of London so elaborately documented. Nor was anyone quicker than he to study the passion for fast money—still far from extinct in the City—that first reached apotheosis in the affairs of the South Sea Company between 1711 and 1720. At twenty-three, not long after he first issued his shop card as an independent engraver, Hogarth was already on the job in a print called *The South Sea Bubble,* in which the effects of greed and speculation could not be more neatly skewered.

At thirty-one, he drew upon his memories of the Fleet Prison when he painted the parliamentary committee that had been appointed to enquire into the excesses of its warden, Thomas Bambridge. In that painting a ghastly light—a veritable halo of iniquity—plays upon the sinister features of Bambridge as he glares at the ragged, hapless, but still erect figure of the prisoner.

At thirty-three, Hogarth decided to work in what he called "a field unbroke-up in any country or any age"—the engraving of "modern moral subjects." It was with engravings of that sort that he made for himself an immense and lasting reputation.

"Modern" was a word well chosen. Hogarth in his prints was up-to-the-minute in ways that keep the social historian in a lather. A new law, a new face, a new fad, a new crime—every one of them gave him an appetite for work.

Decade by decade, his prints spelled out the unacceptable aspect of life in the great City of London. The thief, the swindler, the fortune-hunting suitor, the panderer, the quack doctor, and the bawd were studied over and over again in terms of topicality. The surgeons who operated on mad patients and advertised "No Cure, No Money" did not escape his notice. Nor did the nouveau riche, the arbiter of "taste," and the guardians of the law. Hogarth took on the London of his day in its every detail.

It delighted him if the members of his large and heterogeneous acquaintance wanted to keep up-to-date with what he was doing. They were welcome, for instance, to come by his studio in Covent Garden. (George Vertue, the antiquarian and anecdotal historian of English art, wrote that Hogarth once painted a well-known London magistrate in the act of sentencing a dog to death for stealing a shoulder of mutton.)

He also invented for himself an antic persona that made him notorious for his hostility to foreign painters, foreign singers, and foreign visitors. In the privacy of his studio, and when painting the self-portrait that is now in the Yale Center for Btitish Art, he revealed himself as a tender, vulnerable, and very good-looking young man. But in public, foreigners of all kinds came under his anathema, and he enjoyed telling people that "by God" he was as good a portrait painter as van Dyck.

"Give me my time," he said, "and let me choose my subject." As it happened, he did take his own time—between 1738 and 1743 he made no prints—and quite often he chose his own subjects. Some of the portraits that he painted at that time are among the glories of British art.

They were not "as good as" van Dyck. Nor were they better or worse. The two could not be read as rivals. Van Dyck was a consummate courtier. Hogarth could not imagine himself in such a role. Van Dyck showed the English what they could be. Hogarth showed them what they were. How touching, for instance, is that early self-portrait of his! How handsome he was then, and how blithe, how buoyant, and how free in spirit! In that portrait, the great castigator of men and mores is for once off duty.

In his *Captain Thomas Coram* of 1740 he combined a grand style borrowed from French painting with a direct and unaffected delight in the personality and the achievements of the sitter. In the City of London, Captain Coram stood tall. A man of strong and unpolluted nature, he had made an enormous fortune from trade the world over (witness the globe at his feet in Hogarth's portrait).

But Coram thought of others beside himself. He had worked for nearly twenty years to set up a Foundling Hospital in the City of London under charter from King George II. He was a strong man, a plain man, an unpretentious man. Who else would have been painted in so grand a style while wearing so unfashionable a coat?

We see in *Captain Coram,* just as we see in the straightforward eloquence of Hogarth's portrait of his friend George Arnold, a view of English manhood that is very rarely to be paralleled in his prints. These are big men, true men, men of an unfeigned, unpolished righteousness.

He could find the same traits in women, too. When he painted Miss Mary Edwards in 1742, he knew that she was one of the richest women in England, and he gave due attention to her red dress, her jeweled necklace, and her white ruffles. He counted the carats in the gold of her fob watch. Quite clearly she was no pauper. But Hogarth also tells us that she read Addison in the *Spectator,* and that she was a fiery patriot, a citizen of the world, and a representative of her sex who could be compared with Queen Elizabeth I. That she had married a fortune-hunting brute and forthwith got rid of him is not spelled out by Hogarth, but how readily do we believe it!

When he did not get the portrait commissions for which he had hoped, he blamed "the whole nest of phizmongers, every one of whom has his friends, and all were taught to run down my women as harlots and my men as caricatures." As for the London art dealers, he went into print under the name of "Britophil" and took them apart for peddling "dead Christs, Holy Families, Madonnas and other dismal dark objects."

THE ENRAGED MUSICIAN.

William Hogarth. *Self-Portrait.* c. 1757. Oil on canvas, 16 × 15½″ (40.6 × 39.4 cm). The National Portrait Gallery, London

William Hogarth. *The Enraged Musician.* 1741. Engraving. National Gallery of Art, Washington, D.C. Rosenwald Collection

Like many another extreme opinion, this one had within it a histrionic element. Hogarth knew a great deal about European Old Master painting and did not hesitate to draw directly upon that knowledge when faced with a large-scale subject that would otherwise have given him big trouble.

If confronted with an examination paper on the iconography of gods and goddesses, saints and saviors, he could have passed summa cum laude. (It was not for nothing that he had had a schoolmaster for a father.)

But an ingrown and passive bitterness was not in his nature. If something was wrong with the City of London, he did something about it. From boyhood onward, he had witnessed the plight of the sick, the poor, and the mentally disturbed. He had also monitored the inhumanity of the unlettered "doctors" who preyed upon them.

It was therefore a matter of intense emotional importance to him when James Gibbs was commissioned in 1730 to rebuild St. Bartholomew's Hospital, which had been founded as early as 1123 within a matter of yards from the house in which Hogarth had been born. And I doubt that he ever had a happier day than the one on which he was made a governor of the hospital (and a very active one, as it turned out).

It was one of the more appalling aspects of the City of London in Hogarth's youth and early manhood that large numbers of children, unwanted and uncared-for, were let loose on the streets to fend for themselves. Some were orphans, some were illegitimate, some were turned out for no particular reason.

When it came to painting more fortunate children, Hogarth was one of the most gifted of all English artists. As deftly as any novelist, he could summon up — as in the *Graham Children* — or the *McKinnon Children* — every last nuance of a privileged childhood and a well-filled nursery. And when he saw the human detritus of the London streets, he burned to do something about it.

So, when his friend Sir Thomas Coram at last managed to set up in 1739 a Foundling Hospital under charter from King George II, Hogarth was with him heart and soul. The Hospital was to be a hospital, self-evidently, but it would also be a place in which foundlings would be sheltered and educated.

Hogarth was one of the original governors of the hospital. He gave money. He and his wife adopted more than one of the foundlings. He persuaded his colleagues to give pictures to the new hospital in order that it should be, in effect, the first art gallery in London to be open to all comers. (It is still open, by the way, Monday through Friday, at 40 Brunswick Square.)

In a large painting for the Foundling Hospital called *Moses Brought to Pharaoh's Daughter,* Hogarth brought an exceptional tenderness and, in terms of color, a fine fancy to the situation of the rescued Moses. It was a very long way from the brutish detail of *The Rake's Progress* to the well-filled lap of Pharaoh's daughter and the sweet hesitations of the little boy who had only lately been pulled out of the bulrushes.

Meanwhile, and in his forties, he was very much irked by what he sensed as condescension in the British establishment of the day. The name of *caricaturist* was enough, in itself, to make him boil over. But where another artist might have stayed home and felt sorry for himself, Hogarth had the true City-of-Londoner's resilience.

If he could not support his family as a big-time painter, he would do it as a printmaker. He wouldn't rely on the dealers, either. He would cut out the middlemen, foil the pirates, and act as his own printer, publisher, and distributor. He would function as an independent entrepreneur. Like many another stalwart of the City of London, then and since, he would look to no one but himself for his advancement.

He reckoned, quite rightly, that his prints would find a huge public. This was as true of the Marriage à la Mode series of 1743 as it was of the late and uproarious Election series of 1754. The Marriage sequence was concerned, in his own words, with a series of "modern occurrences in high life." Its subject is a matrimonial exchange, conceived in wickedness and carried through to catastrophe. In *The Election,* Hogarth portrays the course of local politics in Oxfordshire with what was lately described as "a stoical acceptance of the irredeemable wickedness of the world."

Irrespective of age and class, anyone in London who had a shilling to spare could buy one of his prints. They would prove to be addictive, moreover. In this way it came about that, as the Hogarth scholar David Bindman has pointed out, "Hogarth's popular prints were disseminated more widely in society than the work of any other 'serious' artist, perhaps in the whole history of art."

He deserved it. He was a combination of moralist, social observer, and superior gossip. Whenever a new print of his appeared in a shop window, a crowd would gather. They would savor every last allusion to the news of the day and be alert to every telling detail of dress and demeanor. If the print was full of monstrous metropolitans, his followers could put a name to every one of them. In the inferno of London life, he would be their guide and their friend. For that they loved him.

And he deserved that love. The look of Londoners—not the visiting grandees all dressed up for the studio, but true Londoners caught informally at this or that stage in life—has nowhere been better caught than in the *Heads of Six of Hogarth's Servants.*

With the death of William Hogarth in October 1764, a cycle in the life of the City of London may be said to have come to an end. The City had nurtured a great poet, John Donne, who was also a great preacher. It bore the manifold and unmistakable mark of a great architect, Christopher Wren. And it had nurtured a great maker of images, William Hogarth, who was archetypally and irreducibly a City-of-Londoner. These three were the competition that posterity had to face.

The Perpetual President

George Dance. *James Boswell (1740–1795)*. 1793. Pencil, 10 × 7¼″ (25.4 × 17.8 cm). The National Portrait Gallery, London

Sir Joshua Reynolds. *Portrait of Samuel Johnson*. 1769. Oil on canvas, 24 × 29″ (76.2 × 63.8 cm). Collection Lord Sackville, Knole

IN AN ORDERED WORLD, Dr. Samuel Johnson would be president in perpetuity of all thinking Londoners.

Johnson was the complete Londoner. He lived there almost without interruption from 1737 until the day of his death in 1784. He was in London not as a spectator but as an active, participating, germinating, and initiating citizen. Without cease and without stint he put his powers to work. London was the locus of his deepest feelings, his most strenuous endeavors, and his most enduring achievements in friendship. The more we learn about him, the more we realize that he did just about anything that can be asked of a thinking man in a capital city.

Yet he could have done all these things and not have the impact upon us in London that he has to this day—that of a vast, broody, and potentially explosive presence that haunts street after street, square after square, church after church, tavern after tavern, and club after club. Every time we get to London and hear (or don't hear) a new idea, Johnson is with us. And when we read the critics of our own day, it is as often as not the memory of his judgments, not the actuality of theirs, that comes thundering through the page.

Johnson had a difficult start in London. In the second quarter of the eighteenth century, conditions in the city were conspicuously appalling, with deaths sometimes outnumbering births by two to one. There were winters in which, every day at dawn, homeless people were found frozen to death on the streets.

He had been bone poor, with shoes so worn that his bare feet peeped out at the edges. There had been times when he could not afford a candle by which to keep on working after the sun went down. He had been literally in rags, to the point that when he was invited to dinner with a person of consequence he had to eat behind a screen to hide his condition from the other guests. And when he said of his shirts that "I have no passion for clean linen," no one ever contradicted him.

Even in 1763, when his future biographer James Boswell first met him, he was at first disconcerted by Johnson's appearance. "His brown suit of clothes looked very rusty; he had on a little old shriveled unpowdered wig, which was too small for his head; his shirt-neck and the knees of his breeches were loose; his black worsted stockings ill drawn up; and he had a pair of unbuckled shoes by way of slippers." "But," Boswell went on, in words that were to be echoed by every one of Johnson's visitors, "all these slovenly particularities were forgotten the moment that he began to talk."

Johnson had no illusions about London. He knew what it was like to be turned away at the doors of the great when he was at the very height of his powers. But, as was said by an Irish clergyman who knew Johnson well, "Johnson was much attached to London. He observed that a man stored his mind better there than anywhere else. In remote situations a man's body might be feasted, but his mind was starved, and his faculties apt to degenerate from want of exercize and competition. No place (he said) cured a man's vanity or arrogance as well as London. For, as no man was either great or good per se, but as compared with others not so good or great, he was sure to find in the metropolis many his equals and some his superiors."

That same Irishman went on to say that if Johnson had wished to become an Anglican clergyman many a good country living would have been open to him. But "he could not leave the improved society of the capital, or consent to exchange the exhilarating joys and splendid decorations of public life, for the obscurity, insipidity and uniformity of remote situations."

It is this tremendous Johnson, so much of a piece and yet so prone in private to melancholy and self-doubt, who is at our side in London when we walk into a bookshop, library, or publishing house, when we go out to dinner, whether in a friend's house or in a restaurant, and when we decide to walk home, ever so slightly flown with food and drink, at one or two in the morning.

He was, after all, the Johnson who spoke of red Bordeaux as "so weak that a man would be drowned by it before it made him drunk." He was also the Johnson whose fits of laughter, late at night in the street near the church of St. Clement Danes, could be heard from a long way away. And he was the Johnson who had once spent a whole night walking back and forth across St. James's Square, deep in riotous talk with his friend the poet Richard Savage at a time when neither of them had the price of a bed.

It was Johnson's belief that "there is nothing that has yet been contrived by man, by which so much happiness is produced by a good tavern or inn." He also said, to his first biographer, John Hawkins, that "a tavern chair is the throne of human felicity." In that context, as in so many others, he was a past master of his subject. If we manage to find one of the anachronistic London cookshops that does not make do with fast food, we may fancy that Dr. Johnson will come in and sit down somewhere near us. We know from Boswell what would happen, in that case.

> When at table, he was totally absorbed in the business of the moment; his looks seemed riveted to his plate; nor would he, unless when in very high company, say one word, or even pay the least attention to what was said by others, till he had satisfied his appetite, which was so fierce, and indulged with such intenseness that, while in the act of eating, the veins of his forehead swelled, and generally a strong perspiration was visible.

Johnson had weight, and depth, and what was once called "bottom." Few men have fallen so deep into depression, from time to time, but in happier days he had reserves of fun, and energy, and demonstrative private affection that were irresistible. He loved his men friends, but he also knew that somewhere in London there were (as there are today) clever women who were the equal of any man, and he made it his business to find them.

His great friend, Mrs. Thrale, was thirty-two years his junior, but it was not every young wife, then or now, who was perfectly at home in Latin, Greek, French, Italian, and Spanish. (At sixteen, she had translated part of *Don Quixote*.) He also very much liked Elizabeth Carter, who "could make a pudding as well as translate Epictetus, and work a handkerchief as well as compose a poem."

As for Charlotte Lennox, the American-born actress turned novelist, there was

Thomas Rowlandson (after Samuel Collings). "The Procession: Dr. Samuel Johnson and James Boswell followed by Johnson's Negro Servant" from *Picturesque Beauties of Boswell....*" 1786. Etching, 7½ × 9¾" (18.8 × 24.4 cm). The Mansell Collection, London

no one for whom he would more readily put himself out. When her first novel appeared, he gave a dinner for her at the Devil Tavern at which — according to one of the guests — "Johnson had directed that a magnificent hot apple pie should make a part of it, and this he had stuck with bay-leaves because, forsooth, Mrs. Lennox was an authoress and he had prepared for her a crown of laurel with which he encircled her brow."

It was a great evening, and it had an ending that can still be duplicated in London. "About five A.M., Johnson's face shone with meridian splendor, though his drink had been only lemonade, but the far greater part of us had deserted the colors of Bacchus and were with difficulty rallied to partake of a second refreshment of coffee, which was scarcely ended when the day began to dawn."

It was on multifarious errands — by no means all of them as festive — that Johnson made his majestic and unmistakable way around London for almost half a century, initially as nobody in particular and eventually as the man whom "everybody" most wanted to meet. His particular London has very much changed since his day. Fleet Street, for instance, has lost Temple Bar, on which Johnson could have seen the head of Francis Towneley the Jacobite exhibited on a spike in 1746, and in the last few years of our century it has lost its character as the stronghold of London's newspapers.

But I for one can imagine Samuel Johnson coming down at nightfall from his rooms on Gough Square, rolling along Fleet Street on his way to dinner and dropping in for a glass or two at El Vino's, a wine bar long famous for good talk. Not only can I imagine him, but I can almost see him. "When he walked the streets," a contemporary tells us, "what with the constant roll of his head, and the concomitant motion of his body, he appeared to make his way independent of his feet."

Above all, perhaps, we sense him in the air around us whenever we visit the sacred places of intellectual London. One such is the London Library in St. James's

Square. Another is Cecil Court, which runs between Charing Cross Road and St. Martin's Lane. The London Library did not exist in Johnson's lifetime, but ever since it was founded in 1841 by Thomas Carlyle, John Stuart Mill, and others it has been the mainstay of the serious writer in London. Still private, and still offering its members open access to its stacks, the London Library is not only an incalculable resource for readers and writers but a place of calm, and silence, and panoramic rumination. In tone, if not in date, it is eminently Johnsonian. Cecil Court existed in Johnson's day, and the young Mozart lodged there in 1764, when he was eight years old, but its present character is distinctly of the first half of our own century. If it, too, is Johnsonian, it is because it is still the preserve of antiquarian booksellers and print shops. In the great days of Cecil Court, which are not yet quite over, there was hardly a shop in which Johnson would not have felt at home.

Since 1933, moreover, it has been the raft to which refugees from every part of Europe hold fast in ways epitomized by R. B. Kitaj in one of his best paintings, *Cecil Court WC2.* Cecil Court is, he tells us, "the book alley I've prowled all my life in England." If it looks in his painting like a displaced persons' camp, that is exactly what it was. And if the people portrayed are what Kitaj calls "cast in the beautiful craziness of Yiddish Theater," there is not much that is inaccurate about that either.

It would, however, be a great mistake to think of Samuel Johnson in London as only, or even primarily, a bookman. Dipping at random into that great stewpot of vocational miscellanea, the Yellow Pages of the London telephone directory, we keep stumbling over activities as to which Johnson was remarkably well informed.

For unlike so many men of letters, he was a master of many kinds of arcane and practical knowledge. He knew how coins were minted and could describe it in a way that made people think he had been raised in that profession. He could talk with total authority to serving officers in the British army about how gunpowder was made, and he could talk to brewers about brewing, to tanners about tanning, and to butchers about butchering.

To an astonishing degree, he kept abreast of all that was going on in the sciences. An acquaintance of Benjamin Franklin in the 1760s, he was familiar with his electrical experiments. When Richard Arkwright perfected the spinning frame—a machine that was to revolutionize the making of cotton cloth—Johnson was the only man who could grasp its significance at first sight and unprompted.

He was delighted not only to pass on his knowledge in conversation but to suit actions to words, no matter how ill-adapted he might be to the actions in question. Not long after his friend the naturalist Sir Joseph Banks had returned from Australia, Dr. Johnson—then aged sixty-three—told a small but attentive company about some of the marvels that Banks had witnessed.

Not content with that, he insisted on impersonating a kangaroo. One witness recorded that "he stood erect, put out his hands like feelers and, gathering up the tails of his huge brown coat so as to resemble the pouch of the animal, made two or three vigorous bounds across the room."

Even quite late in life, he could not resist physical activity of an unpredictable sort. Walking in the country when well into middle age, he suddenly emptied his pockets, lay down on the bare earth, and rolled down a steep hill. "I have not had a roll in a long time," he said to friends who had tried to dissuade him.

If ever a man was dipped in the dyes of London, it was Johnson, and it is with that fact in mind that we should read once again, and quite possibly for the hundredth time, what Johnson said to James Boswell on Saturday, September 20, 1777. Johnson was sixty-eight years old at the time, and Boswell had been going on and on about how he would like nothing so much as to settle forever in what he called "London, the great scene of ambition, instruction and amusement."

But one thing troubled him. What if eventually he were to tire of London? Johnson had in his arsenal one of the most famous of recorded ripostes. "Why, Sir," he said, "you find no man, at all intellectual, who is willing to leave London. No, Sir, when a man is tired of London, he is tired of life; for there is in London all that life can afford."

If Johnson spoke primarily of those who were "at all intellectual," it was not because he thought of London as one huge campus. (To this day, even the University of London has nothing that can be called a campus.) It was because he prized London above all as a place in which there were clever people to talk to.

He himself had the kind of pure, fervent, unsleeping, many-sided intelligence that comes only once or twice in a hundred years and even then is not always brought to fruition. He was a one-person Academe, a walking encyclopedia, an intellectual locomotive that could haul loads no matter how heavy and never run out of steam. His thoughts, unlike his household arrangements, were never in disorder.

When presented to his first tutor at Oxford, in 1728, he at first kept a respectful silence. But then, and because the conversation seemed to him to need it, he whipped out an apt quotation from Macrobius, the fifth-century grammarian and philosopher. This habit, and this ability, were to be with him for the rest of his life.

His curiosity was never still. When Johnson saw Boswell off to the Netherlands in 1763, Boswell noticed on the way to Harwich that Johnson was passing the time with a classic of ancient geography, Pomponius's *Mela de Situ Orbis*. And when he was sixty-eight Johnson said that "I value myself upon this—that there is nothing of the old man in my conversation."

He personified the life of London in ways that have yet to go out of style. What he was two hundred and more years ago, he is still today—the origin of human types and the progenitor of human activities that remain fundamental to London. If we are sensitive to the University of London in any or all of its manifestations we remember that, quite some years before the university was founded, Samuel Johnson prized above all things the stability of incontestable truth.

"Great thoughts are always general," he said in his life of the poet Cowley, "and consist in positions not limited by exceptions, and in descriptions not descending to minuteness." How far his prescriptions are followed in London University today is not for me to say, but I have sometimes fancied that his huge shadow was beside me in Dillon's University Bookshop on Gower Street.

When foreign visitors walk in a daze through the crowded streets of the City of London at lunchtime, we can remind them of how Johnson urged Boswell "to read diligently the great book of mankind" whenever he arrived in a new place. Passing the Stock Exchange, we can remind our notional visitors that in his great pioneering dictionary of the English language Johnson defined a stockjobber as "a low wretch who gets money by buying and selling shares in the funds."

It was common ground among his friends that he could have excelled at almost anything. Edmund Burke, no mean judge of speakers and speaking, once said that if Johnson had become a Member of Parliament as a young man he would have become the greatest Speaker that the House of Commons had ever had. Walking past the Palace of Westminster, I think of that. And when I look out at the Law Courts on the Strand from the upper deck of a London bus, I remember that although he had never made any formal studies in law Johnson would have made a formidable opponent in the courtroom.

That is why he was able to pull together the series of Vinerian lectures at Oxford to which a younger friend of his, Robert Chambers, had been appointed in 1766 in succession to the great lawyer William Blackstone. Chambers was daunted, as well he might be, by the name of Blackstone. Johnson was deep in one of the pathological depressions that afflicted him from time to time. But he saw to it that Chambers stepped down from the podium undisgraced, just as he had wrought small marvels in earlier years for editors and publishers who needed something in a hurry.

There is no end to Johnson in London, even if there are by now very few places with which he was directly associated. Heading along Fleet Street toward the Strand, and peering into an old-fashioned London druggist's, I think of the mysterious chemical experiments with which Johnson concerned himself, and of how he once sent one of his amanuenses to the chemist's at Temple Bar for "an ounce of vitriol—not spirit of vitriol but oil of vitriol. It will cost three-halfpence."

Nor do I ever look up at a publisher's office, or at the headquarters of a much-talked-of magazine, without thinking of how Johnson arrived in London in 1737, at the age of twenty-seven, as what Boswell later called "an adventurer in literature." Like many another young man in that situation, then and since, he gazed in wonder and awe at the editorial office of the magazine in which he most wanted to appear. There, if anywhere, he would make his name.

In this matter, as in so many others, Dr. Johnson set a tremendous example. *The Gentleman's Magazine,* founded in 1731 by Edward Cave, was the prototype of that great instrument of civilization—the weekly or monthly magazine that keeps its readers up-to-the-minute in concerns that they are either too busy or too idle to study closely for themselves. It was run from St. John's Gate, the gatehouse of a priory suppressed by Queen Elizabeth I—it still stands, by the way, in St. John's Lane in Clerkenwell—and before long Johnson made himself invaluable there. Like most of its successors, *The Gentleman's Magazine* had room for a youngish man who could turn his hand to anything and come up with his copy on time.

In that context, Johnson was the nonpareil. He could do anything. He could translate. He could gut a book in no matter what language and say exactly what was good, and what was bad, about it. He could judge a poetry prize. He could write prefaces and short biographies to order. He could retranslate a classic study of the Council of Trent. He could single-handedly keep the magazine's readers abreast of foreign affairs. He could write fast, and he could write at enormous length without getting up from the table.

To produce eighteen hundred words in an hour was nothing to him. He was capable of writing twelve thousand words—every one of them the right word in the right place—between lunchtime and early evening. And none of this was glib, or secondhand, or in any sense hackwork. It is as compelling today as it was to its first readers, two hundred and fifty and more years ago.

Above all, he could give a completely new and slightly outrageous spin to parliamentary reporting. In London, as elsewhere, the parliamentary reporter in our day is—not least, in his own estimation—a person of importance. Not only does he have access to powerful figures in public life, but he is free to say whatever he likes about them.

Their policies and their manner of presenting them are at his mercy. In rage and in terror do they pick up the morning paper, and in fear and exasperation do they turn on the television news. Known by name nationwide, the parliamentary reporter can make or break the coming men and women, and he can tell their great seniors when enough is enough. He is, or was, or can be, a most tremendous swell.

Front page of *The Gentleman's Magazine,* January 1746 issue. Museum of the Order of St. John, London

In Johnson's years on *The Gentleman's Magazine* there was nothing of that. As of April 1738, it had been decreed by the government of the day that what was said in debate in the House of Commons was privileged and could not be reported in the press. What to do? Then as now, readers wanted up-to-the-minute and authentic political news. How was the new edict to be circumvented?

In *The Gentleman's Magazine* the problem was solved by an ingenious device that Samuel Johnson brought to perfection. Debates were reported at great length. The sense of what had been said was perfectly clear. Fairness and objectivity were preserved. The speakers' names were disguised, but in such a way as to deceive nobody. If we read that on a certain evening someone called "Ptit" caught the Speaker's eye, we would have to be mentally subnormal not to identify him as William Pitt.

Still, there was the matter of what "Ptit" or "Walelop" (Walpole) actually said. What he had said could not be printed. Yet the speeches, as reported in *The Gentleman's Magazine* were exemplary, not to say immortal, specimens of the orator's art. (We learn from Hoover's "Parliamentary Reporting" that as late as 1899 some of them were included in an anthology called *The World's Best Orations* as authentic speeches by the foremost British statesmen of the day.)

Johnson provided the readers of *The Gentleman's Magazine* with elaborate and detailed coverage of twenty-seven parliamentary debates between November 1740 and February 1743. Published in fifty-four installments in the magazine, they amounted in all to half a million words. Everybody enjoyed and admired them — above all, perhaps, the speakers themselves. Even after twenty years, individual speeches thus reported were remembered, quoted from, and ranked by rhetoricians as the equal of anything in Cicero or Demosthenes.

The astonishing fact about those speeches is that, to put it plainly, Johnson made them all up. He had never heard any of them. (Only once had he been in the House of Commons.) Sitting in a tiny top-floor room not far from Fleet Street, he was provided with, at most, the subjects of discussion, the names of the speakers, the order in which they rose to their feet, and a broad outline of what they had said. Thereafter, he was on his own.

As to precisely what was in the notes that were brought to him, no one quite knows. Johnson's biographer Professor Bait tells us that "on many occasions the speeches were spun out of his own head" in ways that showed an intellectual energy, a power of impersonation, a mastery of detail and a familiarity with the events and opinions of the day that will never be rivaled."

As a dying man, Johnson wished that he had never done it. Alone among his writings, they made him feel uneasy and compunctious. Often they had been written, it seemed, "from very slender materials, and often from none at all — the mere coinage of his own imagination." Yet, so far from being essays in deception, they were accepted by the speakers in question as being truer than true.

And apart from that, they had an overall fairness to both parties, even if Johnson characteristically said that "I saved appearances tolerably well, but I took particular care that the Whig dogs should not have the best of it." In an age of sound-bite parliamentarians, we should look back upon Johnson's reporting with awe.

By nature, and no matter how much he enjoyed what he called a "frisk" or impromptu escapade, Johnson was a thinker, a worker, and a doer. But of course he was also a great talker, and one whose talk was recorded by his friend and biographer James Boswell with a stenographic vividness.

Much of what he said in Boswell's hearing has entered the folklore of the

170

English-speaking peoples. Pseudo-Johnsons and would-be Johnsons are a prime hazard of almost any evening in a large company in London. Fathers, grandfathers, chairmen of the board, headmasters, talk-show hosts, and television interviewers—all have known the temptation to bore the hide off the rest of us with quasi-Johnsonian sallies. But how few of them have been, like Johnson, a master of the prompt apology. "Give me your hand, Sir," he once said to a young man who had annoyed him. "You were too tedious, and I was too short."

As has often been said, Boswell's *Life,* once opened, is never quite put down again. But in Boswell's huge, roomy, unhurrying narrative we often lose the sense of Johnson the great professional. Such is the fascination of the *Life* that we may end up thinking not only that Boswell was always in Johnson's company, but that the portrait he gives us is rounded and complete. And, so far from identifying Johnson as England's foremost all-round man of letters, we could believe that this was a man who talked his talents away.

The truth is, first, that Boswell only knew Johnson during the last twenty-two years of life and, second, that during those twenty-two years there were only about three hundred days on which Boswell saw him in London. We hear Johnson, in Boswell's *Life,* as we hear him nowhere else. But anyone who wants to know what

Edward Matthew Ward. *Dr. Johnson in the Ante-Room of Lord Chesterfield Waiting for an Audience, 1748.* 1845. Oil on canvas, 41¾ × 54⅞" (106.1 × 139.4 cm). The Tate Gallery, London

This is history-painting, made a hundred years after the event. But it shows how informed opinion was outraged by the humiliation that was inflicted upon Dr. Johnson in his hour of need by Lord Chesterfield.

William Walker (after a painting by James E. Doyle). *A Literary Party at Sir Joshua Reynolds.* 1848. Engraving, dimensions unknown. The Mansell Collection, London

This, too, is Victorian costume drama, but it makes its point.

he actually did with his life will do better with Walter Jackson Bait's glorious and monumental *Samuel Johnson.*

For Johnson was not only a compendium of English oddities who allowed himself to be completely known. He was a one-man free-form university in which courses beyond number were carried on concurrently. At fifteen, he had been urged by one of his cousins to "shake the tree of knowledge and shake all its branches," and never was advice more firmly acted upon.

He was an intellectual jackhammer that never mistook its target. He was the greatest of English literary critics. As a ghostwriter in his early days of speeches, legal submissions, and learned prefaces he could not be faulted. Virtually the inventor of biography in English, he practiced it with an elegance and a concision that have never been surpassed.

Despite what is sometimes thought of as a life-style of continual and disorderly socializing, Johnson brought every one of his talents to fruition. In his single-handed *Dictionary of the English Language,* and in the historical and grammatical studies that were part of it, he set the pattern for all the great dictionaries of all the great languages that have been published since.

In nine years, virtually on his own, and working in a tiny top-floor apartment in Gough Square, Johnson produced a dictionary that was not to be rivaled in English until, in 1858, what is now known as the *Oxford English Dictionary* was begun. The *Oxford Dictionary* was to take more than a century to take its present form, and well over two thousand scholars took part in it.

Simply to look closely at one of the tall and stately pages of Johnson's *Dictionary* is an awesome experience. When he details forty-two possible uses of the word *from,* we feel a shiver of delight at the limpidity of his procedures. And when he comes to the word *asthma,* he tells us almost more than we want to know about an affliction whose mark is "a frequent, difficult and short respiration, joined with a hissing sound and a cough. . . ."

Johnson was also one of the great English moralists. He believed that there was

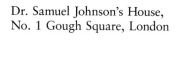

Dr. Samuel Johnson's House,
No. 1 Gough Square, London

nothing quite so terrible that it should not be looked in the face. "Whether to see life as it is will give us much consolation, I know not," he once wrote to a bereaved friend. "But the consolation which comes from truth, if there be any, is solid and durable; that which may be derived from error must be, like its original, fallacious and fugitive." By his example, he taught us how to bear misfortune and how to live with others in love and friendship (or, just now and then, in scorn and contempt).

London had been in no hurry to give him either honor or comfort, but in every other way it had fired and fueled him from the moment that he arrived there in 1737. And toward the end of his life he was recognized as the most remarkable man in London, the greatest all-round man of letters that England had ever produced, and a character as rich and round (and as lopsided) as any in literature. To find a man whom we know as completely as we know Johnson, we would have to go forward nearly two hundred years to Leopold Bloom in James Joyce's *Ulysses*.

For that reason, we often feel in central London that one of the all-time great metropolitans is, if not right there at our side, at any rate around the next corner. Johnson's London is our London, appearances notwithstanding. This is especially true in side streets and narrow alleys anywhere between the Strand, Fleet Street, and Lincoln's Inn to the south, St. James's Square to the west, Oxford Street to the north, and Ludgate Hill to the east.

Outside that irregular rectangle, contact is sometimes broken. Despite all his years as parliamentary correspondent, Johnson was not a Westminster man. Nor was he a Kensington man, or a Hampstead man, or a man who went near the river west of Westminster Bridge.

If Dr. Johnson will not be with us at the Royal Opera House, or at the Royal Festival Hall, it is because music meant nothing to him until, in his seventies, he heard "some solemn music played on French horns" at the funeral of a Freemason in Rochester.

He was not too fond of the theater, either. A failed playwright, he was understandably somewhat envious of the triumphs of his old and once close friend David Garrick. Garrick was a younger man who had been both Johnson's friend and his pupil. But in 1741 and 1742, when Garrick was the talk of the town as Shakespeare's Richard III, and shortly afterward as King Lear, Johnson still counted for little in terms of universal esteem.

When Garrick became manager of the Drury Lane Theatre in 1747, at the age of only thirty, Johnson bestirred himself to write a prologue for the opening of his season. (Garrick passed it off as his own, by the way.) Nor could even Garrick make a success of Johnson's tragedy, Irene, when he put it on in 1749.

So the stage was a sore point with Johnson, and we cannot picture him sitting at our side at the National Theatre, even when the play of the evening is by Shakespeare, of whose virtues and shortcomings Johnson gave many an immortal summation. But he was a man in whom the springs of feeling ran true and deep. If someone spoke ill of Garrick in his presence and called him spoilt, arrogant, and pompous, Johnson would simply say, "Garrick is the first man in the world for sprightly conversation."

And if someone dared to say that Garrick was getting to look old, Johnson said only, "Why, Sir, you are not to wonder at that. No man's face has had more wear and tear." And when Garrick was buried in Westminster Abbey his friends did not forget the sight of Samuel Johnson standing, bathed in tears, beside Garrick's grave, at the foot of Shakespeare's monument.

If we get elected to a London club, or have guest privileges in one, we can fantasize that Johnson has been one of our sponsors. Johnson had not been long in London before he formed a little club of his own in Ivy Lane, Paternoster Row, for purposes of literary discussion. Much later, in the winter of 1763–64, Sir Joshua Reynolds asked him to be a founder-member of an altogether grander and more ambitious adventure—nothing less than the formation of what was to be called simply "The Club." This turned out to be the prototype and original of all the dining clubs, worldwide, in which English is spoken.

It was from a small, privileged, free-spoken world that the membership of The Club was recruited. Dr. Johnson thought that nine was the ideal number for good conversation, but as the fame of The Club grew that number was much exceeded. By the time that Johnson made his last appearance there, in June 1784, the membership had included Sir Joshua Reynolds, then president of the Royal Academy; Oliver Goldsmith, the author of She Stoops to Conquer; Edmund Burke and Charles James Fox, two great parliamentarians; Sir Joseph Banks, the naturalist; Edward Gibbon, the historian; Adam Smith, the economist; Charles Burney, the musicologist; and Sir William Hamilton, the ambassador/connoisseur who is most widely known for having been cuckolded by Admiral Lord Nelson.

These people did not join The Club because it was the thing to do. They joined because they craved the privilege of Samuel Johnson's company. More than any other man of his time—or, perhaps, of any later time—he set the tone and the tempo of London. And if ever we feel, when in London, that Johnson would approve of what we are doing, we may be sure that we are doing something right.

Late in the evening of the day on which World War II finally came to an end in Europe, I found myself sliding on a big silver tray down the main staircase of a great London hotel. The next morning, I might have felt uneasy at the recollection. But I didn't. "Doctor Johnson would have come down on the next tray!" I said to myself.

And he would, too.

Buckingham Palace

UNTIL THE SUMMER OF 1993 the visitor to London had to be told at once that Buckingham Palace was not, never had been, and never would be open to the public. The ceremony of changing the guard could be seen daily, from May through August, and every other day from September through April. The Royal Mews on Buckingham Palace Road could be visited two afternoons a week. In the Queen's Gallery, a few yards along Buckingham Palace Road, rotating exhibitions have been dealing in turn with one aspect or another of the royal collections. But the only way to get into Buckingham Palace itself was to be invited.

As of August 1993, this was no longer quite true. A long and majestic sequence of state rooms could be visited in August and September, when the royal family is never in London. The gate money would go toward the expenses of repairing Windsor Castle, which had suffered grievously (and, some say, avoidably) by fire damage in 1992.

As it happens, the state rooms of Buckingham Palace are really very grand and in general give great satisfaction to those who see them. But Buckingham Palace is not primarily about great state occasions, though it is amply well able to live up to them. It is a palace, as its name indicates, but it is also a private house. It has a forty-acre garden, in which hundreds of guests can stroll around during the Queen's annual garden parties. It has a Grand Staircase that is very grand indeed, and it has state rooms that stun. But much of that dates from Victorian times, and it was never the intention of King George III, King George IV, or King William IV that this should be the first house in England.

Like the 2nd Duke of Buckingham, who bought the house and gave it his name, they wanted it to be, not the first house in England, but the most seductive house. Something of what Buckingham Palace was later to become is already present in Buckingham's ecstatic account of how he lived there.

As former owners go, he was one of the best. A former Lord Chamberlain, he had been the suitor of Princess (later Queen) Anne and had married an illegitimate daughter of King James II. A man of fixed and ferocious loyalties, he had fought with distinction on both sea and land and never hesitated to take the unpopular side in a quarrel. He was also a poet. The National Theatre is unlikely ever to put on his recension of Shakespeare's *Julius Caesar*, but his poems have something of their own. Imperious, plainspoken, and adroit, he was as disdainful of the young woman who denied him her "snowy arms, breasts and other parts more dear" as he was of "feathered officers who never fight."

He was bookish without abjuring the life of action, and he was worldly without ever blocking the springs of true feeling. I know of few lines more succinctly dismissive than his

The Green Drawing Room, Buckingham Palace, with a view toward the loggia. The Royal Collection © Her Majesty Queen Elizabeth II

With tame submission to the will of fate
He tugged about the matrimonial weight.

And there is a fine cogency about two lines of his that Alexander Pope was not too proud to quote:

Of all those arts in which the wise excel
Nature's chief masterpiece is writing well.

This remarkable man just loved the house. To him, it was both town and country in one, and he loved writing to his friends about every detail of it: the avenue of elms along which carriages came out from the city, and the other avenue, grassed between freshly planted lime trees, that served for promenaders; the pilastered brick front of the house, with arcaded galleries that led to the servants' quarters, laundry, and kitchen; the Latin mottoes, indicative of high satisfaction, which told every passerby that this was a happy house; and the six-sided basin in the forecourt, with Neptune and his tritons spouting away from morning till night.

The house inside was truly grand, with a staircase of "eight and forty steps, ten feet broad, each step on one entire Portland stone." The first-floor salon, "35 ft. high, 36 ft. broad, and 45 ft. long," was hung from top to bottom with pictures relating to the arts and sciences. A room of this sort can be pompous and inhuman, but Buckingham—no nouveau riche—was as delighted with the little door that led through to his own apartments as he was with the "niche 15 ft. wide for a Bufette" in the parlour below. What he liked above all was "a little closet of books at the end of that greenhouse which joins the best apartment," and he wished that he had not lost one curious feature of the earlier house: a long gallery fitted up with a small frame of olive wood with holes and pins for the exact computation of walking a mile.

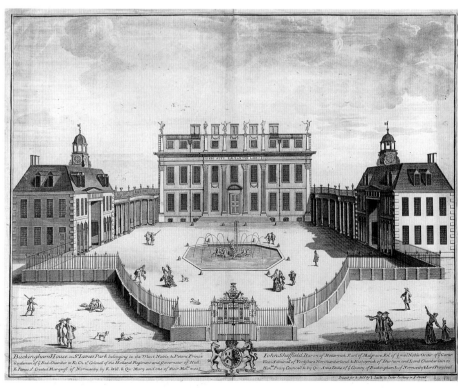

Studio of Thomas Lawrence. *Portrait of George IV*. Date unknown. Oil on canvas, 95 × 61" (241.3 × 154.9 cm). The National Portrait Gallery, London

Opposite left:
John Sheffield (after Sir Godfrey Kneller). *Duke of Buckingham (1648–1721)*. 1779. Oil on canvas, 49¼ × 39½" (125.1 × 100.3 cm). The National Portrait Gallery, London

Opposite:
Johannes Kip and Leonard Knyff. "Buckingham House," for *Britannia Illustrata*, c. 1715. The Royal Library, Windsor Castle © Her Majesty Queen Elizabeth II

Most householders are more interested in looking at the view from their windows than in pacing out a mile indoors, but Buckingham laid such stress on the roses and the jasmine at the back of the house, and on the flower garden, the "bathing-place," and the "kitchen-garden full of the best sorts of fruit," that he may have been as great a walker outside as in.

Much of Buckingham Palace as we know it is already present, in miniature, in Buckingham's account of the house. There are the all-round curiosity, the determination to have the best, the delight in private life, the sense of what is fit and proper, and the care for others' convenience.

The house has of course grown enormously since Buckingham's day, when the main facade mustered only twenty-six windows. George III bought Buckingham House, as it was then called, as a dower house for his consort, Queen Charlotte, and he took great care to play down its importance in the London scene. A contemporary diarist called Mrs. Lybbe Powys, who was used to getting in everywhere, was rather pleased with herself when, in March 1767, she could record a visit to "what is rather difficult to see at all, the Queen's Palace."

Everyone who went there agreed that the house was a delicious affair. But neither inside nor out was it a showy affair. George III liked good books, good music, good clocks, and good furniture, and he knew a great deal about them. Queen Charlotte loved animals—the more exotic the better—and she had the great cabinetmaker William Vile make for her some mahogany stands for her bird cages and "two mahogany houses for a Turkey Monkey." She also had brilliant, reckless, and original ideas about how to do up her house. Wallpaper and matching upholstery bulked large in her household accounts, as did 540 yards of crimson Genoa damask, together with a massive order for crimson silk ropes and large crimson silk tassels for use in picture hanging.

Quite clearly, both George III and his queen adored the house, keying its colors as high as possible and aiming always at the effect of vivacity that Johann Zoffany caught so well in his portrait of Queen Charlotte with two of her thirteen children. We sense at once that they did not go along with the notion, current throughout the eighteenth century, that London simply had to have a big new royal palace. William III had thwarted even Sir Christopher Wren when he preferred Hampton Court to the center of London. And when we look at the models produced by William Kent for a palace in Hyde Park, by Sir William Chambers for a palace in Whitehall, and by Sir John Soane for a palace in Green Park, we can only be glad that London was spared them. England at that time was big in world affairs, and it was to grow a great deal bigger, but there were errors of self-presentation that it never committed.

George IV had his giddy side, and in 1931 he was reproved for being "too well satisfied with the superficial, or romantic, or 'amusing,' too impatient of the platitudes of 'correct' art, to be able to do full justice to the many possibilities when rebuilding Buckingham Palace." This passage from H. Clifford Smith's history of Buckingham Palace was then the standard view of George IV, and it is true that even in his lifetime he was known for enthusiasms that no sooner waxed than waned. "Influenced by caprice," he "had no steadiness," said the painter Joseph Farington, in his invaluable diary.

But capricious or not, George IV both as regent and as king had a streak of wild fancy and a passion for the new and the good. Both traits served the nation well. Even his grand piano, now in Buckingham Palace, was of a kind unprecedented—a "Patent Sostenente Grand," which he bought from its inventor Isaac Mott in 1817. Made of walnut inlaid with brass, it stood not on the traditional legs but on a "monopodium springing from a triangular base." I should like to think, though

I have no warrant for doing so, that it was with the help of this doughty instrument that the composer of the *Barber of Seville* and his admirer King George IV got to sing duets together.

George IV led the taste of the day with his love of chinoiserie, his delight in the very finest French furniture, clocks, and candelabra, and his keen eye for paintings both old and new. Buckingham Palace would be a very different place today without the sculpture of *Mars and Venus* that he had commissioned from Canova, the furniture by Bernard II van Risamburgh, Adam Weisweiler, Martin Carlin, and others that he had sent over from Paris, the long-case clock that he had bought from A.-L. Bréguet in 1825, and the candelabra by Thomire and Gouthière, not to mention the superlative English furniture in what is still remembered as the "Carlton House taste."

When it came to painting, George IV was in the front rank of European

Opposite:
Johan Zoffany. *Queen Charlotte with the Prince of Wales and Prince Frederick.* c. 1766. Oil on canvas, 44¼×50″ (112.4×127 cm). Royal Collection, St. James's Palace © Her Majesty Queen Elizabeth II

The Queen's Return from the House of Lords. Print of summer fashions for 1839, published by B. Read & Co., London. Private collection

Better than many a more formal statement, this fashion plate gives a vivid idea of the changes that came over Buckingham Palace after the accession in 1837 of Queen Victoria. On her way back from Parliament, the young Queen sat sideways in her coach, the better to see and be seen. Her standard flew high above Marble Arch, which at the time served as a place of triumphal entry. And there was nothing incongruous about the young men, women, and children—all dressed to kill in the latest fashions—who larked around in the sunshine.

collectors. He bought singly—often at auction—and he also bought in bulk when the occasion presented itself. The Dutch paintings—nearly two hundred in number—that he bought from the Baring collection were a landmark in the history of royal collecting, whether in England or anywhere else. There was nothing giddy about his espousal of Rembrandt's *Noli me tangere,* Rubens's *Farm at Laeken,* Claude's *Rape of Europa,* Hobbema's *Lane Through a Wood,* and the *Evening Landscape* by Aelbert Cuyp. Equally characteristic was his support for both Reynolds and Gainsborough and his belief in contemporary British painters—Thomas Mulready and David Wilkie among them.

Readers may ask why today's visitors to London should want to hear about collections that they cannot see and that they cannot visit. The answer is that, as has already been said, since 1962 the royal collections have been open to the public on a rotating basis in the Queen's Gallery. This gallery occupies a former chapel—destroyed by bombing during World War II—to which the entrance is in Buckingham Palace Road.

Doubtless for security reasons, the gallery is reached by way of a long narrow L-shaped slit in a thick stone wall. Such, however, are the stately bearing, the stylish red and gold turnout, and the unaffected fine manners of the royal servants that we have a good time almost before we cross the threshold. The exhibitions, when reached, could hardly be of a higher standard.

As for the Palace itself, it remains true that there is no substitute for a privileged intrusion. But there is in the wayward, personal, and wholly un-didactic arrangement and rearrangement of the house something that is specifically English. This is a house in which the owners have always done exactly what they felt like—no less and no more.

When people were on at King George IV to pull down Buckingham House and build a thumping great palace somewhere else, he refused to do any such thing.

"I am too old to build a palace," he said, "but I must have a pied-à-terre, and I will have it at Buckingham House. There are early associations which endear me to the spot."

And that's just what he did. He had John Nash do over the house at colossal expense, and he didn't care at all that the government was furious. No one was going to get the better of him, and in this context no one ever did. What's wrong with that, and all the more so as most of the great houses of Britain have evolved in exactly the same way?

Besides, something had to be done. Looking at the bland, smooth, unprovocative east front that was completed by Sir Aston Webb in 1913 and is familiar to everyone who has watched the Changing of the Guard, it is difficult to believe that Buckingham Palace could ever have been called "desperately dirty." But that is what was said in the 1820s by those who wished to defend Nash and his patrons from the charge of "wanton extravagance."

But there is no doubt that Buckingham Palace had got to be very uncomfortable before Nash went to work on it. The 1st Duke of Wellington was the most respected man in the kingdom, and it had to mean something when he stood up in the House of Lords in 1828 and said that "notwithstanding the expense which has been incurred in building the Palace, no sovereign in Europe—I may add, perhaps no private gentleman—is so ill lodged as the king of this country."

Strong words, from the victor of Waterloo. Is it possible that the great Duke went too far? For it is, on the face of it, an amazing image. Europe at that time mustered many thousands of "private gentlemen," from Finland to the Peloponnese

Aerial view of Buckingham Palace. 1951

The royal family on the balcony of Buckingham Palace, just after the coronation of King George VI, May 12, 1937. From left are the Queen, Princess Elizabeth, Queen Mary, Princess Margaret, and the King.

and from the Carpathians to Cadiz. Could it really be true that every one of them lived better than King George IV?

But nine years later, when Queen Victoria came to the throne and decided to live in Buckingham Palace, it turned out that it really was in terrible shape. Nothing worked. Many things stank. Doors that were open could not be closed. Windows were stuck fast. To find a faucet that ran water took forever.

Outside of *The Sleeping Beauty*, it would be hard to find a greater transformation than the one wrought in this matter by Queen Victoria. Within three months of her accession, she took over Buckingham Palace and at once got the great building to come alive. Within forty-eight hours of moving in, she was entertaining a large party to dinner and listening afterward to "Thalberg, the greatest pianist in the world . . . I was in ecstasy!"

She had the advantage of coming to a palace that for all intents and purposes was hers to inaugurate. One or two survivors of Queen Charlotte's court were still in London. Distinguishable by their bizarre way of pronouncing certain words ("goold" for "gold," for instance, and "yaller" for "yellow"), they managed to make Queen Victoria momentarily uneasy about her command of English. But in no other respect did they affect her. She did what she liked: not for the first time, a very young queen was free to set her own style.

Almost everyone was delighted with that style. Greville found it dull, but then Greville had been struck off the lists because he shouted at table and tried to talk other people down. The Palace quickly became what it is today: discreet and

Eugène-Louis Lami. *The Grand Staircase, Buckingham Palace*. 1848. Watercolor, 15 × 13¼″
(38 × 33.5 cm). Royal Collection, St. James's Palace. © Her Majesty Queen Elizabeth II

Sir Edwin Landseer. *Queen Victoria and Prince Albert.* c. 1842. Oil on canvas, 55¼ × 42¾″ (140.3 × 108.6 cm). Royal Collection, St. James's Palace. © Her Majesty Queen Elizabeth II

The young Queen Victoria loved nothing more than a fancy dress party in Buckingham Palace for more than two thousand people. On this occasion, in May 1842, she and her consort appeared in 14th century dress. Down to the very last button, it was said to be historically correct.

Laurits Tuxen. *The Family of Queen Victoria in 1887.* Oil on canvas, 65¼ × 89″ (165.7 × 226.1 cm). Royal Collection, St. James's Palace. © Her Majesty Queen Elizabeth II

By the late 1880s, Queen Victoria had children, grandchildren, and ever more ramified in-laws all over Europe. Fifty-five people are portrayed in this painting, and every one of them was drawn or painted from life.

effective for the transaction of business, great or small, and the best of accomplices on festive occasions.

There are limits, of course, to the freedom of even a young and strong-minded queen. Queen Victoria did her duty by *les grands,* and invited them in great numbers. But *les grands* are not always very droll, and there were evenings over which boredom hung like a catafalque. What Queen Victoria enjoyed most were the confidential talks with her Ministers, and above all with the delicious, protective, and irreverent Melbourne.

And the dances, of course. She had been fond of dancing ever since King William IV gave her a Juvenile Ball at St. James's Palace on her fourteenth birthday, and during the first years of her reign there was a very great deal of dancing at Buckingham Palace. The costume balls of 1842, 1845, and 1851 were of historic proportions. Though usually hinged to some aspect of the national interest, they gave pleasure of a purely frivolous kind.

Even on the dance floor there were moments when things went wrong: Lord Malmesbury in his memoirs describes how, in 1840, "the Queen danced the first dance with the Duke of Devonshire and valsed afterwards with Prince Albert, but the band played so fast and out of tune that she only took one turn and then sat down, looking annoyed." But in general all went well, and there were many occasions on which a visitor could verify the opinion of King Leopold of the Belgians that "there is hardly a country in which such magnificence exists."

Magnificence does not always make friends for itself, and the curious thing about Buckingham Palace is that gradually it became an ark to which a whole people turned in times of torment or rejoicing. Blore was not a great architect, and no one ever liked the east front that he added to Buckingham Palace. Not only did it look like a station hotel, but it was faced with Caen stone, which quickly crumbled and gave the Palace a mangy and moldy appearance.

But one thing Blore did do. He invented the Balcony. The Balcony is small and narrow and has nothing of grandeur about it. No despot would wish to show himself in so confined a space. But the Balcony works, for English tastes, in a way that even the Scala dei Giganti in the Doges' Palace would not work for this particular purpose.

It was in 1854 that the Balcony was first put to use. Queen Victoria stood on it to watch the the last guards battalion march out of the courtyard on its way to the Crimea. In July 1856 she was back on the Balcony to watch the returning army march past on its way from Vauxhall to Hyde Park; and ever since—and especially in 1914, 1918, and in 1945—the Balcony has been the very center of the nation. Almost everyone who was alive at those times of torment or exuberance will have remembered what happened on the Balcony. Buckingham Palace at such times had an immediate meaning, a face-to-face quality, that neither St. James's nor Hampton Court nor Windsor could have.

This is the more remarkable in that England is fundamentally castle country, and always was. Castles fire the English imagination in a way that palaces do not. Castle people are thought of as bluff, downright, and self-reliant. You know where you are with them. (Shakespeare's Duncan was so moved by the look of Macbeth's castle that he could not believe that any harm could come of his sojourn there.)

Palace people, by contrast, are thought to be intriguers—finicky, fashionable, false. Palace life is contrary to nature. "In palaces, treason" is one of the phrases in *King Lear* that warns us of dreadful things to come. Palace people are corrupt, also: Shelley in *The Cenci* speaks of "that palace-walking devil, Gold." In popular usage, the word long ago took on a facetious, disparaging implication. What are the gin palace, the fish palace, and the fun palace, if not so many attempts to discredit the very notion of a palace?

There may, in all this, be something of foreboding, or of well-founded folk-memory. We may remember, however distantly, what happened to Nonesuch Palace in London (gone without trace) and to Whitehall Palace (burned in 1698 all the way from the Banqueting House in Whitehall to the river). We don't even fancy the idea that any one town house should be very much larger than any other town house; and we think better of Wellington for thinking of his house as simply "No. 1 Piccadilly" than we do of Marlborough for browbeating posterity with Blenheim Palace. We also remember that after the death of Queen Charlotte in 1818 Buckingham Palace was for a time styled simply as "The King's House, Pimlico."

Buckingham Palace has its impersonal side. It is difficult to have tender feelings for an office building, a communications center, a post office, or a catering organization, all of which are secreted somewhere inside Buckingham Palace. But, ever since the Duke of Buckingham's day, almost everything in the Palace has been there not because it was thought to be judicious or correct, but because an identifiable individual liked it.

Some of the things in question have vanished. Buckingham would miss his nightingales. George III might not find his scale models of British harbors where he left them. Queen Charlotte would miss her zebra, and she might also miss her private theatricals, to which luster was lent by Mrs. Siddons, the great actress of the day. Prince Albert, the consort of Queen Victoria, would grieve to know that sixty and more years ago the frescoes that he commissioned for the Garden Pavilion had already decayed beyond recapture.

But enough survives from every phase in the development of Buckingham Palace to make it a monument not only to monarchy but to the way in which a succession of known people have chosen, single-handedly, how they wanted to live. Large parts of Buckingham Palace are like an undestroyed Pompeii in which changes of taste can be detected, one beside another. This is not so much a matter of the state rooms as of corridors many yards long, where it needs only a trick of the light on a summer afternoon for us to see Alice in Wonderland flying in ruched white silk and black patent leather pumps toward tall panels of looking glass.

It is the scale of these undiscovered areas that makes for magic. Doors open where we least expect them, and they lead from rooms in which two hundred people can fit quite comfortably into the kind of fastidious crevice that might have been designed for a particularly spruce young bachelor.

From the Privy Purse entrance, which might be the hallway of a stylish manor house two hundred miles from London, to the topmost and farthest rooms under the eaves, the general tone of Buckingham Palace is one of unaffected amenity. It is enormously *not* the kind of building that could have been arrived at by consensus. At the drop of a latch we move from a genuine India, relic of bygone durbars, to a China fantasticated in the 1820s, and no amount of remodeling has blotted out the fact that strong-minded individuals have had their way with the Palace throughout all its transformations, and that every one of them has left a mark upon it.

Buckingham Palace could be, but is not, the kind of glowering fortress that we find in other European capitals. It relates to London in mysterious, confidential, and unpredictable ways. To look out from one of its windows is to realize that the great house is open to London. Seeing London where, and how, we least expect, the privileged intruder recognizes the truth of what was said by one of the most perceptive of those who have lived there: "I choose to think that Buckingham Palace is not out of the world."

The Other Park: Regent's Park

REGENT'S PARK HAS BOTH an ancient and a curious history, and when it was remade from 1809 onward by John Nash it gave London a new style and a new panache.

London today would not be London without Regent's Park. We need its spectacular and scenographic terraces, the great grassy sweep of its Broad Walk, its well-spaced trees, its elegant little lake, its open-air theater, and (in Queen Mary's Gardens) its apotheosis of the metropolitan rose.

It has a calm, settled, almost predestined look. We might suppose toward nightfall that even the last movement of the last duck on the lake had been choreographed long in advance. Earlier in the day, we recognize what the novelist Elizabeth Bowen—a longtime resident of the park—described as "the slow indignation" with which the Regent's Park swans cruise back and forth.

During World War II, Elizabeth Bowen lived, undeterred, in her house on Clarence Terrace. Later, she gave in her novel *The Heat of The Day* an irreplaceable account of a scene in the park in the summer of 1942. This was one of the bleaker moments of the war. The Open Air Theatre in the park was used at that time for concerts at which a band played marches, waltzes, polkas, popular overtures, and what were then called "medleys."

These attracted large audiences, made up in large part of Londoners for whom a summer evening in Regent's Park was the next best thing to an evening at the then inaccessible seaside. They also attracted Allied servicemen and women, most of whom were far from home. Some had been in London as refugees since the 1930s. Others had arrived during the war—some involuntarily, some prompted by the wish to serve the Allied cause and eventually, with luck, to return to a liberated homeland. They came from all over—France, Germany, Poland, Czechoslovakia, Belgium, the Netherlands, the United States, Canada, and Australia.

An unspoken kinship expressed itself during these concerts. To the beauty and extravagance of the park itself there was added the irresistible and multinational poignancy that fostered memories still vivid and yearnings that might never find fulfillment. This was not a matter of sentimentality. The healing power of music did its work in the open air. Face after face, among those crowded ranks, was the better for it.

This might have been the last great moment of Regent's Park. By the end of World War II the park and its terraces, as John Nash had conceived them, were far gone in dereliction. John Summerson remembered later how in 1945 "the Nash terraces were a shambles of bomb damage and dry rot in structures of very indifferent original construction." In that same year a governmental committee reported that "there are few more lugubrious experiences in London than that to be obtained from a general survey of the Nash Terraces in Regent's Park." There was a faction that would have pulled the terraces down and started all over again in one of the modernist idioms of the day.

James-Jacques-Joseph Tissot. *A Convalescent (A Warrior's Daughter)*. c. 1879. Oil on panel, 14¼ × 8¾" (36.2 × 22.2 cm). Manchester City Art Galleries

In High Victorian times, many a retired soldier took a daily turn round Regent's Park, though not all of them had so pretty a companion.

But wiser views prevailed, and in 1946 it was decided that "the Nash terraces are of national interest and importance, and that they should be preserved as far as is practicable." It was further recommended, in a phrase that in those straitened times was to the honor of all concerned, that the work should be carried out "without strict regard to the economics of prudent estate management."

Regent's Park and its terraces thereby took on a whole new span of existence. The area is neither as grand nor as exclusive, in social terms, as it was originally meant to be, but it is essential to the status of London among great cities. Nash excelled at building big, with an exuberant skyline that has few rivals in Europe. But he also excelled at building small, as in Park Village East, where there is something irresistible about the way in which the linked little houses nestle together. Built in 1829, they marked Nash's farewell to the Regent's Park area. Though now much infringed upon, they are masterpieces of miniaturization.

What we now call Regent's Park was not always a park, let alone a public park. It had its truly pastoral aspect, as is clear from the names (Swan Meadow, Dovecote Meadow, Well Meadow) that once marked out one patch of ground from another in the manifold subdivisions of the area. But insofar as much of it stood on subsoil of heavy London clay and was heavily wooded, difficult to drain, and rather short of water, it was not promising.

To the south, there were springs of sweet water. Vegetation was light. A layer of gravel sat on top of the clay. Something could be done there, in a single-minded way. But five hundred years ago, when London was just a tight huddle of houses quite some way away, rare was the covetous eye that sought it out.

It was after the dissolution of the monasteries in the 1530s, when whatever had been church land became Crown land, that Henry VIII saw the potential of the irregular circle of land that came to be known as Marylebone Park. (*Marrowbone* was Samuel Pepys's name for it in 1668.)

What Henry VIII wanted was a hunting ground within easy reach of his palace in Whitehall. He loved hunting, but he was by then too old and too fat to go far to get it. But he got the mathematics right. With 554 acres in Marylebone Park, he would be no more than a couple of miles from Whitehall. Either he or the royal surveyor is said to have drawn a circle on the map, and that same circle is still the silhouette of Regent's Park.

Where the land that he coveted had been owned by other individuals, Henry VIII paid a decent price. He saw to it that deer did not get out, that poachers did not get in, and that sluices were built to dam the water in times of drought. When important foreign visitors were expected, this would in time be London's Camp David. In 1551, ambassadors from King Henri II of France were invited to hunt and be feasted there. In 1601, the Russian ambassador and his suite hunted in the park, slept over at the manor house, and went back to Whitehall the next day.

Under Queen Elizabeth I upkeep was flawless. Locks and hinges of monumental aspect were made for the park gates. Woodmen, saw men, and painters were kept busy. The properties of several major private landowners bordered on the park. Its thousands of trees—oak, ash, elm, white-thorn, maple—were a great source of potential income, and they were treated as such after the execution of King Charles I in 1649, when the Crown no longer counted for anything and Marylebone Park was leased in lots to private bidders.

It was a brief interlude, but drastic. In her history of Regent's Park, Ann Saunders estimates that "by the time Charles II returned to his throne in 1660, few of the 16,297 trees which were flourishing fifteen years earlier can have been left standing." The park was a different place, therefore, and it was due for a further overhaul of its appearance, its ownership, and its relation to the elegant new city that was growing up to the south and the west of it.

Charles II lost no time in paying off some political debts. In 1666 the Earl of Arlington was granted a thirty-one-year lease of Marylebone Park at a rent of a little over £36 a year. It was probably worth twenty times as much, but Arlington had rendered great services to King Charles II in his hours of trouble.

Two years later, his lease was extended until 1728 and the area was formally "disparked"—made available, that is to say, for parceling as farmland. As Lord Arlington was in that same year granted the whole of St. John's Wood on an indefinite lease for less than £14 a year, his loyalty to the king cannot be said to have gone unrewarded.

He did not, in point of fact, live long to enjoy his new estates. In the eighteenth century, Marylebone Park reverted to small holdings, rented from owners who themselves had only short leases. It was a place of intense agricultural activity. Rabbit and sparrow hawk had their memorial in the naming of this wood or that, but the park was given over primarily to hay and dairy farming, with market gardening here and there.

It made great sense. Without a plentiful supply of horses for every purpose, life in upper-class London would have come to a standstill. Horses had to be stabled, whence the ubiquity in later years of that covert and often voluptuous speciality of London, the pretty little mews house.

They had also to be fed, and it was from Marylebone Park that much of their fodder came. Grasslands in the park were cut, and haystacks completed in May, and again in July, and with luck for a third time in September. During the winter, large herds of cattle were given the run of the meadows. On the hay, grain, and mash thus provided, horses lived well.

Some landlords lived well, too. There was an eager market for clay and gravel. Brick earth was lucrative. Where it went four feet deep, as it generally did, four million bricks could be got from a single acre. There were also "cottage industries" in the original sense. In one cottage, hair powder was manufactured in the heyday of the wig. In another, japan lacquer and copal varnish could be bought and kept in reserve against the superficial damage to coach work that was common in crowded streets.

A place of pleasure called the Jew's Harp had an excellent trade, with its skittle alleys, its rose-arbored areas for refreshment, its willowed pond, and the upstairs room, reached by an outdoor staircase, that could be rented for dances and dinners.

But by the end of the eighteenth century, the busy, useful, and intermittently convivial existence of Marylebone Park was an anomaly in a part of London on which many a covetous eye had begun to focus. There was something almost absurd about the existence of more than five hundred undeveloped and subdivided acres on the very edge of a great city that was being built and rebuilt and rethought. Why should that irregular circle of land not play a vital role in a London redesigned in terms of a grand processional way from Westminster to Regent's Park?

A prime obstacle to that notion was private greed. Speculative builders and at least one great private landlord, the Duke of Portland, would have liked to get their hands on the park and build over its every inch. What we know as Regent's Park would have been turned into streets and squares.

There is nothing wrong with streets and squares, and all the more so if they were built between 1780 and 1830, but the irregular circle of land would have lost the poetical and almost dreamlike quality that the park has to this day.

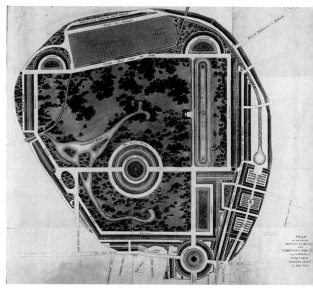

The second obstacle to the rethinking of London was the division of the park into short-term leaseholds, many of which had been fixed at a price that was way below their real market value. But in 1811 this system was due to come to an end. The land would revert to the Crown. With foresight, probity, energy, and the collaboration of an architect and designer of the first rank, the center of London could take on a glorious coherence all the way north from St. James's Park to the north side of Marylebone Park.

Three people, in particular, were needed. The first was a paragon of loyalty, discernment, and fair dealing as the royal surveyor-general. The second was an architect who would think big, see big, and know to how to put bigness into operation. The third was a royal patron who would fight his corner with Parliament.

All three were present and ready. Himself a landowner, with connections by marriage to some of the most powerful men in the country, Sir John Fordyce was the very model of a surveyor-general. He was a hard worker, cast in the great Scottish mold. He was probity personified, he bowed down to no man, and he was a champion elucidator.

The Prince Regent was obsessed with building. If he couldn't build a new

Left:
Sir Thomas Lawrence. *John Nash.* 1824–27. Oil on canvas, 54½ × 43½" (138.4 × 110.5 cm). Reproduced by kind permission of the Principal Fellows and Scholars of Jesus College, Oxford

Top above:
John Nash. *Plan of an Estate Belonging to the Crown called "Marybone Park Farm" Upon a Design for Letting it out on Building Leases.* Engraving from *The First Report of the Commissioners of Woods, Forests and Land Revenues* (London, 1812). The Museum of London

Above:
John Nash. Park Crescent, Regent's Park, London. 1812–22

house, he would turn an existing one inside out. His architect, John Nash, would have rebuilt the whole of London if he had been allowed to. When it became clear that the reordering of Regent's Park, and the clearing of the approaches to it from the south, would involve the design and construction of houses by the hundred, Nash and his royal patron were like schoolboys in a candy shop. There would be terraces to design, and circuses, and villas by the dozen, and new straight streets through which the Prince could drive back and forth in triumph.

Nash dreamed, and he drew, disdaining to indicate the scale on which his drawings were based. He had in mind an audacious mating of park and palaces, in which each would raid the other's spaces. Carefully planted trees would play hide and seek with no fewer than fifty-six villas in the park. There would also be a little palace, or civilized playpen, for the Prince Regent inside the park, with a long strip of ornamental water in front of it. On that strip of water, swans would flaunt their indignation.

News of all this got about, and it reached as far as St. Pancras—a short walk, after all—where in 1818 William and Henry William Inwood, father-and-son architects, won the competition for a church on St. Pancras New Road. As its name suggests, the location was one from which much was expected, now that Regent's Park enjoyed the favor of the highest in the land.

So the Inwoods went to work in the spirit of Regent's Park, as John Nash had set it out in his first proposals in 1811. Inwood junior traveled to Athens, to study the Erechtheum and its caryatids. In this he was up-to-the-minute, given the rediscovery of ancient Greece and the acquisition by Great Britain of the Elgin marbles just a year or two earlier.

But the Inwoods were no less up-to-the-minute in their sense that in the new church, where pew rents would be startlingly high, the congregation would expect a due concern for their comfort and well-being. The pseudo-Athenian caryatids on the exterior were all very fine—they still are, by the way—but they didn't make the sermons seem any shorter.

As to that, I owe to Andrew Saint, the architectural historian, the following extract from a newspaper of the day. The Inwoods' new church was there described as "a very classical, ornamental, Grosvenor-square-like edifice, with pews well-carpeted, pulpits French polished, fanciful green pillars, and windows like those of a conservatory."

The stylish put-down continued as follows: "It is a very elegant sort of a place for a very elegant sort of a party. It will do very well to read prayers in, and would be no bad place in summer to sip lemonade or punch à la romain. But it has little of the appearance, and nothing of the arrangement, which fitness and (we think) policy should have given to a parish church."

Nash saw Regent's Park as an elite operation, and one addressed to "the wealthy part of the public." How could the project not succeed? It was on Crown land, and yet Nash estimated that private money would finance its construction and assume all the entrepreneurial risks. Before long, vast and ever-increasing profits would accrue to the Crown.

There would be "markets, and conveniences essential to the comforts of life," but they would be situated outside the residential area and on the far side of a canal. That canal was to link the Grand Junction Canal in Paddington to the river Thames at Limehouse. It was promoted as a metropolitan miracle that would carry around 800,000 tons of goods a year and be a direct link between the manufacturers of the Midlands and the London docks. How could it not make money?

It was also foreseen that at a respectful distance from the grandees there would be small houses for tradespeople, and markets for meat, vegetables, and hay, all of them tucked away out of sight to the east of what is now Albany Street. To bohemians and subversives, the park would be off-limits. Furthermore, and not by accident, a regiment of soldiers would be quartered within reach.

Access to the park would be by one entrance only—from Portland Place, to the south. Every window in the terraces would face inward, onto a scene of unflawed pastoral. The villas within the park would be so laid out that everyone who lived in them would have the impression that the park was theirs alone.

As for the grand design—the triumphal way that would lead from Carlton House to Regent's Park by way of an arcaded Regent Street, up Portland Place, and in through Park Crescent—the Prince Regent was quoted all over London as having said that it would make Napoleon's Paris look like nothing at all. Nash talked big, too, but in a way that was rather endearing. "Mr. Nash is a very clever, odd, amusing man," one shrewd observer reported, "with a face like a monkey's, but civil and good-humored to the greatest degree."

It was thanks to the Prince Regent, to Sir John Fordyce, and to John Nash that Regent's Park had the immunity from commercial interference that we prize in Kensington Gardens, Hyde Park, the Green Park, and St. James's Park. Meanwhile, "the Regent's Park" (as it came to be called) had to be made new. There would be no cows, no timber industry, no rose-arbored dance hall, no lucrative haymaking.

The buildings that would surround Regent's Park had also to be made new. They would be required to wreak magic, and magic of a new kind. It was a great adventure, and it was in the right hands. As Sir John Summerson said in his *Georgian London,* "Once, and only once, has a great plan for London, affecting the capital as a whole, been projected and carried to completion."

There was nothing innovative about the interior layout of the terraces. Despite the enormous length of Cumberland Terrace (around 275 yards) and Chester Terrace (well over 300 yards) each of the houses within it was in essence a classic London terrace house, narrow and tall. Houses in London had always been built upward, rather than sideways, and this was not the moment for change.

But then Nash was not proposing, or building, or selling, a new kind of house. He was building a standard London house that would be dressed up in an unprecedented way. And the people who put down their names for one of those houses would be paying, in part, for the privilege of having the future King of England as their near-neighbor.

The houses were not masterpieces of the builder's art. Where the exteriors were concerned, the builders and the contractors, and the investors who were financing the scheme, had to stick with Nash's instructions. Indoors, it was a different matter. But in the last instance, it was for John Nash to make sure that the work was properly done.

When things went wrong, as they sometimes did, Nash would be called upon to testify that—to take one instance only—the mortar had been made with the right proportions of lime and sand. People complained that stucco was not stone, but Nash could not afford stone. And, in any case, he preferred to work with stucco, which can be molded like a meringue, than with stone, which would be more resistant to the histrionic fancy that reached apotheosis in his Regent's Park terraces.

The men with whom Nash dealt on the job were basically speculators. He was not always a good judge of men. One of his closest associates—a pseudoarchitect and all-round scoundrel called Charles Mayor—turned out to owe large sums of money all over town and went bankrupt. It did the scheme no good at all that the six

Thomas Hosmer Shepherd.
*Macclesfield Bridge, Regent's
Park*. 1823. Watercolor,
9⁹⁄₁₆ × 14⅛″ (24.3 × 35.8 cm).
The Museum of London

houses that Mayor had half-built stood for month after month open to the sky and overgrown with grass.

Nor did it look well for Nash that after one of the houses collapsed in 1818 surveyors reported that Nash and his clerk of works had not done "a tenth part of what was necessary to be performed" before a house could be passed as properly completed.

He had trouble with Regent Street. Progress with the great new street was so slow as to be—as one surveyor said later—"a common subject for laughter among the profession." Without Regent Street, the charm and the convenience of Regent's Park, as a location, would evaporate. Of the potential householders who had shown such a lively interest in 1812, not one took up his option.

Those were trying days for John Nash. The Regent's Canal, of which he had had great hopes, was also in deep trouble. Neighboring landowners threatened to sue. The stink of the canal water was touted as a danger to public health. The canal diggers faced physical opposition from those whose lands they crossed. The Grand Union Water Company refused to supply water for the canal. Reportedly fertile springs, found and bought elsewhere, were of no use at all. Yet Nash needed that canal, not only as a source of revenue, but to feed his ornamental lake in Regent's Park.

On top of all this, when the Regent's Canal Bill was debated in the House of Commons in 1812, the project was described by one speaker as a dishonest attempt to use Crown property for the personal advantage of Nash and his friend and co-investor Lord Glenbervie.

Even worse befell Nash in 1815. The canal had first been mooted in 1802 by a speculator named Thomas Homer. Nash had been persuaded in 1811 by Homer that the canal would be in every way a good thing for London, for Regent's Park, and (not least) for the shareholders. A capital sum of £254 thousand was raised. But, in 1815, Homer made off with a large amount of that capital sum. It was never recovered. To save the situation, Nash (by his own account) put up £110 thousand in his own name, and in those of others, to keep the work going.

Not only that, but in 1818 he assumed all the wharf leases for the Regent's Park basin, since nobody else was willing to do so. And in 1824 he leased the land that

was still available along the banks of the canal and earmarked it for Park Village East and Park Village West.

The canal had been dug, the villas had been marked out on the map, and Regent Street—thanks to many a compromise—was inching northward. Yet Nash was staking a huge amount of his own money on projects which might come to nothing. But he held on. Other architects—Robert Smirke, for one, who designed the British Museum in 1823—were superfine technicians, impeccable builders, and models of sobriety and maturity. Nash, by contrast, was a gambler, an improviser, and a man who lived for adventure.

He was at home with money and with moneyed people. He had as his patron a man who had never in his life counted the cost of anything. It was not his ambition to come in under budget. So he simply went ahead with all his plans, trusting that everything would come out all right in the end.

And, to a remarkable degree, they did come out all right. In 1816 he joined forces with an investor/builder called James Burton who was to build Cornwall, York, and Clarence terraces. (Burton was one of the first men in London to be a full-fledged master-builder, and to have in his permanent employ a work force that could build anything, anywhere, in short order.)

In 1818 a man called John Farquhar, who had made millions out of gun-powder, guaranteed the money that was needed for the development of the circus that was to stand at the main entrance to the park.

Others came forward to build Sussex Place, Hanover Terrace, Kent Terrace, Chester Gate, and Gloucester Gate. Regent Street was more or less completed by 1824. Chester Terrace and Cumberland Terrace were finished by 1828.

The canal had been opened in 1820, to general acclaim, and it became an integral part of the canal network of the country. By the end of 1823, every site had been let. There were in all 1,233 building sites in Regent's Park, and they were originally let out in 365 leases to 220 leaseholders, of whom 17 were women. It is also significant that 40 percent of the leases were owned by 11 individuals.

So it was a great success? Yes, it was, but not quite on the terms that Nash had originally envisaged. The King never came. Of Nash's projected fifty-six villas within the park—each of them invisible to all the others—few were built and fewer still survived into our own day. He was forbidden to proceed with either the two crescents at the north end or the double inner circus with its villas facing inward and outward. The projected church and the projected Valhalla were likewise abandoned.

Nash himself put a good face on what another architect might have seen as cruel reverses. He had lost his streets, his squares, his circuses, and his villas. But he had secured what he called "a greater variety of beautiful scenery." He had also managed to parry the insinuations of Lord Brougham, who had said in Parliament that the proposed Regent's Park was a device for "trenching on the comfort of the poor for the accommodation of the rich." And, not least in the scale of importance, fewer leaseholds meant higher prices.

What might, therefore, have been a garden city, planned and defined in its every detail, instead became Regent's Park as we know it—a place at once majestic and informal, poetical and practical, in which a certain natural wildness still coexists with an architecture that sets a very high value on theatrical effect.

As with all other forms of theatrical effect, maintenance was essential. Fresh paint does not last forever. Some tenants are more reliable than others. But even after bomb and fire damage during World War II those terraces could still command the imagination. At all seasons and in all weathers, something prodigious survives, and something dreamlike also.

It was at the very apex of his success that Nash was painted by Sir Thomas Lawrence, who had painted many of the great men of his time at the Congress of Vienna. He saw Nash as pink-cheeked, half-smiling, and at ease with himself. Neither ascetic nor puritan, bookkeeper nor precisionist, Nash had taken enormous risks, both for himself and for others.

But when he sat for Lawrence, all those risks seemed to have paid off. His genius may have been, as was said lately, "essentially opportunism writ large." But genius it was, all the same. And what did Sir Thomas Lawrence seize to perfection in his portrait? The sense of generosity and shared enjoyment that we get when John Nash is on top form in Regent's Park.

He still had his enemies, one of whom said of the Regent's Park terraces at that very time that they showed "an inconsistency between the affected grandeur of the design and the poverty, in many instances, of the detail that excites no small degree of disappointment in the beholder."

It is to the credit of Victorian London that it did not seek to disparage, let alone to discard, an architectural ensemble that in its lightness of hand and implicit gaiety was so distinctly un-Victorian. That kind of disparagement went out with Maria Edgeworth, who wrote in 1830 of "plaster statues and horrid useless domes and pediments crowded with mock sculpture figures which damp and smoke must destroy in a season or two."

Before long, it became known that the terraces were really very agreeable to live in. Contrary to the sponsors' original expectations, the area did not become a theme park for the English aristocracy, though at one time the 3rd Marquess of Hertford lived in a villa in the park and carried on in ways that got him into Thackeray's *Vanity Fair* (as the Marquess of Steyne) and Disraeli's *Coningsby* (as the Marquess of Monmouth). In general, the Vicomte d'Arlincourt was way off course when he wrote of Regent's Park in 1844 that it had become "the perfumed abode of the aristocracy" and that "nothing less than the habitations of princes" were to be found there.

Nor did it ever have the equivalent of a hot line to the Houses of Parliament, as

William Radcliff (after T. H. Shepherd). "Park Village East, Regent's Park." Steel engraving for J. Elmes' *Metropolitan Improvements*, 1829–32. Yale Center for British Art, New Haven. Paul Mellon Collection

had been hoped. Rare was the cabinet minister who received the red boxes peculiar to his office at an address in Regent's Park. Rare, likewise, was that phenomenon of central London, the political dinner party. The people who loved the park, and lived there in happiness for thirty, forty, and even fifty years, were not (and did not aspire to be) the tribunes of the people.

The park was always peculiar in its dispositions. Alone among the London parks, it fostered in Victorian days the ancient skills of archery, for which a thirty-one-year lease had been granted to the Toxophilite Society in 1831. (Very active it was, too.)

In 1836, a retired wine merchant called George Bishop began a second career, when already over fifty, and set up a private observatory in the Inner Circle. It was not a matter of idle gaping at the skies. Bishop made himself into a qualified man of science, who was perfectly capable of making observations and calculations at a professional level, which he went on doing until his death in 1861.

Though planned as a playpen for high-level conviviality, Regent's Park soon became, and can be still, a haven of civilized quiet in which the long haul of scholarship can go forward without distraction. There was the thirty-three-years' residence of George Bellas Greenhough, president of the Royal Geological Society and a founder of the Royal Geographical Society. Also, and more conspicuously, there was the establishment of the London Zoo in 1826 and of the Royal Botanic Society in 1836.

Zoology as a subdepartment of science had long had its place in the ambitions of the Royal Society, but until the Zoological Society of London was founded in 1824, as an offshoot of the Royal Society, it had none of the amenities, or the status, or the headquarters, of a learned society. There was nowhere to meet, nowhere to look up a book, and not so much as a place to hang a hat, let alone a fruit bat.

Regent's Park was clearly and from every point of view the ideal location for a London zoo, and it was duly opened in 1828 for the enjoyment, primarily, of members of the Society. Everybody loved the zoo, which was opened to the public as a whole in 1845. Though prized above all as a fun place in which to go and peer at the Cuban bloodhound and the dreaded man-eating hyena, it never lost its high status in the hierarchies of learning.

It was in early Victorian times that Londoners took their collective revenge on the elitist prospectus of Regent's Park. A key event in that regard was the acquisition by the Crown of the neighboring eminence called Primrose Hill. In 1841, it was inaugurated as a public park. A second key event, in that same year, was the opening to the public of 180 acres within the park itself. Not long after, it was reported that "the Park is always full, but on Sundays and holidays it really swarms with pleasure seekers. During the summer months, a band plays on Sunday afternoons on the greensward by the side of the long avenue, and is the means of attracting thousands of the working classes thither."

This classless kermess was the very antithesis of the Regent's Park scene as it had been described by the Vicomte d'Arlincourt. Foreign visitors often get London wildly wrong, of course. It is also possible that the English friends of the French grandee were putting him on. Either way, I am more inclined to believe James Elmes, the author in 1829 of *Metropolitan Improvements: or London in the 19th century*. Elmes said that the majority of the houses in the park "are the retreats of the happy, free-born sons of commerce, of the wealthy commonality of Britain, who thus enrich and bedeck the heart of their great empire."

It is also relevant that speculation in real estate reached a point almost of frenzy in the mid-1820s. (In 1829 the Select Committee on Crown Leases heard it said that in the mid-1820s "there had been such a speculating spirit abroad that persons would have built upon almost any terms.")

This notwithstanding, the park in later Victorian times was occupied by serious people of every kind. Included among them were soldiers seasoned by long service overseas, retired colonial governors, a president of the Royal Academy, Wilkie Collins, the novelist, J. G. Lockhart, the son-in-law and biographer of Walter Scott, and a wonderful specimen of that perennial species, the endearing English freak.

The freak in question was Sir Goldsworthy Gurney, a retired eye doctor who had taken over the lease of the little hospital that Nash had built as one of the park's more reputable neighbors. Sir Goldsworthy was obsessed by the potential of steam on the open road. Nothing would calm him until he had built and perfected a steam carriage in which he would function as owner, driver, conductor, navigator, and sole passenger.

Behind the closed doors of his yard, weeks passed, and months, and maybe even years. But eventually, and with doubtless a warning toot and a puff of white steam, the steam carriage came out and made the tour of Regent's Park.

People watched it in awe. The tour of the park became a daily affair. Imperfections in the carriage were banished, one by one. Time and patience paid off when, in the summer of 1829, Sir Goldsworthy for the first time left the confines of Regent's Park, made a turn to the west, and set off for Bath, where he arrived without mishap and was doubtless a seven days' wonder in a town that was always eager for novelty. As for his carriage, it had no successor in the park.

Regent's Park became the haven of civilized choice in which the long haul of scholarship could go on without distraction. The case of higher education for women was championed in Regent's Park by Elizabeth Jesser Reid, the founder of Bedford College, later to be housed within the park itself in 1913.

In no time at all there was established an American garden, a garden laid out in homage to Linnaeus, and many another ingenious and arcane attractions. It was in the botanic gardens in Regent's Park that Queen Victoria peeled and ate her first banana. It was there, too, that the secretary of the Royal Botanic Society sat in a chair on the leaves of a gigantic Amazonian water lily that had been brought back to England by Sir Joseph Banks, the explorer, naturalist, and longtime president of the Royal Society.

The Crown Commissioners are, no doubt, bound in duty to make as much money as they can from the rents in Regent's Park. But given the intense pleasure that the Society's gardens gave to many thousands of people, it seems in retrospect no less than deplorable that in 1932, when its lease came to an end, the Society was booted out of Regent's Park and left to fend for itself elsewhere. Its eventual home in Kew Gardens is a wonderful place, but it is not in the middle of London. Nor does it have what Regent's Park has — a tradition of disinterested study in many disciplines, carried on in part by learned societies and in part by independent scholars.

I may have overstated the propriety of life in Regent's Park during the reign of Queen Victoria. Many was the eminent Victorian who led a secret life. One of them was the poet Algernon Charles Swinburne. He never lived in Regent's Park, but he was a regular and purposeful promenader up the Broad Walk at all seasons. Neither zoologist nor botanist, archer nor partisan of women's higher education, he nonetheless had a look of high excitement. And why was that? Why did the little redhead press on at so brisk a pace?

Plain words are best. Swinburne was on his way to be whipped, by appointment, in St. John's Wood. Thereby he gratified an inclination widespread in Victorian times and not, I believe, yet extinct. Money was never better spent, he thought, and a sharp walk through Regent's Park was just the thing to get the circulation going. On misty mornings I have often fancied that I saw his ghost half-walking, half-running up the Broad Walk.

The Broad Walk has a predominance in the park today that it would not have had if Nash had been allowed to build as many villas as he had originally proposed. Nor has any one of his villas survived in anything like its original state. The prettiest of them may well have been Holford House, designed by Decimus Burton in 1832. It was destroyed during World War II, but we cannot hope that after long service as Regent's Park Baptist College it was in anything like pristine condition.

One or two oddities in the surviving villas must be signaled — among them the French Empire decoration attributed to a member of the famous firm of Jansen in Paris. It dates from 1935 and apparently survives in The Holme, in the Inner Circle. The view across the park from Winfield Lodge, now the residence of the United States Ambassador, will not be forgotten by those lucky enough to see it. The Islamic Cultural Centre, built in 1977 at Hanover Gate, has an exotic air that John Nash — no foe to the dome — would have savored.

But when all this is said, it remains true that there are large stretches of Regent's Park in which landscape has got the better of architecture. The equality that Nash had in mind has gone forever. Villas are out. Trees are in.

For that matter, trees have always been in, except for a ludicrous period, during the run-up to Nash's great adventure, when the Treasury attempted to grow potatoes and mangel-wurzels in Regent's Park and to make money by selling them.

As of 1812, Dr. Saunders tells us, this project was abandoned and large orders were placed for "eight-foot oaks, Spanish chestnuts, mountain ash, Turkey oaks, sycamore and tulip trees." Nash had asked for plantations in October 1811, and their lordships of the Treasury were pleased to agree.

Walking through the park toward nightfall, we do not see the lights go on in the fifty-six villas (cut back to twenty-six in 1811) that Nash had envisaged. Had his ideas been acted upon, we would see house after house come into view among the trees, ablaze with light and yet well hidden from the others.

But today, lights are very few, and long shadows almost ubiquitous. The big apartment houses along Prince Albert Road, which looked so modern in the 1930s, may still command our attention as they sit on the edge of the park like cruise liners that have gone aground. But if we turn our backs on them, we can stroll this way and that and not think ourselves too far from the Swan Meadow and the Dovecote Meadow that were so carefully marked out here close on three hundred years ago.

The Regent's Canal is another casualty of progress. Nash's notion of a large and lucrative two-way traffic along its entire length vanished in the railway age. As for the surviving towpath, there are those who find it a seductive anachronism. To others, this particular waterfront is dingy, stagnant, and sometimes dangerous.

Sociabilities can still be found here and there in the terraces. But many of the lights go out at the end of office hours. When I lived for some years in Regent's Park, the weekend with its three evenings and its two long days was not a convivial time. The more memorable, therefore, was the occasional coming out party when nobody went home until the summer sky began to blue up at four in the morning.

At other times, nostalgia struck. I thought for instance of Hanover Terrace, which at one time or another had harbored a great novelist, Charles Dickens, at no. 3, Ralph Vaughan Williams, a sizable composer, at no. 11, and H. G. Wells, a many-sided and invaluable irritant, at no. 13.

But perhaps the most fun evening ever to occur in Hanover Terrace was at no. 17 in 1852. Wilkie Collins, the author of *The Moonstone,* and his brothers William and Charles (both very good painters), were the hosts at a dance presided over by their mother. No fewer than seventy writers and artists crowded into the house, and Charles Dickens stood behind the buffet, carving and ladling.

I cannot pretend to welcome the change by which Sussex Place now houses the London Business School. Business can be taught anywhere. Those delicious houses, with their ten pointed domes, their fifty-six Corinthian columns, and their three-sided bow windows, were not intended as classrooms. Their heyday may well have been after World War II, when Cyril Connolly, the editor of *Horizon* magazine, made Sussex Place the address of first resort for visiting writers (not all of whom were admitted). Not even the Collins dance in 1852 can have stood higher in the annals of hospitality.

I suggested earlier that in a mysterious, unbidden way society had taken its revenge on the original plan for Regent's Park as a place from which so many of its members would be excluded. Regent's Park is all very fine, as a spectacle, and the Crown Commissioners have done a good job of saving it from destruction. But the life by which it once distinguished itself has quietly been draining away, and it is around its perimeter that an idiosyncratic and irreplaceable form of metropolitan activity now flourishes.

It has been so for quite some time. It was not inside the park, but on Albany Street that Anthony Powell, the foremost English novelist of his day, and Constant Lambert, composer, conductor, and author of *Music Ho!,* lived the life of the imagination. Never did either say a dull word.

It was north of the park that after World War II V. S. Pritchett, storyteller and critic, set up house. Jonathan Miller, neurologist and theater director, Alan Bennett, playwright, Sylvia Plath, poet, Kingsley Amis, novelist, and Peter Quennell, biographer, were soon niched in the nearby streets that had once played host (though not concurrently) to both Friedrich Engels and W. B. Yeats.

What makes this area so agreeable is not great architecture. It is the undestroyed hamletlike quality of streets in which life goes on at an easy, unhurrying pace. This is not Hampstead, with its glorious past and its air of cultivated leisure. It is not Highgate, with its alpine breezes and its air of distinguished withdrawal from the metropolis below. It has graces (mainly indoors) but no airs. The shops are run by the people who own them. This is a genuine, working, kindly, unspoilt, and inconspicuous piece of London. And it is in such places that the spirit of London resides.

The Center of the World

William Powell Frith. *The Railway Station*. 1862. Oil on canvas, 46 × 101″ (117 × 256.5 cm). Royal Holloway College, University of London

In High Victorian days, the train station, large or small, was the fulcrum of London life. It was in the station that hopes were fulfilled or dashed, careers began or ended, and romances burgeoned or ended in despair. Before the airport, and before the motorway, the train station had a paramount importance.

IN LONDON DURING WORLD WAR II, my secret pleasure at lunchtime was to go and stand in front of the facade of Blackfriars train station and read off the European place names that were cut in stone there. Every one of the cities in question had been beyond our reach since September 1939, and many of them would shortly be destroyed. But as an honor roll of prewar Europe they had a memorable presence.

"What were they doing there?" is a natural question. Blackfriars Station today is of no account whatever in the international scene. Even if you just want to get to the other side of the river Thames, it's quicker to walk.

As a terminal, it was always in the junior league, with none of the heft of Paddington or Waterloo, Victoria or King's Cross. In looks, it could not compare with Marylebone or Liverpool Street, let alone with the waterside majesty of its neighbor Cannon Street. Pevsner gave it exactly nine words: "Opened in 1886. Weak Italianate, of red brick, two-storeyed."

But, with those place names, and during World War II, Blackfriars held its own. The city that it called "Leipsic" would before long be in ruins. "St. Petersburg" was enduring one of the most terrible of all sieges. Yet, within living memory, people had been able to walk into Blackfriars Station, take a ticket to one or both of them, and be sure of getting there.

Murray's Foreign Handbooks told them exactly how it would be, and did it in a way that spoke for a specific idea of civilization. Of that civilization, the City of London was the center. Once inside that stumpy little station, the rest of Europe was ours for the asking.

This, for instance, is what Murray's guidebook had to say around 1990: "By taking the route via Calais, Bleyberg, Aix-la-Chapelle, Elberfeld, Kreiensen, Berlin, Kovno, Vilna and Pskof, St. Petersburg can be reached from London in 3 days, inclusive of a stoppage for one night in Berlin." A first-class one-way ticket cost a little over £13.

Travelers were advised that "the carriages throughout are comfortable and roomy" and that "in case of fatigue" they could pass the night at Königsberg, a city made famous by Immanuel Kant. Buffets were "frequent and good." Russian customs officers were models of politeness. At Wierzbolow, 560 miles short of St. Petersburg, there was a "good buffet kept by a Frenchman, with plenty of time for refreshment" and bedrooms for those who fancied them. Travelers could get down as often as they pleased and stay on for as long as they liked.

Toward the end of World War II, when conditions in the places named were worse than appalling, there was a heartrending quality about the leisurely and luxurious journey thus described. What happy days were those, when a side trip from Königsberg to the seaside town of Liebau would offer the traveler a choice of excellent sea bathing, wildfowl shooting on a nearby lake, and pretty public gardens with restaurants and music as well as a theater!

And to think all that was available on demand to anyone who presented himself

Ford Madox Brown. *Work*. c. 1852–65. Oil on canvas, 53 × 77″ (134.6 × 195.6 cm). Manchester City Art Galleries

It was the paradox of the great nineteenth-century City of London that although a vast amount of work was done there, hardly anybody was ever actually seen to be doing it. The office was all. The painter Ford Madox Brown was the archetypal concerned citizen, but when he painted his panoramic vision of the role of work in society, he had to set it out of doors, in Hampstead.

202

at Blackfriars in springtime, wearing for preference a *demi-saison* overcoat of the kind attributed to Gaev in *The Cherry Orchard* and carrying a custom-built leather suitcase and "a light game-bag, or gibecière"!

Fired up by these notions, I saw myself as a precocious continental traveler in the 1870s or 1880s, rather than as what I actually was—a replaceable bit-player in a just but terrible war. For half a century, and quite possibly forever, that war was to deprive us of the kind of journey that Murray recommended.

But then I remembered that trains do not only go in one direction. For every English traveler who got to trundle across the Thames on the three-day journey to St. Petersburg, there were people from all over Europe who stepped aboard the trains and boats that in due time would bring them directly to the City of London.

There were legendary figures among them—the International Spy with his pocketful of stolen state papers, the Adventuress bent upon lucrative seductions, the Innocent from a far country who would be swindled out of his last penny. Beyond a doubt there were mainline crooks among the mainline passengers, and beyond a doubt some of them did very well.

But fifty years after my initial epiphany in front of Blackfriars Station, I prefer to think of the honorable and ambitious traders who headed for London with every confidence of doing well. Present to me are the bankers from Frankfurt, the silk merchants from Lyon, the silver dealers from Augsburg, and the azalea specialists from Ghent. I dream, likewise, of the wholesalers of figs and tobacco from Smyrna, the lace men from Brussels, the wine makers from Bordeaux and Cadiz, the diamond merchants from Amsterdam, the watchmakers from La Chaux-de-Fonds, and the Siberian furriers.

Before the telegraph, the telephone, the telex, and the fax, business was best done face to face. And what better place for business than the heart of a great empire? Addison himself could not have wished for either a more motley or a more motivated company, nor the City of London for more promising recruits.

Was this romancing? Not at all. Those were the glory days of the City of London. It had no rival as the most important of the world's commercial and financial centers. It had the Empire. It had the port. It had the ships. It had the capital. It had the banks. It had the markets, both domestic and international. As an insurance market it engendered trust the world over.

London was the world capital of entrepreneurial adventure. It was also the center of the world's money market and the heartland of investment. What a nineteenth-century enthusiast called the "nerval juices" of credit flowed more freely there than anywhere else. Who could forget, in that context, the glorious simplicity of what was said in the *Key to the London Money Market,* first published in 1877. The role of the London banks, it said, was "to collect money from those who do not want it, and lend it to those who do, to the profit of all."

"To the profit of all" is not, of course, entirely true. There were lots of winners in the High Victorian City of London. This was a place and a time at which virtually no commercial transaction—overt or clandestine, rascally or straightforward—could not be carried through in the City.

But there were lots of losers too. Giddy and ferocious are the ups and the downs of the City. In 1876 an American observer, William Purdy, listed the firms that had failed in 1875 in his book *London Banking Life.* There were well over two hundred of them, nationwide. Unpaid debts amounted in all to over £37 million. Hosiers, jewelers, "railway spring manufacturers," spinners, ship merchants, gunsmiths, cheesemongers, copper smelters, sugar brokers, umbrella makers—all had failed to meet their obligations. Myself ever in dread of penury, I trembled to read of a grain merchant called John Russell who had owed £60 thousand and could not pay it.

Ups and downs notwithstanding, the City in Victorian times had the physical trade—the moving in and out of London, at the right price, of whatever goods were most wanted at any given time. It also had the office trade, in which physical production played almost no part and what mattered was diplomacy, experience, quick-wittedness, personal contacts, and high-level paperwork.

How could the City in late Victorian times not be in enviable shape? On the south bank of the Thames, just below Tower Bridge, wharf and wharfer were doing terrific business. Big steamers from all over waited in line for a berth in the London docks. (The London docker was a formidable human being, by the way—competitive, tireless, built as if of granite and ever ready with his fists.)

Warehouses in the City had gone up by the hundred, year after year, and every one of them was full. As for the market for precious metals, it was as lively as it had been in the 1690s, when English coins came in real gold and real silver and were much in demand, by fair means or foul, in foreign parts.

Britain in High Victorian days had a great empire as its backyard. Thanks to that empire, it had an effective near-monopoly of trade and services over a large part of the world. The Royal Navy ruled the seas. The London docks were bigger than many a European city. The new railroads and the strategic network of canals were in full service.

Britain was a great manufacturing country. As an importer, it was second to none. The City of London was famous for its centuries-old store of experience, its openness to new people and new ideas, and its ability to adapt. It was also famous for a commercial intelligence network that could rarely be faulted.

There was almost nothing movable that could not be handled in London. Whether the consignments were of furs, feathers, rubber, tea, chemicals, platinum, diamonds, or quicksilver, London had the expertise to look them over, gauge their quality, sell them on the spot, or send them on their way to the place that most wanted them.

There were single-minded specialists in the City. A plainspoken poetry still sings out in their names. Goad, Rigg & Co. traded in nothing but hair and did very well with it. If you were after ebony, cedar, satinwood, rosewood, or walnut, Churchill & Sim had trees, some place, that were as if already marked with your name. For ships in the sugar trade, Erlebach & Co. were the people to go to. Gellatly's had all-purpose agencies in Khartoum, Jeddah, Suakin and Port Sudan. Given these resources, and hundreds more like them, why should the primacy of London among the cities of the world ever come to an end?

Besides, there were new countries, if not new worlds, to conquer. The entrepreneurial genius of London was not confined to the British Empire, colossal as that then was. New York had long been free of the British Empire, but when the time came to build the East River tunnels, it was a British firm, S. Pearson and Son, that built them.

Pearson's were active—hyperactive, some would say—in bringing the benefits of electricity to Spain, Greece, and Chile, none of which could be classed as British fiefs. Was there a Sennar Dam to be built on the Blue Nile? Would Mexico be the better for the Tehuantepec Railway? Guess who would make the best tender for them.

It was with all this in mind that the new arrivals at Blackfriars Station stood in awe before the sight of St. Paul's Cathedral at the top of Ludgate Hill. As much as on the day of its completion, St. Paul's was the flagship of the City of London. But the City that new arrivals went on to explore did not look like an ancient city.

It looked, on the contrary, like a city that not long before had discovered the economic potential of real estate. That potential was enormous. To the readers of *The Builder* magazine, in 1866, for instance, it was divulged that a big new house on Lombard Street could be built for between £10 and 15 thousand.

After the owners' own needs had been amply met, there might well be three complete floors available for rent. Each of them could be let for up to £2 thousand a year. The City was in full ebullition, with building and rebuilding in progress on every hand, and monumental construction works under way both above and below ground.

New ambitions bred new needs. This was a time at which the Italian concept of *bella figura* had its way with the City of London. The banks, the insurance houses, and the developers of office blocks and warehouses who were changing London almost by the hour—all wanted buildings that would double as public relations touts.

This was something new for the City. When the East India Company was all-powerful, its five-acre warehouses were not built for show. "Bare red brick, with a minimum of classical stone detail below," was how Pevsner described them. But in the 1850s and 1860s, designer warehouses were the thing.

Banks had to be emblems of stability. Insurance houses had to propagate (here I quote from John Summerson) "the image of upright, prudent men banded together to arrest the cruel hand of fate." Office blocks welcomed the magic wand of whatever was newest and most inventive in architecture. Warehouses could take on a frisky look that was contrary to expectation.

In terms of prestige, it was important to have an architect who was also an artist. That commercial architecture could be seductive had never been thought of before. But the High Victorian City of London was a highly competitive place, in which looks were all-important.

New buildings had to engage the passerby in a mating dance. If our new arrivals at Blackfriars Station had dreamed of a City still steeped in the past, they were soon corrected. In street after celebrated street—Threadneedle Street, Lombard Street, Bishopsgate, Eastcheap, Lothbury, Cheapside, Leadenhall Street—building after building was of recent construction.

It might have been supposed that all these recent buildings would be in roughly the same style. That had been the case just a few years earlier, in the second quarter of the nineteenth century, when the Grosvenor Estate in Belgravia was developed under the supervision of Thomas Cubitt. The stuccoed terrace houses, with their subtle variations of scale and prominence, were cut from the same cloth by a single distinguished hand—that of George Basevi, the pupil of Sir John Soane. To walk round Belgravia is to hear Basevi's well-spoken voice. And what we see there—alleyways and back passages included—is one of the great metropolitan achievements.

In the City of London, the exact opposite happened. Competition ruled. Dog ate dog. It was one against all, and all against one. The sole unifying factor was that the elevator was not yet in current use and there was a limit to the number of stairs that busy men cared to climb. With this one proviso, the architect/artist, as distinct from the journeyman, had a free hand. This was a time when fancy was unrestrained and the client would run with it, hoping to outshine the neighbors.

They had steady nerves, those clients. If Crown Life Insurance wanted to build on a narrow site on New Bridge Street, where unaffected Georgian houses had

George Elgar Hicks. *Billingsgate Fish Market.* 1861. Oil on canvas, 27 × 49″ (68.6 × 124.5 cm). The Worshipful Company of Fishmongers, London

George Scharf. *Crooked Lane at the Time of the Construction of the London Bridge.* 1830. Watercolor, 20½ × 30¾″ (52 × 28 cm). Guildhall Library, Corporation of London

minded their own business for generations, they did not hesitate to hire Thomas Deane and Benjamin Woodward, whose most recent achievement was the heaven-scaling interior of the Museum of Natural Science in Oxford.

The Crown Life building went up. By the standards of the City, it was not large. Same height as its neighbors. Same number of floors. But, thereafter, vroom! This was a new kind of building for the City of London. To be precise, and as John Summerson said, "The new Crown Life Office was, more or less, Venetian, with a delicate polychromy of Portland stone, brick, red and grey granite and Sicilian and other marbles." An important part was played in it by "naturalistic carving by the famous Shea brothers of Oxford."

Inside were "ceiling and friezes with foliage, birds and animals painted by the minor Pre-Raphaelite John Hungerford Pollen." The building's "round-arch pointed-extrados medievalism" was followed by many an awed junior colleague of Deane and Woodward. But still—this was an insurance office! In the City of London! In 1860! People couldn't get over it.

Charles Robert Cockerell. *Westminster Life and British Fire Office, London* (destroyed). 1831

Insurance was one of the great promoters of architectural energy in the early Victorian City of London. Thanks to the newly passed Joint Stock Companies Act, insurance from the 1840s and early 1850s onward was a growth industry in which company after company craved a new headquarters in the City of London. Once again, looks counted. Quiet buildings in quiet streets stood for quiet little deals that would never make anybody rich. The new vogue was for big-name architects who could tackle corner sites on crucial streets.

Charles Robert Cockerell, a major architect much underused in the City, proved himself a master of the corner site when the Sun Life Assurance Company commissioned him in the 1840s to build for them on the corner of Threadneedle Street and Bartholomew Lane.

The trick with a corner site is not to get stuck with the corner, but to sashay round almost imperceptibly from one street to the other. Cockerell solved the problem, first by canting the corner and then by flanking it with two tall Tuscan columns that might have enshrined a conventional main entrance.

But what Cockerell put between those tall columns was not a door at all, but a segment-headed window that gently told strangers to keep on going, to left or to right, until they found a door. The whole building responded to this, the way a skilled waltzer would have responded at that time to the signal to reverse.

This was one of the great insurance buildings. In 1890 Frederick Leighton, painter and for eighteen years president of the Royal Academy, used to come and gaze at it whenever (so he told a friend) he wanted to "revivify himself with the sense of the beauty of Greek work." But by 1970 the City had had enough of it. A newer building on so choice a site would make more money, people said, and that was the end of Charles Robert Cockerell in the City of London.

As time went on, flagship buildings in general became heavier and more emphatic, with that particular blundering coarseness that recurs throughout the centuries in commercial buildings in the City of London. When making an official choice, in a major context, the City blew it as often as not. This was especially the case in 1841, when Sir William Tite prevailed over Cockerell in the competition for the new Royal Exchange, right across from the Mansion House.

Had Cockerell won the competition, his Royal Exchange would have spoken for brilliance, festivity, and a soaring imagination. But the prize went to Tite, who held fast to preexisting formulae. It was to commissions in the private sector, between 1840 and 1880, that the City of London had to look for diversity, for a certain wild wit, and for the readiness to try anything.

Could the Travellers' and Reform Clubs in Pall Mall set a new tone for insurance buildings in the City? John Gibson proved that once and for all in 1849 with the building he designed for the Imperial Assurance Company on Threadneedle Street.

Was Venetian Gothic a valid guide for office building in London in the 1860s? It was in the City that G. Somers Clarke answered "Yes" to that when in 1866 he built in Lothbury for the General Credit Company.

Was it permissible to introduce English country ways to Leadenhall Street? The question would have seemed almost too silly to ask until in 1873 Richard Norman Shaw designed an office building called New Zealand Chambers and showed a drawing of it in the Royal Academy summer exhibition.

As New Zealand Chambers was destroyed during World War II we cannot judge it at first hand. But what Shaw did was to import from the High Street in Oxford a fantasized and much enlarged version of a shop front, with rooms above, of the early or mid-seventeenth century. In Leadenhall Street it was an outrageous newcomer—out of place, out of style, perverse, and over-ornamented.

Sir Thomas Lawrence. *Sir Frances Baring BT, John Baring and Charles Wall.* 1806. Oil on canvas, 61 × 89″ (154.9 × 226.1). By permission of the directors of Barings

In 1958, the American architectural historian Henry-Russell Hitchcock saw it not as an anachronism but as an early and covert trial run for the glass-walled, iron-framed office buildings of the future. Shaw's contemporaries had been so dazzled and so piqued by the ornamentation of spandrel and cove that "they hardly noticed the way in which the bold articulation of the facade by the brick piers, with the areas between nearly all window, frankly reflecting the internal iron construction, provided most satisfactory lighting for the offices."

There was something irreducibly English about it. Among its other virtues, it brought into the hyperactive, soot-ridden City of London a strange, countrified, almost folkloric vision. Much of its color was owed to Cawte's of Fareham, a firm established not long before, whose bricks gave an apple-red flush to much of London in the 1870s. This was a case in which the apples looked fresh from the tree.

It was the paradox of the High Victorian City that although the big money came (or was hoped-for) from the development of big sites, the power of London to reinvent itself also resided in small, clear, and unpredictable statements. One of these was the warehouse on Upper Thames Street of a drysalter named Skilbeck. It was remodeled in 1865–66 by William Burges.

Burges had colossal ambitions. He was eventually to excel as castle builder, cathedral builder, college builder, church builder, large-scale decorator, furniture designer, stained glass designer, ceramicist, mosaicist, and artist in jewelry and metalwork.

He could design anything, from a pair of hairbrushes for the Duke of Norfolk to an art school in Bombay and a cathedral in Brisbane. And he was as much at home with a projected replanning for the city of Naples as with his "Narcissus"

George Elgar Hicks. *Dividend Day at the Bank of England*. 1859. Oil on canvas, 35½ × 53″ (90.2 × 134.6 cm). Courtesy of the Governor and Company of the Bank of England

washstand (later given by a poet, John Betjeman, to a novelist, Evelyn Waugh).

Burges could have been simply one of the all-time great pasticheurs. When he submitted drawings for the cathedral in Lille, in northern France, they were so perfectly in style that Viollet-le-Duc, the great French arbiter in such matters, refused to believe that they were nineteenth-century drawings. Only when he spotted the Whatman watermark on the double elephant paper did he bow to the evidence.

But his ambitions went way beyond that. He wanted to make a nineteenth-century world with thirteenth-century syntax. When he undertook the relatively footling job of remodeling the Skilbeck warehouse in the City of London he did not see it simply as a notch above designing the organ seat for Worcester College Chapel, Oxford (1865), or the cope for the Bishop of Honolulu (1862). It was no more than a little slot on Upper Thames Street. Burges could not pull it down and start all over. But it had potential.

What Burges did was fraught with poetry. This was industrial architecture, but it had elements of symbolism and inspired miscellany. Burges's biographer, J. Mordaunt Crook, tells us what he did to the original plain facade. "The ground floor became an essay in glass and iron: plate glass windows, wrought iron guards and a massive cast iron beam, exposed and stencilled. Above, pulleys, crane, ropes and loading tackle festoon, without embarrassment, the symbolic sculpture of the facade."

It made work look like fun. Smaller packages were drawn up to the top floor from the street. Those pulleys were supported by stout little lions, way up near the gables. As for the big crane, it was supported by a corbel "which was carved into the

Detail view of the City of London, from *Philips' Picture Map of London*. Courtesy Peter Jackson

bust of a fair Oriental maid, symbolizing the clime from which so many of the drysalter's materials are bought."

This was once a City in which buildings like the Skilbeck warehouse could be put up and savored, not as aesthetizing fantasies, but as constructions that served commerce as much as they served art. Everyone loved it. Some people admired it because, as the *Building News* had said, it was "a piece of genuine 13th century construction."

In a building of that sort, we sense a society that fears no rival. We also sense a City of London that for centuries had harbored exceptional human beings and paid due attention to them.

And yet, even in High Victorian times, there were buildings in the City that played down the importance of their owners. One was in Bishopsgate, where the facade of Baring Brothers' bank was designed in 1881 by Norman Shaw. "Very domestic and not at all for display" was Pevsner's verdict, and it was one that very few banks would have coveted in the 1880s. It related, rather, to the days when the partners of Barings' were painted by Sir Thomas Lawrence in civilized, unhurried colloquy.

Better than any novelist or playwright, and as well as any biographer, Lawrence in this portrait group puts the case for the London private banker as the epitome of civilization. Sir Francis Baring, Bart., Mr. John Baring, and Mr. Charles Wall come across as men of concern, men of bearing, and men of weight. So far from passing the day in privileged idleness in what looks more like a curtained loggia than an office, they are getting down to business.

It is not perfunctory business, either. The man on the right has papers in his right hand, and is gearing up to say something important about them. The man in the middle has papers on the table, within reach, but is waiting for a lead. On the right, at the head of the massive, un-ornamented table, is Sir Francis Baring.

Leaning with his two hands on a monumental account book, Sir Francis has the look of a practiced chairman who will observe the courtesies but is not going to waste his time. Though not staged, the scene rings true. (Almost too true, one might say. The next generation of Baring sons complained that they "did not like to have their Father exhibited with a Ledger before him.")

It was not, by the way, as an awestruck hack that Lawrence faced his sitters. He had been first painter to the King of England since he was twenty-three. He was perfectly at home with persons of consequence, and he would have spotted the interplay between his three sitters almost before they got into the studio.

It is for these reasons that the Baring group stands out as a masterpiece in a City where the incidence of bad portraits per square foot of wall space is as high as it is anywhere in the world. He showed the Barings as big men in their field, which they certainly were—Baring Brothers had been around since 1763—but he did not flatter them. The subtext of this picture is that making money is anxious work, and keeping it almost more so.

Someone who knew that very well was Walter Bagehot, who in the 1870s was the most lucid, the best-informed, and the wittiest of commentators on the City of London. As the son of a country banker, Bagehot was born to the business. As the editor of *The Economist* magazine, he had as many contacts in the government as in the City. He was, by all accounts, an incomparable talker. And in his book *Lombard Street,* which he finished in 1873, he gave an unforgettable portrait of the City of London at what seemed to many to be its apogee.

Others dwelt on the darker side of this phenomenon. The year 1873 was also the time in which Anthony Trollope in his novel *The Way We Live Now* gave a detailed and still relevant account of how a great swindler, in that same City of London, can take a great fall. But—in terms almost too famous, but not often quoted in full—Bagehot described the City at that time as "by far the greatest combination of economical power and economical delicacy that the world has ever seen. Of the greatness of the power, there is no doubt. Money is economical power. Everyone is aware that England is the greatest moneyed country; everyone admits that it has much more immediately disposable and ready cash than any other country. But very few persons are aware how much greater the ready balance—the floating loan-fund which can be lent to anyone and to any purpose—is in England than it is anywhere else in the world."

Bagehot was also fired up by the City's private bankers. He knew, and he admitted, that the paradisal state of affairs that he outlined might not last forever. But meanwhile the name of "London Banker" had "a charmed value. He was supposed to represent, and often did represent, a certain union of pecuniary sagacity and educated refinement which was scarcely to be found in any other part of society. In a time when the trading classes were much ruder than they now are, many private bankers possessed a variety of knowledge and a delicacy of attainment which would even now be very rare."

London had then, and has still today, private banks that seem to have been there forever. Over the names of Baring, Rothschild, Hoare, Coutts, Fleming, and Hambro, the dust has never gathered. The banks that bear their names may, in fact, be more active and more inventive than ever. Yet you might sometimes imagine from the partners' behavior at lunch that they were a bunch of undergraduates who had decided to cut a lecture.

"Their position is singularly favorable," Bagehot went on to say. "The calling is hereditary; the credit of the bank descends from father to son; this inherited wealth soon brings inherited refinement." At that point, Bagehot seems in the 1990s to have taken off like a hot-air balloon.

212

"Banking," he said, "is a watchful, not a laborious trade. A banker, even in large business, can feel pretty sure that all his transactions are sound, and yet have much spare mind. A London banker can also have the most intellectual society in the world if he chooses it. There has probably very rarely ever been so happy a position as that of a private London banker; and perhaps never a happier."

It must be said for Bagehot that he saw this state of affairs as already on the wane and quite possibly doomed. Like many another, he was haunted by the misfortunes of Overend & Gurney, a once-great firm that had been brought to ruin in 1852 in a single generation in spite of the "hereditary calling" that he so prized in others.

Conditions today are such that, according to a recent authority, "financial institutions, faced with strong competition, need both to keep all their funds employed constantly and to maintain a position of liquidity." This can best be achieved "by operating on a global market on a 24-hour basis."

The "24-hour basis," with its continual juggling of news from New York, Frankfurt, Tokyo, and elsewhere, is the very antithesis of Bagehot's view of private banking. Conscious as he was of the element of risk in banking, it would never have occurred to him that there would come a time when a moment's lapse of attention at three A.M., London time, might have a terrible importance.

A landmark in the history of the City of London as Bagehot knew it was the foundation in 1842 of Gresham's Club. Named after that great cutter of corners, the sixteenth-century financier and high-level go-between, Sir Thomas Gresham, this was a companionable warren of rooms in which men had lunch together. It did not serve dinner, since there was no demand for it. It had no bedrooms, since none of its members would have dreamed of sleeping over in the City of London. It was not a lunch club, either. It was a long lunch club.

Membership of Gresham's was confined to "merchants, bankers and professional and other gentlemen of known respectability." It was not a club in which business was transacted—all business papers had to be given up at the door—but it was a place in which a decisive word could be dropped.

The day's routine was as follows. Principal partners in companies of good standing would arrive about 12:30 P.M. In their demeanor, Bagehot's pages lived again for many years. By 12:30 they would have done their day's work and delegated its implementation to others, none of whom would ever cross the threshold of Gresham's.

They would move to the dining room. If ever it turned out that there were thirteen men at table, a fourteenth-chair was pulled up and a bright blue teddy bear set upright on it to make up an acceptable number. They would take a long lunch, not without lubrication. They would then adjourn to the smoking room, where they drank port till about 5:30 P.M. After a short and honorably steady walk back to the office, they signed their letters and left for the day.

Thereafter, they had—so Bagehot said—the run of the "most intellectual society in the world." Some of them doubtless never missed a conversazione at the Royal Society. Others, maybe, preferred to drop by at a superior whorehouse, well away from the City, or at one of the long-running places of amusement at which dogs were set to kill rats by the dozen and men laid money on the upshot of it. Either way, we may assume that they left in good spirits.

Gresham's Club closed for lack of trade in 1992. If Bagehot were to stroll along his favorite Lombard Street and its neighbors, he would still find, by name, the banks that he knew, and the shipping lines, the insurance companies, and even an occasional now-distant echo of Empire.

William Logsdail. *The 9th of November, Sir James Whitehead's Procession, 1888.* 1888–90. Oil on canvas, 73¾ × 107" (187.3 × 271.8 cm). Guildhall Library, Corporation of London

The annual Lord Mayor's Show was until World War II a moment of genuine festivity in which care was put aside for an hour or two and the City put on a show that gave pleasure to many thousands of people.

But he would have trouble recapturing the look and the scale of London in High Victorian times. All over the City, the stocky and sometimes almost jaunty rhythms of the Victorian heyday have been discarded and can never be put together again. The skyline of the City in the 1990s is like nothing that Bagehot could ever have imagined, let alone wished to see.

One or two shifts of emphasis might surprise him, also. As a profession, accountancy did not rank high with him. (Annual audits were not even mandatory until 1900.) He might even have thought that the Institute of Chartered Accountants went rather too far with the splendidly assertive headquarters in Great Swan Alley that it commissioned from John Belcher in 1880.

"Eminently original and delightfully picturesque in its free Baroque" were Pevsner's words for it. Devotees of late-Victorian idiom may regret the removal in 1971 of the stained-glass windows by Henry Holiday in which could be seen, among much else, a possibly apocryphal figure of a sixteenth-century auditor.

But what matters more is that the most recent extension to the Institute (by William Whitfield, completed in 1970) does more for the dignity of the City than almost any other building of its date. It is, in fact, the visual equivalent of the greatly enlarged importance of accountancy in the postwar City.

From being thought of primarily in terms of auditing, the major firms emerged by the 1970s and 1980s as general financial advisers whose back-room expertise on taxation, mergers, flotations, and acquisitions was invaluable. A profession in which the fee income of a major firm could rise from £90 thousand in 1945 to £148 million in 1988 is entitled to be pleased with itself.

Bagehot would grieve, on the other hand, to know of the ups and downs—some of them grisly—that have befallen many a name that he knew well and must have regarded as virtually immune to change. When trustful pensioners by the thousand have been ruined by a scoundrel, when Morgan Grenfell's is taken over by Deutsche Bank, and when even Lloyd's of London has been in deep trouble, the sage of Lombard Street would hang his head.

Meanwhile, and for a sense of late-Victorian London that in terms of actuality is dead and gone, almost the way Persepolis is dead and gone, I recommend above all the fourteen-minute portrait that is to be found in Edward Elgar's overture *Cockaigne*.

The absolute rightness of *Cockaigne* is the more remarkable that no one could call Elgar a true Londoner. By temperament he was to the end of his life a country dreamer. But he used London. He looked at London. He walked about London. And he hoped to do business in London, at a time when the annual income from his *Enigma Variations* could barely climb into the low two figures.

London gave him major musical experiences. At a time when he himself had just written a part song called "Why So Pale and Wan?," he was bowled over by the animal spirits and the innovative orchestration of Berlioz's overture *Les Francs Juges*. (Not long after, he bought and studied Berlioz's treatise on orchestration.) In 1881 he went to London to hear Clara Schumann play her husband's *Etudes Symphoniques*. In 1889, he was in London and went to Wagner's *Die Meistersinger* three times in a fortnight.

London for its own sake never seemed to make much of an impression upon him. Yet in 1900 he began to think about writing an overture in which there would be something of *Die Meistersinger* and something that he described as specifically "cheerful and Londony, stout and steaky." *Cockaigne* was the name he chose for that overture, which as a concise portrait of London life has never been equalled in music. *In London Town* was the subtitle that he added when it became clear that a lot of people didn't know what Cockaigne was, or where it was, or anything about it. In April 1901, he told the conductor Hans Richter that his overture *Cockaigne* "was first suggested to me one dark day in the Guildhall: looking at the memorials of the city's great past, and knowing well the history of its unending charity, I seemed to hear far away in the dim roof a theme, an echo of some noble melody."

He loved the name of *Cockaigne*, which had been the source of the adjective "Cockney." It is the City of London Cockney, not the grandee or the alderman, who laughs and struts his way through *Cockaigne*. London would not be London without its Cockneys, and there are still a great many of them around.

Cockneys are observant, quick-witted, buoyant, un-envious, and disrespectful of authority. Long before radar was invented, they could spot a pompous ass before he (or she) came round the corner. The stuffed shirt gets nowhere with them, and about their very footfall there is something larky. In all matters pertaining to life as it is really is, they know the score. Society has never done them any favors, and they don't expect any now. (As for the "unending charity" that Elgar attributed to London, their views would be worth hearing.) But they are London's leaven, and in a curious but unmistakable way they are also its touchstone of truth.

To a remarkable extent, Edward Elgar in *Cockaigne* succeeded in portraying

Herbert Lambert. *Sir Edward Elgar (1857–1934)*. 1933. Gelatin silver print. The National Portrait Gallery, London

the inner City of London, the way Richard Wagner portrayed a fifteenth-century Nuremberg in the overture to *Die Meistersinger.*

Elgar himself never forgot that John Florio, the first English translator of Montaigne, had called Cockaigne "the land of all delights: so taken in mockery." When it was first performed in 1901, good judges at once spotted what Ernest Newman, the great Wagnerian, called the whistle of the "perky, self-confident, unabashable London street boy." And Donald Francis Tovey, a musical analyst who was also one of the best prose writers of the day, noted that in the first theme of the piece there was "a magnificent Cockney accent in that pause on the high C."

There were those who thought it vulgar when Elgar went slightly over the top in his introduction of a brass band that blew its heart out in ways then familiar. Tovey wouldn't hear of that. "I cannot find vulgarity in Elgar's brass band as it comes blaring down B flat Street," he said. Edwardian London had its rowdy, well-fleshed, "stout and steaky" aspect, and Elgar got it exactly right.

Horses' hooves are there, too, and hansom carriages kept in tip-top condition, and a sense of people beyond number going about the business of the greatest empire the world had ever seen. But Elgar also excelled at aspects of the City that have thus far proved to be perennial—church bells not always attuned to one another, the flash and flicker of stained glass reflected on old stone floors, the shared feeling among lovers that London is on their side, and the sudden blast of sound when the King of Instruments is given its head in an organ loft.

We should add to all this the gift for musical characterization that Elgar had shown a year or two before in his *Enigma Variations,* and contrapuntal skills in which mockery had a role, and a conviction (not always justified, alas) that London is a place in which just about everything turns out well.

Cockaigne does not make Elgar a true Londoner, but as a guide to the City on the very edge of its long decline it has a dead-center quality. It inspires belief, just as Walter Bagehot inspires belief. And the truth? Well, the truth lies somewhere between the two.

There's Always the Theater

WHEN VISITORS TO LONDON start to count their blessings, there is a moment at which they say "And, thank heaven, there's always the theater." They are quite right, too. London is a theater town. It always was, and it always will be. Something in the blood, the heart, and the folk-memory of the Londoner demands it. The theater is there to amuse, to amaze, and to entertain. But it is also there to serve London as conscience, sounding board, and touchstone of truth. Concurrently, it functions as classroom, safety valve, and pleasure ground.

Not every great city is, or can be, a theater town. Rome will never qualify. Nor will Washington, D.C. Athens dropped out 2,400 years ago. To make a great theater town, several things are needed. Great plays have to have been around, since the day they were written, as a fact of everyday life and everyday speech. There have to be theaters, and plenty of them. There have to be actors and actresses who redefine the potential of theater every time they come on the stage. And there has to be a committed public that renews itself, generation by generation.

All these preconditions have long been fulfilled in London. Close on two hundred years ago—in 1817, to be precise—William Hazlitt gave the keynote address, when he said that, "Wherever there is a playhouse, the world will not go on amiss." And he went on to say of actors and actresses that they show us "all that we are, all that we wish to be, and all that we dread to be. The stage is an epitome, a bettered likeness of the world, with the dull part left out."

In all these respects, the last fifty years have been one of the golden ages of theater in London. What is Tom Stoppard's *Arcadia*, first performed in 1993, if not "a bettered likeness of the world, with the dull part left out"? This is a theater in which words are on the wing, with ideas hanging on for dear life.

The golden age began small, but it began very strong. World War II was not long over when the twenty-one-year-old Peter Brook came to the tiny (347 seats) Arts Theatre Club, just off Charing Cross Road, and directed Jean-Paul Sartre's *No Exit* (*Huis Clos*). It is a short play about three badly assorted people who are sealed up forever in one small windowless room. The thirty-two-year-old Alec Guinness gave terrifying expression to the author's somber message, which was that "Hell is other people."

In 1955, Peter Hall, then twenty-five, directed Samuel Beckett's *Waiting for Godot,* which gave a completely new spin to the concept of human pairings—how they come about, what they feed upon, and why they sometimes persist, open-endedly.

Along the way, in *Godot,* indispensable conclusions were advanced by Samuel Beckett with a stoical concision rarely equalled. They did not bring comfort, but they had a finality that confounded cant. No attentive listener will ever forget Pozzo's unsparing summation of our life on earth, that, "They give birth astride of a grave, the light gleams an instant, then it's night once more."

Then, and at other times, that almost clandestine little playhouse reaffirmed the role of the London theater. We were reminded that things can be said there, seen there, and felt there that would otherwise go unsaid, unseen, and unfelt. To people

Walter Richard Sickert. *Gatti's Hungerford Palace of the Varieties: Second Turn of Katie Lawrence.* c. 1887–88. Oil on canvas mounted on hardboard, 15 × 18⅛″ (38.1 × 26 cm). Yale University Art Gallery, New Haven. Mary Gertrude Abbey Fund

218

who are harassed and fragmented by the traffic of everyday life, the London theater at its highest brings wholeness, oneness, and a heightened sensitivity. In this city, theater is at home.

Other plays, not new, but as yet unplumbed, pertinent, were to speak to us as confidants. When Harold Pinter directed the Royal Shakespeare Company in *Exiles,* by James Joyce, at the Aldwych Theatre in 1971, a new and disconcerting view of human entanglements was presented to us by one who is himself a master in such matters.

In its presentation of Beckett and Sartre, as later of Eugene Ionesco's *Bald Soprano* (1956) and Eugene O'Neill's *The Iceman Cometh* (1946), the Arts Theatre Club tapped into a widespread, unformulated, and quite possibly half-unconscious craving for serious theater.

Other cravings were there, too, and at least one of them was amply satisfied. It turned out, for instance, that the English musical—above all, in the hands of Andrew Lloyd Webber—was to have a phenomenal success not only in London but the world over. But these were times of abundance, also, for those who see theater as a word-centered, high-risk activity. After the *Bald Soprano,* silly conversations in so-called real life never sounded the same again. In *The Iceman Cometh,* there was foreshadowed the disinherited society that would soon be trapped in derelict inner cities, worldwide.

In the convalescent London of that time, the audience for theater longed for a collective experience that would leave them changed, once and for all. The movie house was by comparison a place of darkness and alienation. As for the rented movie of today, it can never generate that collective awareness.

The difference is total. When the theater reaches deep into our inmost being, buried memories are unblocked. Connections unknown to us are suddenly reestablished. What is crooked in our lives is made straight. The theater tells us who we are, and where we come from.

William Hazlitt had all his priorities right. He knew, for instance, that without actors and actresses of the first order even the finest repertory will be a beached leviathan. "When an author dies," he said, "it is no matter, for his works remain. When a great actor dies, there is a void produced in society, a gap which requires to be filled."

Just such a "void in society" might have been followed by the recent deaths of Edith Evans, Peggy Ashcroft, Sybil Thorndike, Laurence Olivier, Ralph Richardson, and Rex Harrison. There was, meanwhile, a rare poignancy in the knowledge that John Gielgud, who was born in 1904, was not likely to be seen on the London stage again.

From players of this class, a large public took its tune for half a century. Edith Evans *was* the nurse in *Romeo and Juliet,* just as she was Lady Bracknell in Oscar Wilde's *Importance of Being Earnest.* Hers was an achievement that would last as long as there were people alive who had seen it. The young Peggy Ashcroft's achievement as Shakespeare's Juliet was of that order, as was Sybil Thorndike's as Saint Joan in the play that George Bernard Shaw had written for her in 1924.

Neither age nor serious illness could deter Laurence Olivier from taking the main parts in Strindberg's *Dance of Death* at the National Theatre in 1967, and in Eugene O'Neill's *Long Day's Journey Into Night* at the same theater in 1971. For the London public, he made these parts his own.

These were not players who would have dreamed of early retirement. In the 1990s there were veteran playgoers who still marveled at the memory of John Gielgud's first Hamlet in the Old Vic Theatre in 1929. By the mid-1970s, Gielgud

Thomas Rowlandson. *Jack Bannister in his Dressing Room at Drury Lane.* 1783. Pen and brown ink with gray wash, 8⅝ × 6½" (22 × 16.5 cm). Yale Center for British Art, New Haven. Paul Mellon Collection

and Ralph Richardson could have coasted along on the classics and given universal delight. Instead, they teamed up in 1975 in Harold Pinter's *No Man's Land,* a play that never spells out quite where it is going.

"There isn't any plot," Richardson said on television in 1975. "But that never bothers an actor. And the characters are never really rounded off. They don't quite know who they are. But that's rather natural in a way. We don't know exactly who we are, do we? We hardly know anybody else, really completely.... We're a mystery to ourselves, and to other people."

As so often with Pinter, we feel that, at any moment in *No Man's Land,* human identities may blow up in our faces. The play includes some of the longest, most haunting, and most wayward speeches ever written for the contemporary stage. As an inventory of London mores in the 1970s, this play will be valid forever.

Once again, Hazlitt spoke true. *No Man's Land* is indeed "an epitome, a bettered portrait of life, with the dull bits left out." It was one of the great theatrical adventures to see Gielgud and Richardson play off one another, night after night, in *No Man's Land,* picking up the conversational ball on the rebound and sending it back to bounce in a dark corner.

And it should be remembered of Rex Harrison that, even when he was half blind and within a week or two of his death from cancer in 1991, he was still on stage in *The Circle* by Somerset Maugham.

Nothing could have been more beautifully delayed than his first entrance. And, before he had even said a word, he convulsed his audience, seven times a week, by feigning to blow his nose in a gigantic yellow handkerchief.

For those who had grown up and grown old with them, these players were irreplaceable. They had served as landmarks in human experience. Without them, we felt both bereft and disinherited. The trust that we had placed in them could never be duplicated.

But it is the great strength of the London theater that every generation of audiences has its own "take" on great plays and great acting. Concurrently, new ways of behaving on the stage come into being. New expectations abound, and new responses, also. The very notion of theater changes.

In all those matters, the London audience has always had a part to play, and actors and actresses know it. Ralph Richardson made some good movies, but he was preeminently an actor who had to be seen on the stage. "Acting is never boring," he said in 1975, "because audiences are always different. In music, the punctuation is absolutely strict. The bars and the rests are absolutely defined. But our punctuation cannot be quite strict, because we have to relate it to the audience. In other words, we are continually changing the score."

Until the day of his death, almost, Richardson had that quality. As old Werle in Ibsen's *Wild Duck,* he had a long walk onto the stage of the National Theatre before he got to say anything. During that walk, he was almost palpably taking the pulse of the audience. They in their turn were adjusting to the look of immense wonderment with which he gazed around him. By the time he opened his mouth, the audience knew more about old Werle than they usually do by the end of the evening. And Richardson, in his turn, knew a lot about them.

There has been a great deal to sort out, these last fifty years. The stockpile of plays available to the London theater has become consistently more and more rich. It includes the native English repertory, the Irish repertory, and the American repertory, together with theater that originated in, or bears directly upon, one part or another of the former British Empire. If we add the foreign classics that have lately lent themselves to an altogether nimbler style of English translation, we have a total corpus that offers a lifetime of exalted enjoyment.

Jules Bastien-Lepage. *Sir Henry Irving (1838–1905).* 1880. Oil on canvas, 17 × 18″ (43.2 × 45.7 cm). The National Portrait Gallery, London

Pierre Corneille, for instance, wrote some of the greatest verse-tragedies in the French language. Those tragedies—*Le Cid, Horace, Polyeucte*—defy translation. That Corneille could also be very funny was a secret well kept from the English public—until, that is, Corneille's *The Liar* was done at the Old Vic in 1990 in a new translation by Ranjit Bolt. As directed by Jonathan Miller, with Alex Jennings in the main part, this was permeated by a comic energy that swept the audience along with it.

At no time since the death of Shakespeare have more good new plays been written in English, or more good old ones brought back to vivid life, than in the second half of the twentieth century. During that same time, fundamental changes came over the London theater and gave it a flexibility and a freedom of movement that it had long been hungry for.

For centuries, the London theater had been privately owned and run. At one time the great actor-managers—above all Henry Irving, from 1878 onward, and after him Herbert Beerbohm Tree, George Alexander, Martin Harvey, and Donald Wolfit—made theater in their own image.

Each was master in his own house. They did not work for change in the theater, or in themselves. But they knew exactly what they could do, and what the public liked, and they did it till they dropped.

And audiences loved them. When Henry Irving toured the English provinces—a week here and a week there—the audience couldn't stop calling him back and back. "It wasn't that we wanted him to *do* anything more," a veteran of the period once said to me. "It was just that we couldn't bear not to see him again."

The alternative was the all-purpose management that acted as a kind of broker between the available actors and actresses and the public who wanted to see them. ιn the years before and after World War II a company called H. M. Tennent had enormous power in the London theater, and often that power was well used.

Theater after theater was in Tennent's hands. Its director, Hugh ("Binkie") Beaumont was no friend of the avant-garde, but when it came to acting and stage direction he had a sense of quality. He also delighted in casting, matching and mating players to parts, and eyeing the result the way a gourmet eyes a menu. Though starstruck by nature, and partial to big names, he knew when to harden his heart. Nor could he be pushed to put on a play that he didn't like and couldn't believe in. He liked a well-made play, full of actors and actresses whom he already

Sir Joshua Reynolds. *Garrick Between Comedy and Tragedy.* 1761. Oil on canvas, 58½ × 72″ (148 × 183 cm). Collection the Royal National Theatre, London

knew, and produced in a way that was irresistibly and reassuringly stylish. A historic example of this was the production in 1956 of Georges Feydeau's classic French farce, *L'Hôtel du Libre Échange.* Adapted and directed by Peter Glenville, and renamed *Hotel Paradiso,* it was performed with matchless dexterity and split-second brio by Irene Worth and Alec Guinness, among others. Here, if ever, was a rebuttal of Laurence Sterne's celebrated remark that "they order these things better in France."

But Tennent's was never going to be a force for change in the London theater. After the end of World War II there was an ever-growing demand for a theater in which room would be found for the anger of those who felt themselves disregarded and disinherited by the comfortable "West End" productions. They wanted a political theater in which the status quo would be held up to ridicule.

A key event in this context occurred in 1956 when George Devine's English Stage Company took over the Royal Court Theatre in Sloane Square and encouraged young nonconformist playwrights—among them John Osborne, Arnold Wesker, John Arden, David Storey, and David Hare and Edward Bond. Their activities served to thicken and strengthen the almost universal dream of a genuinely national theater. In that theater, the great classics of world theater would be available, year-round, in repertory, while chances would also be taken on the new and the unproven.

Such a theater would have its pick of what was already an exceptional work force. It would have the prestige of the Comédie Française at the time of its foundation in 1680. It would have the innovatory genius of the company formed and paid for in the 1870s by the Duke of Saxe-Meiningen. (The standards of ensemble playing set by that company have rarely been equalled.) And playwrights would be at home there, the way Anton Chekhov had been at home in the Moscow Art Theatre during his years of maximum activity.

At the same time, there was an almost equally widespread feeling that good theater did not necessarily need a big traditional playhouse, or official status, or a ramified bureaucracy. It could be made anywhere, and at any time, and on a purely inspirational basis. This was an international view, and it was to persist well into the 1990s.

When Gérard Philipe was the most charismatic young actor in France, he thought nothing of appearing in French seventeenth-century tragedies in a factory in the suburbs of Paris. Peter Brook was already feeling his way toward a concept of theater that in 1985 found apotheosis in a disused quarry near Avignon, in southern France, with a version of an Indian epic, the *Mahabarata*, that lasted nine hours.

In London in the 1960s, there was that same drive toward informality. Plays did not have to be any particular length. There was lunchtime theater in Soho. There was the Almost Free Theatre, where the audience paid whatever they thought the show was worth. There was, in fact, an imaginative energy that began even before the curtain went up. (And, by the way, in most cases there wasn't a curtain anyway.)

This was also the time at which the director began to get top billing in conversation. People spoke of Zeffirelli's *Romeo and Juliet*, of Peter Brook's *King Lear*, of Jonathan Miller's *Three Sisters*, and of Ingmar Bergman's *Faust*.

This was something quite new. In the earlier great ages of the London theater, there was really no such thing as "the director." The chief actor, or the actor-manager, lavished a lifetime of savvy stagecraft on getting the company to talk right, stand right, and move right. Thereafter, the prompter and the stage manager between them did their best. "Direction" was vestigial. (There was a famous and long-hardened old actor who toured England for years. When faced with a new recruit as Lear's Fool, he said, "All I ask of you is that when you are on stage you never come within six feet of me.")

There had been a visionary English designer called Gordon Craig, but it was in Moscow, not in Edwardian London, that Craig got to stage *Hamlet* in a way that made history. There was a Frenchman called Michel St. Denis who came to London in 1935 and brought a matchless unity of tone to Chekhov's *Three Sisters* and Shakespeare's *Romeo and Juliet*. And there were professional directors (or, as they were then called, "producers") who could be relied upon to pull a production together.

But the director as poet and visionary was something else altogether. Joan Littlewood in London and Ariane Mnouchkine in Paris were directors who left their mark on whole generations of playgoers. They didn't have to have a fancy theater, either. Littlewood went to Stratford East in London. Mnouchkine went to a disused cartridge depot in the Château de Vincennes, near Paris. Even when the new directors had traditional theaters at their disposal, as was the case with the Royal Shakespeare Company both in London and in Stratford-on-Avon, there was imaginative energy to spare. Little groups would fan out all over the town and put on plays that didn't suit elsewhere. (They even toured them, too, till the money ran out.)

The new golden age was born in part of huge and lengthy undertakings, in which many gifted people took part and the audience likewise was put to the test.

In 1963, the Royal Shakespeare Company at the Aldwych Theatre performed the *Wars of the Roses* cycle of Shakespeare, directed by Peter Hall in versions edited by John Barton. Audiences sat through them, one and all, without a cough or a yawn. In 1977, the National Theatre performed *Henry IV*, Parts I and II, and *Henry V*, with Alan Howard. Audiences more than once came to see all three plays in a single day and went home happy.

In 1968, the Royal Court Theatre in Sloane Square performed what was, in effect, the Selected Plays of D. H. Lawrence, thereby adding to its repertory a singular depth and grandeur of feeling. In 1982, the Royal Shakespeare Company performed a two-part version of Dickens's novel *Nicholas Nickleby* that lasted in all seven or eight hours and did not seem a minute too long. (It, too, could be seen in a single day.)

These monumental operations made history in terms as much of quality as of size. But when a great living playwright is on top form, history can be made equally well by one actress in just a few minutes and with vestigial stage action.

With productions like the ones just mentioned, the theater reassumed its place as a locus of deep and true feeling in a society that was much in need of it.

But monumentality was not indispensable. A single voice, heard for just a few minutes, can be quite as telling. That was the case in 1973, when Billie Whitelaw at the Royal Court Theatre performed Samuel Beckett's *Not I*. As the stage directions required, nothing could be seen of her but her mouth. Nor could any voice but hers be heard. The play was built with fragmented sentences. The wild whirling of the language held meanings not easily seized. But, by the end, the potential of theater had been fulfilled. Something new and decisive had happened in the domain of human understanding.

Why should good theater of every kind not be concentrated under a single roof, and with a single banner floating overhead? It seemed to take forever. But in the 1970s the dream of a truly national theater began to come into being on the south bank of the Thames. The National Theatre had not one, but three theaters in one on that incomparable site. It was as if the formal and the informal had been mixed and mated.

Walking toward the National Theatre at nightfall, across Waterloo Bridge, we see the pacific fortress, designed by Denys Lasdun, that was opened in 1976. On its amiable battlements, the program for the evening comes up in colored lights. And when we get to the door, we stand on high ground and look back across the river to where St. Paul's Cathedral exerts its ancient magic on the skyline and the recent and provocative building designed by Richard Rogers for Lloyd's of London is picked out in candy colors. It is a moment that does not stale.

One of the triumphs of the National Theatre is that it does not have the institutional feeling that can deaden a subsidized theater. There is no sweeping, drafty foyer, no grand staircase, no preordained stratification in regard to class, or status, or pocket.

Interior spaces, though large, are easy and companionable. There is a proscenium theater, a forestage theater, and a tiny little space, part cockpit, part operating theater, in which directors can cut loose. (Not so long ago, *A Midsummer Night's Dream* was staged there in a sea of mud.) All kinds of theater, and all sizes of theater, can be found at one time or another.

Bookshops turn up where we least expect them, and are very well stocked. There is plenty to eat, and enough to drink, and time to stroll around. Musicians work the crowd before curtain time. But where once they would have been sitting in black tie in the orchestra pit, at the National Theatre they are simply there — round the corner, up the stairs or on the floor, heard if not seen.

This is a national theater in which risks are taken. Almost from Day One, it has had its great successes. The most unpredictable of these was Peter Brooks' production of Seneca's *Oedipus,* with John Gielgud as Oedipus and Irene Worth as Jocasta. Those who thought of Seneca as a long-forgotten chore were proved wrong from the moment at which they walked into the theater and found that members of the cast were already lashed to the columns of the auditorium. Thereafter primal terrors ran free, and a familiar story bit deep with a new set of teeth.

But the National has also fallen on its face. Plays not worth exhuming were dragged up from an encyclopedia of world theater. Peter O'Toole, in 1963, and Daniel Day-Lewis, in a later generation, are performers with virtually unlimited potential, but neither was at ease as Hamlet in the National Theatre. But then what is the theater, if not a place in which terrifying risks are taken?

We never feel about the National Theatre company that they are civil servants who have opted for a safe job with tenure. Somewhere near at hand are strolling players as they were portrayed by Daumier, and actresses as Hogarth saw them, undressing and dressing in a barn with a raucous and exacting audience almost at the end of its patience outside. Playacting is integral to London life, and the young actor making up for his debut at the National is one with Betterton, as Rowlandson portrayed.

It has been fundamental to this continuity that London has always had theaters that will be famous as long as there are plays to perform and players to appear in them. Some of them are beautiful. Simply to see the facade of the Haymarket Theatre gives us an appetite for acting. The recent restoration of the Savoy and the Criterion cannot be overpraised.

But even a theater that was never a true theater can claim our awed attention, as when we step into Middle Temple Hall. Though largely rebuilt after bomb damage during World War II, Middle Temple Hall is the place in which, on the evening of February 2, 1602, *Twelfth Night* was first performed. If we like to think that

It was on Bankside that the London theater established itself from the 1580s onward. In an area formerly best known for bear baiting and brothels, Shakespeare's plays (and Shakespeare himself) found a home in the Globe Theatre.

Shakespeare himself was on the stage that evening, no one can contradict us. In the case of the vestiges of the Rose Theatre that were discovered on the south bank of the Thames in the late 1980s, and of the nutshells that were somewhere among them, we are once again free to fantasize.

Among theaters of later date, the most purely stylish was undoubtedly the Theatre Royal, Drury Lane, as it was remodeled inside, and given a facade outside, by Robert Adam in 1775. Engravings show that the interior was light, clear, elegant, and festive. It had ornamentation that could have doubled as costume jewelry. It had broad and hospitable boxes, and it was held up by slender, square-shafted wooden columns whose practical function was given a dandified air by being covered with plate glass over colored foil. If the auditorium and its attendant corridors were a sub-department of debauchery, as Rowlandson suggested in some of his most evocative drawings, we cannot wonder.

The facade, likewise, could hardly have been more distinguished. But such was the volatility of taste that after no more than eight years the theater was done over again. More than once, in later years, fire put an end to it. The race to stay one step ahead of fashion led to endless remodelings of one kind or another. Drury Lane as it stands today is the scene of many an archetypal evening on the town, but it has nothing to do with the Drury Lane that once upheld, almost single-handedly, the honor of the London theater.

The interior today is post-Edwardian in style, stiffened and held together by steel and reinforced concrete, but still aspiring to opulence. Though appropriate to the long-running middlebrow entertainments that now keep it open all year, Drury Lane is no longer the theater of David Garrick, or Mrs. Siddons, or Edmund Kean, or Henry Irving, or Ellen Terry. Neither is it the relatively intimate theater

Thomas Rowlandson. *An Audience Watching a Play at Drury Lane.* c. 1785. Watercolor with pen and black ink over pencil on laid paper, 9⁷⁄₁₆ × 14³⁄₈″ (24 × 36.5 cm). Yale Center for British Art, New Haven. Paul Mellon Collection

in which Diaghilev's Ballets Russes first appeared in London. But as a big, busty entertainment-factory it does a good job.

Elsewhere in London, the business of the theater is often carried on in buildings that almost without exception are shabby, inconvenient, comfortless, and designed for a public that has not existed since 1914. The heyday of the London theater, in popular architectural terms, was between 1880 and 1914, and most of them show their age.

When still new, they were both gaudy and ostentatious. Heavy on gilt and red velvet, kitted out in plaster with putto and bacchante and herm, they were rich in small private spaces that favored a precipitous courtship. You were expected to look your best. For men, white tie and tails. For women, a long dress (stylish, if possible) and a jewel or two that had been brought out of a safe for the occasion.

I owe to Victor Glasstone's *Victorian and Edwardian Theatres* the exact date on which that particular era showed signs of ending. In the year 1908, the Queen's Theatre was opened on Shaftesbury Avenue. It was in every way a model of ingenuity, practicality, and simulated splendor, with boxes here and there that could almost double as *chambres séparées*.

But it was also the first new theater in which the words *dress circle* did not mean exactly what they said. In the first three rows of the circle, white tie and tails were still obligatory. But the management made it known that in the remaining eight rows "evening dress will be optional." (The price was correspondingly reduced.) In those five words, the passing bell was sounded for a certain kind of theater.

Before the curtain went up, and again during the intermissions, a live band gave a sense of festivity by playing "medleys" and "selections." In the afternoon, tea and biscuits were served between the acts. In the evening, coffee and chocolates, eaten from a box lined with crinkled paper, were the thing.

The public in London knew what Honoré Daumier, Edgar Degas, and Edouard Vuillard had known in Paris—that in the theater the audience can be as compelling as the play. In London, Walter Sickert proved that in paintings and etchings that are as pertinent today as ever they were.

Sickert was very good at what happened on the stage, too, both in those early days and when, in the 1930s, he worked from photographs. Some of the scenes that he set before us no longer exist. Like many another free spirit, Sickert loved the London vaudeville—the music hall, as it was called—and he knew it at its apogee. The cheapest seats at the music hall were very cheap indeed, but that is not to say that they attracted an easygoing public.

Where the performers were concerned, there was no way to fake it in the London music hall. There was no prepacked hyperbole, no hidden microphone, no asinine mechanical spectacle, no mind-blowing amplification. It was one man, or one woman, against the many. You walked out on the stage by yourself, and you did it. (If you couldn't do it, the audience would soon tell you.)

At the turn of our century, the great music-hall performers made local theater, popular theater, irrepressible theater of a kind that has gone from the world. Single-handed, they tapped a great geyser of feeling that offstage was repressed or reprobated. It was a magical experience. One man, or one woman, walked on from the wings and a thousand people said, "Come on, then—speak for us!" And the woman, or the man, knew how to do it.

It was an experience to which even the most unlikely people responded. In 1891 the nineteen-year-old Edward Gordon Craig—later to become the lost leader

George Clint. *Edmund Kean as Sir Giles Overreach in "A New Way to Pay Old Debts."* c. 1820. Oil on canvas, 11 × 9″ (27.9 × 22.9 cm). By courtesy of the Board of Trustees of the Victoria and Albert Museum, London

Walter Lambert. *Popularity: The Stars of the Edwardian Music Hall.* 1901–3. Oil on canvas, 64 × 150⅜″ (160 × 375.9 cm). The Museum of London

of a completely new movement in stage direction and stage decoration—went to see Albert Chevalier, a great comedian then at the outset of his career.

It was the speciality of the very young Chevalier that he spotted the theatrical potential of that archetypal figure, the London costermonger. He was the incarnation of the unlicensed multipurpose London street salesman with his irrepressible patter, his speed of wit and capacity for mischief, his handbarrow, his stock-in-trade of everything from oysters and Dutch eels to baked potatoes, and his Sunday-best suit ornamented with pearl buttons by the hundred.

"Chevalier it was," Craig wrote many years later, "who brought to life the one British Mask which, with John Bull, could have taken its place in the groups created by the Italians in the sixteenth century and the French in the seventeenth century. This mask was the Coster—a good companion to Arlecchino and Pierrot. It was a very strange thing to see and to hear, all of a sudden, this new being among the dudes, the tarts, the cabmen and the White-Eyed Kaffir of this glittering stage.

"And this is strange, too—that the public at once gave him an open-armed welcome. Chevalier swept the town just as, nearly a century earlier, Edmund Kean had done with Shylock. The face, the figure, the voice, its words and its singing tunes, all this delighted us. Especially wonderful and lovely was the rhythm of the whole thing, a rhythm made up of tune and swinging limbs and of face, of buttons and tilted bowler—and of delightful words, full of fun and of power too. Never a moment's pause—all joy."

In the world outside the theater—and it is the magic of the London theater that it sometimes persuades us that no such other world exists—there are no more costers now. (On a regular basis, that is: one or two veterans can still put on a fine show on special occasions.) There is no longer the huge, united, single-voiced underclass that was the mark of London before 1914. Nor is there the eager, exacting, and insubordinate audience with whom the great music-hall performers had to deal. Of that audience, T. S. Eliot said in 1923 that "it was in the music-hall comedians that they found the expression and dignity of their own lives. . . . The working man who went to the music-hall and saw Marie Lloyd and joined in the chorus was himself performing part of the act."

Alvin Langdon Coburn. *Bernard Shaw Rehearsing Androcles and the Lion.* 1913. Collection of the George Eastman House, Rochester, New York

Today, the variety bill is virtually extinct. The days when Louis Armstrong would play the Holborn Empire every evening at 6:30 P.M. and again at 9 P.M. are gone. So are the supporting performers—the dog act, the sea lion act, the magicians, the conjurers, the dancers, the balladeers, and the warm-up comedians who so relished the brief luster of being on the same bill as the Boswell Sisters or Duke Ellington. So is the Holborn Empire itself, pulled down in 1961 after many years in dereliction.

They are missed, those great-hearted and single-handed performers. I should count my life a smaller thing if I had not heard Harry Champion, well into his seventies, sing a song called "Any Old Iron" on a bare stage and follow it with a song called "Boiled Beef and Carrots."

Well-named Champion had a turn of speed that would have been the envy of any Italian buffo baritone. He had diction that slammed every last syllable against the rear wall of the theater. Energy personified, he accompanied his every song with a wild but never untidy dance. His every footfall clicked into place, and when at the end of his act he pulled off his wig and revealed himself as totally bald the house rose to him.

"The end of an era," therefore. But even after the end of World War II, the music-hall audience could put aside its inborn rowdiness. When Mistinguett appeared in London in the late 1940s after more than half a century of triumphs in Parisian vaudeville, she was a very old woman and terrified to the point of not being able to make a sound.

A great silence fell. Her anguish was our anguish. Then suddenly there came a shout from the topmost row. "Carry on, Miss—we're with yer!" And she did carry on, as best she could, and people applauded as if it were the best thing that they had ever seen or heard. But then the London theater audience—when not bored to extinction—has a quietness, a sense of community, and a nose for the true and the good that are peculiar to itself. It is in part for this reason that London is a theater town.

It is, of course, important to know that the London theater is not simply a matter of the National Theatre, or of the Royal Shakespeare Company, or of the Old Vic (more than once left for dead, but forever coming back to most welcome life) or of the theater as it exists on and near Shaftesbury Avenue. Peripheral London has made a perennial contribution, and one that has never been either more widespread or more effective. So far from being put out of business by the movies, or by television, live theater has never been more important to London. It turns up,

Marie Lloyd, music hall performer, c. 1923

Above left:
Samuel Beckett's *Waiting for Godot*. Photograph by Houston Rogers, from the collections of the Theatre Museum by courtesy of the Board of Trustees of the Victoria and Albert Museum, London

Godot was at the Arts Theatre Club in 1955, directed by Peter Hall. In our photo Timothy Bateson (Lucky) is on the left and Peter Bull (Pozzo) is on the right.

Above:
Ralph Richardson and John Gielgud in *No Man's Land* in the National Theatre at the Old Vic, 1976. Photograph by Anthony Crickmay, from the collections of the Theatre Museum by courtesy of the Board of Trustees of the Victoria and Albert Museum, London

Left:
Laurence Olivier as Othello in Shakespeare's *Othello* at the National Theatre, 1964. Photograph Harvard Theater Collection, Cambridge

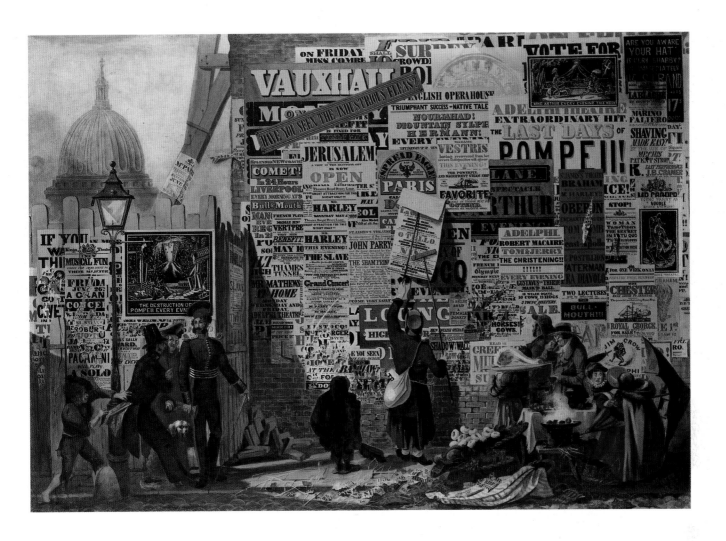

John Orlando Parry. *A London Street Scene*. 1835. Watercolor, 27⅝ × 39½" (70.2 × 100.3 cm). Collection Alfred Dunhill Ltd., London

moreover, in places that have never had live theater before.

In this, too, there is continuity. It was not in the West End, but in the Theatre Royal in Croydon, that in 1897, for one performance only, Max Beerbohm had a wordless, walk-on part in a play called *The New Magdalen*. It was in Fulham, in 1903, that Ellen Terry (then aged fifty-six) played Beatrice in *Much Ado About Nothing*, and her thirty-one-year-old son, Edward Gordon Craig, played Benedick, and Henry Irving sat in the back of a box all afternoon to see what came of it.

If you wanted to see Harley Granville-Barker—producer, playwright, and sometime actor—on stage in *The School for Scandal* in the summer of 1897, Kingston-on-Thames, not Shaftesbury Avenue, was the place. And where was it that in 1926 John Gielgud appeared in, and Theodor Komisarjevsky directed, a play by Leonid Andreyev called *Katerina*? In Barnes, by the river.

In Hampstead, just a few steps from the Underground stop, there is the Everyman Theatre (now a movie house), where in 1921 Chekhov's *Uncle Vanya* got one of its first and, by all accounts, one of its best productions in London. Noel Coward's *The Vortex* had its first performance there, in 1924, and it was on behalf of the Everyman that scouts would go to New York every year in the 1920s, snap up two or three of the new season's plays, and come back well content.

In my own distant days as a drama critic, many was the foray that I made to points west, north, and east. A midweek matinee in Walham Green did not deter me. Sent to Swiss Cottage, on a hillside that rises toward Hampstead Heath, I enjoyed the Alpine air. Hammersmith I knew well as a schoolboy, and remember

232

best for the ease and grace and wit of Jack Buchanan in the last performance, on a Saturday night, of a musical that he alone could make bearable. For that matter, Shepherd's Bush is still present to me, and Sadler's Wells to the east, and Stratford East, further still, and Greenwich.

Theaters in central London, now vanished, have also played their part. The Little Theatre, not far north of the Thames, was well named. It was also the place to go to for plays in which subjects then largely taboo were touched on. When *The Seven Who Were Hanged* by Leonid Andreyev was given by a company of Yiddish players in 1924 James Agate—no pushover, as a critic—wrote that "I do not propose ever to forget anything which happens in this play." That performance was in the long-lost Scala Theatre, just off Charlotte Street.

As for the history of performance in the British theater, it is usually written in terms of men and women who were at the top of their profession for twenty, thirty, forty, or fifty years. It is they, after all, who were talked up by writers whom we still read with pleasure. Some of them were painted, or drawn, or caricatured, or photographed over and over again. (In the 1920s, two hundred different postcards of Gladys Cooper were said to be in circulation.) They kept the repertory in being. When there were good new plays to be performed, they appeared in them (with some exceptions).

But of course they were not the whole of the British theater, then or now. From time to time, the great stars astound us. But the enduring strength, and the necessary strength, of the London theater is not only in the great stars. It is in character acting that the London theater excels. In acting of that kind and class, the players are not selling their own sole selves. It is by abrogating those permanent selves and coming forward as someone completely different that they keep the theater alive as a place of wonder and surprise.

The great players have always known this, too, and they delighted in taking (though not too often) unexpected and vastly rewarding small parts. Not long after World War II, Alec Guinness had a triumph with the small role of Abel Drugger in Ben Jonson's *The Alchemist*. There was a great precedent for that: David Garrick was as happy, from time to time, to play Abel Drugger as he was to bring out his fabled Richard III. When Ralph Richardson was working all evening long as Peer Gynt, in London just after World War II, Laurence Olivier came on toward the end of the play as the Button Moulder and made the whole audience lean forward in their seats.

Great plays are full of supporting parts that are also great parts. Who would not wish to be Enobarbus in *Antony and Cleopatra,* Feste in *Twelfth Night,* the Second Murderer in *Macbeth,* Chebutykin in *Three Sisters,* Firs in *The Cherry Orchard?* What better role for a debut on the stage than the manservant in the opening scene of *The Importance of Being Earnest?* Did not Kenneth Tynan, in his early days as a critic, appear onstage as the Player King when Alec Guinness was Hamlet?

In plays such as these, there are no small parts. And if sometimes there are small actors—well, it is not given to everyone, or even to everyone with a true gift, to sustain a lifetime on the stage. In our day, as in every other day, there have been wonderful performers who for one reason or another burned out, dropped out, drank or drugged themselves out, or were simply too difficult, too unreliable, or too scared.

Other, simpler factors could also play a part. Sometimes, actors and actresses were too tall, too short, too thin, too fat, too plain, or too pretty. Sometimes they talked in a modish way, and then the fashion changed, and they couldn't adapt to the new one. Acting is a very hard way to make a living, and there were stars of the 1920s and 1930s who ended up begging for tiny parts in a Christmas pantomime, or being let go because in old age they couldn't learn their lines.

So I want to end with a little pitch for actors who never quite made it into the big time. One of them was Robert Cox, an actor who was doing quite well in London before the theaters were closed in 1642 by the Puritans. Other actors obeyed. He did not. He would do almost anything to appear in public and amuse even one or two people.

He did rope-dancing at country fairs. He did conjuring tricks. He did comic turns of his own devising and hoped that they would not be mistaken for plays. But the Puritans caught up with him when he was acting in the Red Bull playhouse in 1653 and sent him to prison. Two years later, he died.

That's the kind of person a theater town needs. He may not get famous. He may not even be very good. But nothing—nothing—will stop him going onstage. The older one gets, the more moving it is to think of the dead-center, unselfish, unstressed mastery of the actors and actresses who lived long in London and were loved and honored for it. But Robert Cox is, or was, the London theater too. Watch out for his descendants when next you settle into your seat.

George Dance. *A Man Doing Splits*. c. 1760–90. Pen and gray and brown ink, 7⁵⁄₁₆ × 5¹¹⁄₁₆″ (18.6 × 14.5 cm). Yale Center for British Art, New Haven. Paul Mellon Collection

A tiny image? Yes. An isolated moment? Yes. An unknown performer? Yes. But in this little drawing the spirit of Robert Cox lives on, intact and undeterred.

The Great Outdoors

THERE COMES A TIME when newcomers to London sit back and say to themselves, "Well now—I think we've got this place pretty well licked." The diplomat, the executive on a long-term posting, the scholar on a foundation grant, the foreign correspondent—all know the feeling. So do their spouses.

They know where they most like to go, and how to get there. Their address books bulge. Somewhere in London there is a High Street in which every shopkeeper knows them by sight. They have their habits, their inclinations, and their lawful privileges.

Something in this may be owed to the latent conviviality of Londoners. This was best expressed as long ago as 1912 in a novel called *Tenterhooks* by Oscar Wilde's close and loyal friend Ada Leverson. "It is only in London," she wrote, "that people meet for the first time at a friend's house, and then, if they take to each other, practically live together for weeks after. No matter what social engagements they may happen to have, these are all thrown aside for the new friend. London people, with all their correctness, are really more unconventional than any other people in the world."

Even if they have not experienced that almost conspiratorial closeness, foreign residents can get to know the calendar of London hour by hour, and week by week, and season by season. They know about the Prime Minister's question time in the House of Commons, about how to get in to see the tennis at Wimbledon, and about the Chelsea Flower Show and the newest multiplex movie house. Their clothes all come from London stores, they eat where London eats, they move to London's rhythms, and sometimes they wonder if London has any more surprises to spring.

This is a state of mind that calls for drastic action. Visitors thus afflicted should take London, shake it, and turn it inside out. One way of doing that is to stop thinking of London as the antithesis of "the country." They should think of it, instead, as a vast countryside, several hundred square miles in extent, that is subject from time to time to metropolitan intrusions.

Well-watered, bird-loud, much beflowered in season, and blessed with tall and often ancient trees, this countryside has still a little something of its original character, which was that of forest and fen, hillside and trickling stream, market garden and Iron Age earthwork. Once the home ground of deer and duellist, smuggler and itinerant preacher, shepherd and cricketer, vagrant and orgiast, it counted nothing human as alien to it—and nothing in nature, either.

In the matter of turning London inside out, the unquestioned pioneer was the naturalist W. H. Hudson. With *The Naturalist in La Plata, Birds in London, Green Mansions,* and many another book, Hudson eventually established himself as traveler, scholar, and storyteller. But when he arrived in London for the first time from South America at the age of thirty-two, in May 1874, he was nobody.

Initially that did not deter him. Where others would have hurried out to see the sights of the town, Hudson by his own account

Edward Dayes. *The Promenade in St. James's Park*. 1790. Watercolor, 15½ × 25½″ (39.4 × 64.8 cm). Victoria and Albert Museum, London

put up at a City hotel, and on the following day went out to explore, and walked at random, never enquiring my way of any person, and not knowing whether I was going east or west. After rambling about for some three or four hours, I came to a vast wooded place where few persons were about.

It was a cold wet morning in early May, after a night of incessant rain; but when I reached this unknown place the sun shone out and made the air warm and fragrant and the grass and trees sparkle with innumerable raindrops. Never had grass and trees in their early spring foliage looked so vividly green, while above the sky was clear and blue as if I had left London leagues behind.

Given Hudson's antinavigational bias, it is difficult to say where he was. But wherever it was, he loved it.

As I advanced farther into this wooden space the dull sounds of traffic grew fainter, while ahead the continuous noise of many cawing rooks grew louder and louder. I was soon under the rookery, listening and watching the birds as they wrangled with one another and passed in and out among the trees or soared above their tops.

How intensely black they looked among the fresh brilliant green of the sunlit foliage! What wonderfully tall trees were these where the rookery was placed! It was like a wood where the trees were self-planted, and grew close together in charming disorder, reaching a height of about one hundred feet or more.

The existence of so noble a transcript of wild nature as this tall wood, so near the heart of the metropolis, surrounded on all sides by miles of brick and mortar and innumerable smoking chimneys, filled me with astonishment.

Thomas Rowlandson. *Showing off in Rotten-Row.* c. 1875–90. Pen and ink and watercolor over pencil, diameter 12⅛″ (30.8 cm). The Museum of London

Hudson at that time had traveled wildly in far places, living outdoors for months at a time, shooting his own food, and cooking on a fire of bones and thistle stalks. (Rhea and armadillo were his favorites.) But he said of his first morning in the rook-loud London forest that "I have seldom looked on a scene that stamped itself on my memory in more vivid and lasting colors."

His was, of course, both an extreme and a special case. But even today, to walk across the 635 acres that lie somewhere between Orme Square in Bayswater and Apsley House at Hyde Park Corner is to invite a total disorientation. That this should be so is odd. Are not Kensington Gardens and Hyde Park in the very center of a great city? Where in the world are parklands open to the public more perfectly looked after?

And yet, toward nightfall, we can lose ourselves in those two huge contiguous metropolitan spaces. Though we are in the middle of London, we can neither hear it nor see it. Its noises are subdued, hooded, and seemingly directionless. The pinkish light in the sky seems to come from no particular quarter. And when hotels and apartment houses form up on the skyline on a clear night their crocketed and castellated outlines take on a wild poetry, as when in Tennyson "the splendor falls on castle walls."

When a solitary and anachronistic horseman heads for the stables, we feel ourselves deserted by humankind. Steeples turn to silver. Distances multiply themselves, as oceanic grasslands are flattened by the failing of the light. We look for landmarks, but find none.

The last of the radio-controlled model boats on the Round Pond has been lifted clear of the water and taken home. The lights have gone out in the Serpentine Gallery. The bone-white outline of Henry Moore's eighteen-foot-high sculpture, *The Arch,* is hidden by a fold in the shelving ground. The sculpture called *Physical Energy* by G. F. Watts would put fresh heart into us, but it is miles away. So is the naked figure of Achilles by Sir Richard Westmacott.

Jacob Epstein's figure of *Rima*—erected in 1925 as a memorial to W. H. Hudson, and more than once defaced by vandals—is nowhere to be seen. Of the glorious zigzag of clearly marked pathways that André Derain painted when he was in London in 1906, there is never a sign.

More and more at a loss, as we cast around for a landmark, we would settle for the seated figure of Dr. Edward Jenner, the pioneer of vaccination, or even for George Frampton's statue of Peter Pan. Thinking of the lighted doorways, on all

four sides of the park, that are being flung open at this moment to greet an honored guest, we may even compare Hyde Park to Thomas Hardy's Egdon Heath. Are we not in the very center of the "vast tract of an unenclosed wild" that was like "an instalment of night which had taken up its place before its astronomical hour had come"?

Thus wracked, we empathize with the lonely and dejected situation of Harriet Westbrook, the first wife of the poet Percy Bysshe Shelley, who is said to have drowned herself in the Long Water in Kensington Gardens in 1816.

Rumors of that kind get about, and they lodge themselves in the folk-memory of London. In 1820 Princess Lieven in London wrote to Metternich that Kensington Gardens had once been a little paradise in high summer. "But," she said, "for some years that lovely garden has been annexed as a middle-class rendezvous, and good society no longer goes there, except to drown itself. Last year," she went on, "they took from its lake the body of a very beautiful woman, expensively dressed, who had probably been a whole week in the water."

When darkness comes, tales of that kind linger in the mind, even if we cannot as much as find the Long Water. Gladly, at such times, would we wish ourselves back in the age when King William III had three hundred oil lamps hung along the southern carriage drive toward Kensington and guards patrolled the park after nightfall.

We are not being stupid, either. The Royal Parks in London have a long history of violence. There were deaths by duelling, sometimes with pistols and sometimes with swords. Respectable people who strayed into the parks by night were often set upon, robbed, and left unconscious.

No one was safe. When walking in Kensington Gardens, King George II was relieved of his purse, his watch, and his silver buckles. It was deferentially done, but nonetheless exasperating for that. As for Horace Walpole, who was delicacy personified, he was held up in broad daylight. "One is forced to travel even at noon as if one was going into battle," he wrote afterward. "What a shambles this country is grown!"

Things are better now? Yes. But, like Central Park in New York, like the Bois de Boulogne in Paris, and like virtually every metropolitan park of any size, Hyde Park at night can be dangerous. How should it be otherwise in summer, when darkness, long grass, and deep shadow are as irresistible to criminals as they are to lovers?

It is for good reason that Highgate Cemetery is now closed to visitors, even in the daytime, and that parts of Hampstead Heath are known for nighttime satur-

Carel Weight. *The Moment.* 1955. Oil on hardboard, 24 × 72″ (61 × 183 cm). Castle Museum, Nottingham

As to the mysterious and irresistible terrors of being alone in London, a poet in paint called Carel Weight got them just right. What is there to be frightened of, in this everyday scene? Nothing, and everything.

Thomas Gainsborough. *The Mall in St. James's Park*. 1783. Oil on canvas, 47½ × 57⅞" (120.7 × 147 cm). The Frick Collection, New York

nalia to which even Martial—unexcelled as a connoisseur of urban depravity— would find it hard to put a name. "On such a night as this. . ." is one of the all-time great passages in Shakespeare, but nighttime in Cosmopolis, London style, has other connotations.

Great is our relief, therefore, when the question "Where are we?" at last finds an answer and we breast one of the diminutive slopes in which Hyde Park abounds. There before us, near or far, is the electric necklace of light that signals a metropolitan intrusion upon this wayward countryside.

Of those diminutive hills, in daylight, Claude Monet gave a wonderful account when he was in London in 1871. Better than anyone else, he brought the shifting terrain of Hyde Park to life. He immortalized the distant fringe of housetops, the human figures that suddenly stand tall where we least expect them, the echoing groves and the treetops high in the air. Looking at his paintings of Hyde Park, we can almost imagine ourselves on one of the lookout towers that were built there in the sixteenth century, when deer were pursued by privileged huntsmen across those same shelving slopes.

When Henry James first went to live in De Vere Gardens, on the southwestern edge of Hyde Park, he mentioned the "unobstructed sky" as one of the great advantages of his new apartment. Today we take that sky for granted. That Hyde Park could be sold up and built over does not occur to us, even if we have read somewhere that it was not opened to the public until 1637, was sold under the Commonwealth in 1652, and was later recovered by King Charles II.

London without Hyde Park, without Kensington Gardens, without Green Park, and without St. James's Park would simply not be London. Green Park and St. James's Park are models of civilized contrivance.

They are delicious to walk in. They are delicious to look down upon. They are delicious to listen to when the regimental bands play, the impeccable horses go clip-clop, and we can hear the taxi meters tick, and Big Ben is within earshot.

On every side we hear a brisk, purposeful footfall as the great ones of the earth steal a quarter of an hour from the House of Commons, the Foreign Office, and nos. 10 and 11 Downing Street to check on the birdlife in St. James's Park. Where else would prime ministers take time to go birding and write to the *Times* about the debut of this or that annual visitant?

It is the distinction of Green Park and St. James's Park that they have a purely aesthetic purpose. There is nothing to buy. Barely a shop front can be seen even in the far distance. These parks do not function as the shortest route from one place to another.

They are very grand, but so subtly that nobody feels upstaged. If you know your way around and can slip into Green Park or St. James's Park on the way from one engagement to another, you will think better of the world, and of yourself. If you have nothing particular to do and feel like lying on the grass and looking up at the trees, no one will ask you to move on. In a quiet way, these two parks are the very crown of central London. King Charles II knew that, and it was his particular pleasure to get up early, when the dew was still heavy on the grass, and go walking with his dogs. He did not have to have security men with him, either, for nobody pestered him.

When these parks negotiate for precedence with the great city that surrounds them, it is with the manners of Old Diplomacy. There are palaces, hard by, but they feign to be amiable backwaters. (St. James's Palace does not put on airs, and never will.) There are great houses, with big gardens, adjoining the parks. Marlborough House, Lancaster House, Apsley House, and Spencer House are very grand indeed, but they do not overwhelm the parks on which they look down.

Carlton House Terrace, overlooking St. James's Park, is as beautiful as almost anything in St. Petersburg, which is saying a great deal, but it minds its own business. The Duke of York's Steps, with the Duke himself at the top of the column, might be overbearing. But it is with exhilaration, not with awe, that we walk up those steps.

Elsewhere, discretion still prevails. A little street, niched among palaces, can radiate an ageless, timeless, fashion-free civility. It can be within a hundred yards of the Great Outdoors, and have privileged access to it, and yet not be known even by name to the strollers in the park. Cleveland Row, between St. James's Palace and Green Park, was rightly described by Nikolaus Pevsner as "the paragon of distinguished retiredness in the West End—a close, of sufficiently intricate shape to defeat those who are not familiar with its topography and thereby keep them out."

To have been a regular visitor to Cleveland Row is to have known the very center of civilized London. It is a secret place, as Pevsner implied, but it is an open secret—not hidden, not cordoned off, in no way forbidding. Give or take an occasional toot from the soldiery in St. James's Palace, never a metropolitan sound can be heard. Cleveland Row at its best is so narrow that we can almost lean out and shake hands with the owner of the house across the road. It has been that way since 1700, with the invisible and inaudible nearness of Green Park as fundamental to it.

The houses on Cleveland Row are right in themselves, and right in their location. But we prize them above all for the reticence, the subtext of human confidentiality that underlies them. As a street, Cleveland Row is undemonstrative. But as a human statement it brings great reassurance.

There are, of course, many memorable sights in the great outdoors of London that are not at all confidential. Above all, perhaps, there is the apparition of the Horse Guards Parade as we walk toward it through the ordered acres of St. James's Park. On a moonlit night, with blossom on the trees, the Horse Guards Parade has a look of faery that gives no hint of its sober daytime aspect.

And what has art made of the London outdoors? It is both spasmodic and definitive. There are large and sometimes delectable areas of London that art has passed by, leaving no trace. But when major art has touched the outdoors of London, however lightly, we treasure what came of it. Pacing the wooded slopes above Greenwich, we remember how Eugène Delacroix went to work on his sketchbook there—not far from the Old Royal Observatory, built by Wren in 1675—when he was in London in 1825.

Thomas Gainsborough in *The Morning Walk* caught to perfection the moment at which the amorous potential of London reached its apogee. (His feathery touch with an outrageous hat will never be rivaled.) Thomas Rowlandson got the simpler but universal pleasures of Greenwich just right when he made a watercolor of a lot of people rolling downhill on the grass and roaring with laughter as they went.

Minor art can also do well by London. I remember a little print of a nouveau-riche servant of the East India Company riding along Rotten Row in the year 1797 as if the devil himself were behind him. I also remember a very small painting called *First Love*, in which G. F. Watts took a nondescript patch of London park and turned it into the very bower of romance.

The view downriver from the top of Richmond Hill can speak for itself, but J. M. W. Turner gave it a spin all his own with the echoes of Claude Lorrain in his *Richmond Hill on the Prince Regent's Birthday* that he showed at the Royal Academy in 1819. And when the great thunder clouds are on the move above Hampstead Heath on a squally summer afternoon we see what John Constable saw when he looked northeast, at three P.M., toward the Spaniards inn on July 20, 1822.

Since Gainsborough's day, the gloss of high fashion has gone off the Royal Parks in central London. But it held up well for a very long time. In a long story called "Lady Barbarina," first published in 1884, Henry James sets the tone with his very first single sentence: "It is well known that there are few sights in the world more brilliant than the main avenues of Hyde Park of a fine afternoon in June."

The avenues in question were, respectively, the Carriage Drive and the Row (which was open to horsemen and horsewomen only). Couples not smart enough to play a conspicuous part in the scene were welcome to sit "under the great trees in a couple of armchairs (the big ones with arms, for which, if I mistake not, you pay twopence)." Thus installed, they sat "with the slow procession of the Drive behind them, while their faces were turned to the more vivid agitation of the Row." And what did they see? "The riders, the horses, the walkers, the great exhibition of English wealth and health, beauty, luxury and leisure."

That particular social scene has gone forever, and seasoned walkers in the great outdoors of London now have quite different memories to store away in their memory box. There are the strange, spiky, uncongenial thickets of Putney Vale,

Claude Monet. *Hyde Park, London.* c. 1871. Oil on canvas, 15¾ × 28⅞″ (40 × 73.3 cm). Museum of Art, Rhode Island School of Design, Providence. Gift of Mrs. Murray S. Danforth

where we might imagine (and not be too far wrong) that a crime worthy of Agatha Christie in her heyday has just been committed. There are ponds, canals, disused harbors, hillsides, cricket grounds in full use, and miniature wharves.

As we walk toward Marble Arch, the sound of political speeches may come to us, downwind. In park after park, outdoor statuary leads its mostly lugubrious life, and here and there we stumble upon a necropolis in which the tombstones chart London lives by the thousand.

The outdoors of London comes in all sizes, from the tiny One-Tree Hill in Honor Oak, much prized by John Betjeman for its glorious views, to the 2,358 acres of Richmond Park. There are parks that are places of learning, as much as of delight. Kew Gardens is the most famous among them, but for intimacy nothing in London can rival a quarter-acre patch of ground, not far from Lambeth Palace, south of the Thames. That patch of ground is the sanctuary of a tradition that goes back to a father and son, both named John Tradescant, who were gardeners to King Charles I.

Camille Pissarro. *View Across Stamford Brook Common.* 1897. Oil on canvas, 21¾ × 25⅝″ (53.4 × 65 cm). Private collection

Spencer Gore. *Harold Gilman's House at Letchworth*. 1912. Oil on canvas, 25 × 29⅞" (63.5 × 76 cm). Leicestershire Museum and Art Galleries, Leicestershire

As for the new-built villas in Letchworth, they were to Gore and his friend Gilman what the village houses of Provence had been to Vincent van Gogh.

Spencer Gore. *Letchworth Station*. 1912. Oil on canvas, 62 × 72½" (157.5 × 184.2 cm). By permission of the Keeper of the National Railway Museum, York

Just before the outbreak of World War I, and thanks to an assiduous train service, the outer suburbs of London were thought of as an earthly paradise. Spencer Gore, for one, backed up that idea.

The Tradescants would go anywhere, at no matter what cost and trouble, to bring back a new plant to England. North Africa knew them, and Russia before the age of Peter the Great, and Virginia when it was still a royal colony and loyal to King Charles I.

Visitors to the Tradescant garden should not mess with the poisonous monkshood, which stands nine feet high. Elsewhere, no harm will come to them. The Tradescant Trust is in full operation in ways that would delight the original Tradescants, and there is an elegant continuity in the fact that the present garden and the adjacent Garden History Museum were brought into being between 1976 and 1983 by the same family—the Cecils—that had employed the two Tradescants more than three hundred years before.

A little homework will convince the visitor that there is no limit to the number of ways in which London can be turned inside out. Even the sightless visitor is not forgotten in Waterlow Park in Highgate, which was given to the people of London by Sir Sydney Waterlow as a "garden for the gardenless" and includes a small scented garden for the blind.

The idea of London as a sub-department of the great outdoors has from time to time been given a fresh focus. There were, for example, attempts to re-create the great outdoors on the very edges of central London. As early as 1876, Bedford Park in Chiswick was laid out by the architect Norman Shaw as a self-contained little colony in which "artistic people of limited means" would live in pleasant surroundings. Houses were sharply personalized in an inconspicuous but endearingly arty way. Private gardens were fenced, rather than walled, with the result that Bedford Park had an almost American openness.

In 1903, Hampstead Garden Suburb was begun on 243 acres of land adjacent to Hampstead Heath. As in Bedford Park, the primary object was to slow down, if not to arrest, the mercenary development of London. A scale model of the countryside was to be brought to the frontiers of central London, thereby propagating a civilized mode of life that would be easygoing, unpretentious, and not too expensive.

And then, later, there was talk of Metroland—an inspired invention on the part of the general manager of the Metropolitan Line—as a scene of pastoral straight out of *As You Like It* and yet no more than half an hour from Baker Street station. Thanks to the Metropolitan Line—so the posters suggested—you could find affordable housing in a countryside without blemish.

Even more to the point was the Green Belt, much talked of in the 1930s, which was to keep the great outdoors as a statutory ingredient of Greater London. Within a zone that was to encircle London in perpetuity, farmland, parkland, and recreation land were to be watched over and new building strictly controlled.

The adjective "Green" had not at that time its present connotation. But there is to this day the Green Line bus, still in operation, and its very name speaks for destinations that are (or were) grassy, leafy, unspoiled, and unpolluted. Posters of the 1930s backed up this idea with both charm and wit.

Before World War I, it was the sheer difficulty of getting in and out of London that kept the city within bounds. The local trains did their best, puffing and chuffing and whistling toward wayside stations at which half a dozen people at most would get down. Later, the Green Line buses likewise did their best, setting off from Hyde Park Corner (or, nowadays, from the Victoria bus terminal) toward destinations marked in small print on the map.

Journeys were reliable, if slow, and visitors often had the sensation that, some way back, the city had run out of city. At both station and bus stop, tiny knots of parents, children, business associates, lovers and would-be lovers would gather at the peak hour to greet, or to despatch, the favored visitor. But even they often looked as much amazed as delighted that journey's end had arrived.

There was something very soothing about the train stations in question. For much of the day, bird song was clear and continuous. The station staff had time to plant flowers, and to look after them. Pony and trap had not vanished from the streets. There were machines that for a penny would print one's name (or someone else's) on a long strip of tin. There were all-weather metal billboards that bore rhymed messages. (My favorite told of how "The Willow, the Owl and the Waverley Pen/ They come as a Boon and a Blessing to Men.") For every signal on the not-much-frequented line, there was a signal man in a glassed-in box way aloft. And at every level crossing a uniformed official stood ready to raise and lower the gate by hand.

The effect of all this was undoubtedly to suggest that there was no point in being in a hurry. A car would have been more convenient? Maybe. But at that time even the Great Bath Road felt like a two-lane affair. What everyone wanted, but not everyone could afford, was a house within twelve miles of Hyde Park Corner in a setting for which "demi-paradise" would not be too strong a word.

A house of that kind was what Soames Forsyte built for himself in John Galsworthy's novel *The Man of Property*. Though begun in 1902, *The Man of Property* is set firmly in the 1880s when Galsworthy was still very young.

As social history, the episode in question cannot be faulted. Soames does not just want a country house. He wants an archetypal English scene that will be his alone. He finds it. And when he feigns to think the site too expensive, his architect says, "Hang the cost, man. Look at the view!"

"Almost from their feet," Galsworthy goes on, "stretched ripe corn, dipping to a small dark copse beyond. A plain of fields and hedges spread to the distant grey-blue downs. In a silver streak to the right could be seen the line of the river.

"The sky was so blue, and the sun so bright, that an eternal summer seemed to reign over this prospect. Thistledown floated round them, enraptured by the serenity of the ether. The heat danced over the corn and, pervading all, was a soft insensible hum, like the murmur of bright minutes holding revel between earth and heaven."

That was the dream of the moneyed Englishman of the day: a piece of English perfection within an hour's drive from Hyde Park Corner. The London parks were perfection too, in their way. But anybody could march across them, sprawl on the grass, light a cigarette, and vandalize the view. What was money for, if not to buy a piece of heaven on earth, just a few miles from London, where the words "Trespassers Will Be Prosecuted" meant what they said?

But gradually the idea got around that virtually every Londoner should be able not merely to nibble at the great outdoors but to own at any rate a few square yards of it. As a place to live in, so much of London was so unredeemably awful that pilot schemes for a humane alternative were undertaken in a spirit of high earnestness. "From hell-hole to haycock!" was the general idea.

In retrospect, that scene has a timid but authentic poetry. There is something to be said for a world in which two-lane roads meander past genuine hedges, and butterfly and ladybug are the fastest things in sight. A countryside slowed and intact is still an English dream.

Yet even the Green Belt had its limitations. It was the outdoors, all right, but it was not the *great* outdoors. It was undeniably suburban at a time when people rather made fun of suburbia. (At the very mention of the word in a new play by Noel

Coward, the audience cracked up.) The kind of location which had been a plus for Soames Forsyte was getting to be a minus in the 1930s. Nibbling at the countryside was not enough, in other words.

As to that, a historic shift has occurred in the last quarter of the century. If you love London and yet want to get out of it on a regular basis, there is virtually no limit to where you can find a house. (Money helps, of course). The open road is truly open, and you need never again say that somewhere is "too far."

The little Thames-side town of Maidenhead is no longer your maximum. Nor need you hanker after the dinky little villages in Surrey that play so large a role in the novels of E. M. Forster. You don't even have to dream of the Cotswolds as Titian once dreamed of the blue hills of Cadore. You can go anywhere.

This is due primarily to the postwar system of motorways. Though much contested at the time when they were clawing their way across the countryside, those motorways now make it possible to drive to south Wales, to Shropshire, to Norfolk, or to Somerset in time for a late lunch. The English have thereby acquired not only an American freedom of movement but an American belief that everything is possible. In that sense, the Londoner's backyard is now "as big as all outdoors," even if the banks no longer throw money at their customers.

This has brought about a historic shift, whether conscious or not, in every Londoner's attitude to his city. It does not in any way downgrade the London parks. Nor does it make Syon House or Kenwood or Hampton Court any the less

Sir Stanley Spencer. *The Vale of Health, Hampstead.* 1939. Oil on canvas, 24 × 32″ (61 × 81.3 cm). Glasgow Museums, Art Gallery and Museum, Kelvingrove

Eric Ravilious. *Train Land-scape*. 1940. Watercolor on paper. 17½ × 21″ (44.5 × 53.3 cm). City of Aberdeen Art Gallery and Museums Collection

The notion of the Great Out-doors was summed up once and for all by Eric Ravilious just be-fore World War II. There was the super-comfortable third-class carriage, with its buttoned upholstery and the stout strap that worked the window.

Through that window, and on a green hillside, the mam-moth figure of a horse had been cut in chalk long, long ago. It still sets the imagination racing.

Times have changed. So have habits. But that figure in chalk was worth leaving London to see, and so it is today.

memorable as examples of great English houses in a great English setting. But (for this former Londoner, at least) it relieves the slight sense of oppression that comes from an incapacity to get up and go.

As a result, many Londoners now see London in a new way. Though long regarded as the antithesis of the countryside, it now looks more and more as if to live in London is to serve an apprenticeship for life in the country. Looking at the three houses within Regent's Park that survive from John Nash's original plans, we recognize them at once as prototypical English country houses that we should love to relocate in our remote and newfound country acres.

If we are looking for the beau ideal of a seventeenth-century village, barely touched by time and exemplary in its relation to rolling countryside, we don't have to go chasing all over England to find it. It is right there in London, with "The Grove, Highgate" as its address. And if we have in mind a little private zoo, somewhere behind high country walls, it was Dante Gabriel Rossetti, poet and painter, who had the best ideas for that when he lived on Cheyne Walk.

If we want to see a country cottage that in season is smothered with bluebells over an area of thirty-seven acres, we can find it in the far corner of Kew Gardens that harbors the little house that was once owned by Queen Charlotte. The Londoner who wants to go skating in deep winter need not make the ritual run from Cambridge to the cathedral city of Ely. He has in the Serpentine in Hyde Park a lake which, when iced over, has for centuries been a scene of uproarious enjoyment. It was on the Serpentine and not on the river Cam that in 1826 a skilled vansman drove his van and its four monumental horses across the iced-up water for a bet.

With criteria such as these, the Londoner will be nobody's fool when he goes looking for "a place in the country." In this, as in so much else, London will have been his school and his guide, and when his apprenticeship has been completed, and the irresistible house comes on the market, he and his wife will in no time at all be master and mistress of the great outdoors.

Index

Photograph Credits

The publisher and author wish to thank the museums, galleries, and collectors named in the captions for supplying images; other credits are listed below. Numbers refer to page numbers.

Aerofilms Limited: 80, 180; Agnew's, London: 43, 69; Arcaid/Richard Bryant: 59 right; Art Resource, New York/The Tate Gallery, London: 17 above, 69, 170; Bildarchiv Preussischer Kulturbesitz, Berlin: 148; Bridgeman Art Library, London: 38, 200 above, 213; Christie's, London: 21; Courtauld Institute of Art, London: 119, 121; Michael Dyer Associates: 96; Greater London Council: 206; Hulton Deutsch Collection Limited, London: 12, 181, 229; E. T. Archive, London: 29, 73 bottom; Fine Art Society, London: 72; A. F. Kersting, London: 104, 110 above, 116, 172, 190 below right, 194; Lime Tree Photographic Studio: 162; Photothèque des Musées de la ville de Paris: 25; Jo Reid and John Peck: 97; Service Photographique de la Réunions des Musées Nationaux, Paris: 39; E. V. Thaw and Co., Inc., New York: 56, 77; Jeremy Whitaker/© Her Majesty Queen Elizabeth II: 174